THE INWARD GARDEN

When it is enclosed, a garden such as this one in Sussex feels like a sacred realm—set apart in time and space.

THE
INWARD GARDEN

CREATING A PLACE OF BEAUTY AND MEANING

BY JULIE MOIR MESSERVY

PHOTOGRAPHS BY SAM ABELL

LITTLE, BROWN AND COMPANY

BOSTON • NEW YORK • TORONTO • LONDON

First Edition

Portions of this text were originally published in *Connoisseur* and *Garden Design*, and some photographs appeared previously in *National Geographic* and *Contemplative Gardens*.

Library of Congress Cataloging-in-Publication Data
Messervey, Julie Moir.
   The inward garden : creating a place of beauty and meaning / by Julie Moir Messervy ; photographs by Sam Abell. — 1st ed.
           p.   cm.
   Includes bibliographical references and index.
   ISBN 0-316-56792-2
   1. Gardens—Design.   2. Gardens—Pictorial works.   I. Abell, Sam.
II. Title.
SB475.M47 1995
712' .6—dc20   94-27802

10 9 8 7 6 5 4

IMAGO

Design by Marilyn Fowles Appleby

Published simultaneously in Canada by Little, Brown & Company (Canada) Limited

Printed in China

CONTENTS

ACKNOWLEDGMENTS

WRITING *THE INWARD GARDEN* has been a source of great joy in my life. To create it, I have had to clearly map out the imaginative world in which I live as a designer and a thinker. I have journeyed within myself, to understand my own creative process as it applies to garden design and writing. The result is what I hope will be a delightful hybrid: part personal memoir, part design manual, and part philosophy text.

For the past two years, I have been given a precious gift by my editors, Catherine Crawford and Roger Donald—that of time and of trust. Their words of wisdom and consistent support have urged me to look ever more deeply inward, to elevate the text yet make it personal throughout. My agent, Lew Grimes, brings another kind of joy into my life—that of clear-seeing adviser, steadfast guardian, and ever-present friend. Gael Love at *Connoisseur* and Cheryl Weber at *Garden Design* first published many of my ideas as essays. Marilyn Appleby, my graphic designer, together with Sam Abell, photographer extraordinaire, provide a wonderful visual interpretation of the book's imagery. Kirsten Gay drew up garden plans and helped give graphic form to my descriptions of the archetypes.

Other designers and friends have influenced me as well. First always is Kinsaku Nakane of Kyoto, Japan, my Japanese garden master. Collaborations and discussions with design professionals including Ed Allen, Sheila Brady, Margaret Hensel, Jack Myer, Shiro Nakane, Gunter Nitschke, Susan Ryley, David Slawson, Marco Polo Stufano, Elizabeth ten Grotenhuis, Jere Trask, Jan Wampler, and especially A. E. Bye, Gary Koller, Nobby Mawby, Tom Paine, and Peter Welanetz, have helped outline my thinking about our field. Thanks also to my friends Callie West and Steve Harris for providing a writing retreat when I most needed it. Landscape contractor Donald B. Curran and his crew have taught me as I worked alongside them in the field over the past fourteen years. I hope my many wonderful clients and students will recognize their part in creating this book.

A working, writing, gardening mother can only do the things she loves because of the support, patience, and devotion of her family. My husband, John Messervy, is a fellow designer, a loving critic, and my best friend. Our children—Max, Lindsey, and Charlotte—provide the constant interruptions, activities, and delight in the world that inspire my thinking and bring me my greatest joys. My sister, Allison Moir, listened always through thick times and thin.

My mother's creativity—in her garden, her paintings, and her life—has nurtured my sense of spirit; my father's sensitivity—to his children, his grandchildren, and the values by which we live—has nourished my sense of self. I dedicate *The Inward Garden* to my parents, with love.

Twists and turns allow a change of pace, orientation, and anticipation in your garden. A path's destination point should be shrouded in mystery, piquing the visitor's interest and creating delight in the events along the way.

PREFACE

SHOW ME YOUR GARDEN
AND I SHALL TELL YOU WHAT YOU ARE.

ALFRED AUSTIN, *THE GARDEN THAT I LOVE*

I INVITE YOU TO JOIN ME ON A JOURNEY. A joyful journey; a collecting expedition that will take you into many places you have loved in your life, from your earliest childhood, to the present day, and even into your dreams for the future. The voyage's departure point is this book; its destination is a garden, composed of personally satisfying images, one that will flourish both in your mind and in the ground.

The purpose of these travels is to map your "inward garden" and to re-create its features upon your land. I am your guide; you will choose the itinerary. Together, we will embark upon a fascinating set of excursions off the beaten track, into known but sometimes uncharted territory.

Building a garden is a lifelong endeavor, not something that can be accomplished in several weekends, or even over just a few years. Your inward garden is your very personal dreaming place, which you will continue to refine as you grow, change, and gain wisdom over the span of your life.

This dreamy landscape of a misty watercourse becomes part of our visual memory, providing an image that helps us know how to design our gardens. Environmental psychologist Robert Sommer wrote, "For the sensory thinker, the world of the mind bears a direct physical resemblance to the world outside."

Little Thakeham, Sussex, England.

INTRODUCTION

DEEP WITHIN EACH ONE OF US LIES A GARDEN. An intensely personal place, this landscape grows from a rich blend of ingredients—imagination, memory, character, and dreams—that combine in wonderful ways in our innermost selves. Throughout most of our lives, this garden remains hidden from view save for brief glimpses during moments spent daydreaming or in quiet contemplation. But many of us long to make this imaginative garden real: to sit in it, stroll in it, to palpably possess it on our land. We seek to give form to our inward garden as an ornamental landscape—an outward garden in our own backyard.

Your inward garden exists in your imagination; your outward garden lies upon your land—a private landscape for wandering, for dancing, for daydreaming. Both gardens represent your personal paradise—a beautiful place designed specifically to capture the most positive and refreshing landscape memories; a place that is both a sanctuary from the stress of everyday life and a place of rejuvenation; a place available to you at all times.

My own inward garden grows from my earliest memories of childhood, the places I have lived in and traveled to, as well as influential intellectual, emotional, aesthetic, and spiritual experiences. Added to this is my particular character, my preferences, my dreams.

I grew up as one of seven high-spirited children in a midwestern suburb with forests, ponds, and fields around our house. I learned early to stake my place in this world, to roam to the fringes of our vast grassy lawn, to escape by climbing high up in a locust tree, or by crouching low in a soft brown blanket of needles under a favorite pine. When I was eleven, we moved east to a landscape of rock-strewn hillsides, streams, and waterfalls, and we bought a house with a formal garden. At seventeen, I went to rural Austria as an exchange student; there I fell in love with the rolling hills and dales, churches in the mist, and forest dances.

I came to realize my latent fascination with the visual world while in college. After a solid grounding in undergraduate art history, I went on to architecture school, where I was taught design process and theory, and the practice of making buildings upon a landscape. One day, for an assignment in a course on East Asian architecture, I opened a book on Japanese gardens, and suddenly knew my destiny. These visions of perfected nature resonated with my childhood memories and flooded me with good feelings. Although I had enjoyed learning the craft of building, I knew now that all I wanted was to learn to design upon the land.

So I went to Japan. I was taken on as an apprentice in a traditional Kyoto landscape design firm—perhaps the first female ever in such a male-oriented profession. There, over two years, I learned the art of gardenmaking from a true master. My first assignment was to visit eighty gardens and to "open my heart to their beauty and spirit." Thereafter, I was assigned to the construction crew, learning the art of pruning maples, placing moss, wheeling wheelbarrows, and serving tea.

It was arduous work. But I learned in the best way possible: through my body as I built, through my mind as I studied, and through my heart as I absorbed the cultural traditions around me. I studied the Japanese language, practiced Zen meditation, took tea ceremony lessons, and resided in a Buddhist nunnery. The result was the beginning of an understanding of what constituted the soul of a garden, the aesthetics of rock placement, and the abstraction of nature into very small spaces: the glimmerings of a vocabulary that changed the way I perceived the world.

Upon my return, after finishing architecture school, I began teaching design and building gardens in order to continue my apprenticeship in my own way, in my own culture, and on my own landscape. After five years in the field I returned to the master for several months' more work and research, and some five years later the master came to me. Together we created Tenshin-en, the Garden of the Heart of Heaven, at the Museum of Fine Arts in Boston—he as designer, and I as coordinator and design associate. What delight to watch him work with my materials, my crew, my land!

For the past fifteen years, I have built gardens for residential and institutional clients, most of them with moderate budgets and small pieces of land. Although many clients originally came to me for a "Japanese garden," I soon learned that what they wanted was something else: a natural setting for daydreaming in their own backyards. They longed for what I came to call a contemplative garden, a personal place, far away—in feeling if not in form—from the hectic schedule of their busy lives.

I developed the idea of the contemplative garden in my first book, exploring our need for places of reverie and reflection in the form of a garden. To demonstrate the universality of this idea, I traveled to seven different "garden realms" around the world to show a range of geographical, historical, and cultural conditions wherein contemplative gardens have been built. I found that, despite the diverse expressive qualities of these settings, they all held common design elements: archetype, enclosure, path, viewing position, focal point, and frame, to name a few. This first publication expanded my own understanding of garden design and forms the basis for the ideas in *The Inward Garden*.

In my work as a teacher and garden designer, I have come to appreciate the unique process involved in creating a garden. This book will guide you step by step through the design process, from the form in your imagination—your inward garden—to the outward garden on your land. Each chapter represents one step in a seven-part process:

—In chapter 1, I explore *the meaning of a garden* in our lives. Here, I articulate goals that may clarify your purpose in building a garden as you start the design process.

—In chapter 2, I ask you to visualize your *archetypal places,* the first gardens of your life. By exploring these universal spatial images, you will understand the most fundamental feelings and forms that you seek to build in your garden.

—In chapter 3, I help you gather information for your design by analyzing your *inward and outward sites.* Here, you make an inventory of attributes and qualities that will inform the design of your garden.

—In chapter 4, I discuss the seven *primary elements* that make up the building blocks of a garden. In this section, you will begin to give form to the attributes and qualities identified earlier.

—In chapter 5, I explain the two different forms of *garden composition*—the "stroll journey" and the "mind journey." Here, you will learn how to organize the different primary elements into a coherent structure.

—In chapter 6, using a series of case studies, I suggest a range of "big ideas" that will help you transform your qualities, elements, and compositional structure into an *inward garden design*. By means of certain imaging techniques, you will begin to visualize your garden space as a complete design.

—Finally, in chapter 7, I suggest perspectives for building your inward garden design as an *outward garden on your land*. With a clear understanding of the process, the actors, the materials, the money, and the maintenance involved, you will find that gardenmaking is a joyful pursuit that evolves and changes over time.

Designing a garden is always a journey of discovery. As you follow these seven steps, you will open yourself up to the world within and all around you, finding meaning in heightened feelings and perceptions, and long-lost memories. You'll discover, as I have, that no matter what your background, no matter what size or shape your piece of land, you have the creativity within to make a work of garden art. I have written this book for the gardener in us all: for those who own a garden, and for those who might not ever; for those who have tried and failed, and for those who were afraid to begin; for those who want some new ideas, and for those who just like to dream.

As you read, I suggest that you keep a journal or sketchbook close at hand and record your ideas and images for use in your own design. Throughout the book, I will ask questions, suggest exercises, and list techniques that I employ in my teaching and design practice. Garden plans at the end of the book illustrate a graphic process that will lead you, step by step, to a finished design. Photographs will give you images to ponder and make visual connections between ideas in the text and your own site. An appendix includes a bibliography for helping you construct the garden and select the specific plantings. By the end of the book, you will have learned how to become an artist in your garden.

The Persian poet Rumi wrote, "This outward spring and garden are the reflection of the inward garden." Designing your inward garden is one of the most creative things you will ever do. I hope to give you the confidence to transform your backyard into a place of respite for your soul. It requires that you elicit your memories, so that you can re-create the most emotional—the most joyful, the most comforting, the most meditative, the most transcendent—places of your life. Along the way, you will make a garden of structural integrity, sensory delight, and spiritual significance.

A water lily (Nymphaea sp.) *floats across a reflecting pool.*

Built by my garden master, Professor Kinsaku Nakane, the garden of Korin-in, part of the Daitoku-ji Temple complex in Kyoto, hosts a bell-shaped window that acts as a picture frame, focusing viewers' attention upon its mossy mounds, plucked pines, and carefully placed boulders. Inside, a miniature landscape of rocky islands, mountains, harbors, and promontories is revealed, surrounded by a raked gravel sea.

CHAPTER I

THE ART OF THE GARDEN

I WILL NEVER FORGET my feelings the day I started building my first garden—a half-acre Japanese-style landscape for a client's summer home high on a bluff overlooking the ocean. Although I had helped construct several gardens during my stay in Japan, I hadn't yet built one of my own design. I had never decided—by myself—where to set the rocks and place the plants.

I was terrified that first morning. The contractor had been selected by the client. The materials were already on-site, boulders left behind by a previous designer who had placed them all in two huge mounds that looked nothing like the creations I knew and loved in Kyoto. So it was left to me to create a landscape out of a pile of unset stones.

I came armed with a plan. On a previous visit to the site,

I had learned that the owner needed a path that led to the front door of his contemporary house, and that he had several viewing positions from which he hoped to see an attractive scene. He had a limited budget and no experience as a gardener. His site sloped gently down from a parking lot above the house, and was flat directly in front of it. Those were my clues—the rest was up to my creative imagination.

My plan was to work in the *karesansui*—dry landscape—style, eliminating water both for ease of maintenance and to accommodate the tight budget. Instead, I would give the impression of water by the way I set my rocks and raked the gravel. I would construct a rocky staircase that stepped down the hill next to a stony waterfall, terminating in a pond with a tortoise and a crane island—traditional Japanese garden features—that would provide focal interest from the client's house. I explained my ideas to the contractors, showed them a rough plan, and we began our work.

First, I selected each focal rock and decided where to place it. The men would then chain, lift, and drive it with the backhoe to the location I had selected. There they dug a hole just deep enough to expose the part of the stone I wanted revealed. Next, we lowered the rock into its hole, shimming it so that it sat just right, and returned to the pile for the next stone. It was dirty, intense, and exhausting work.

But I had never felt so exhilarated. To create a powerful miniature landscape where a rockpile had been is heady stuff indeed. To build—stone by stone, plant by plant—a composition that possessed beauty and meaning, not only for me, but for my client, was thrilling. In that first long, dusty, and hot summer's day, my life changed. I became a garden designer.

Since that day, for more than fifteen years, I have

An ever-flowing spring seems to emanate from the gap between two stones in this small private garden near Boston. Recirculated water also flows from a tiny hole drilled through the mossy rock to the left, adding its trickle to a man-made streambed strewn with rocks that flows through the garden.

Once the summer home of landscape architect Joseph Henry Curtis, Thuya Garden in Northeast Harbor, Maine, possesses this formal walled garden that forms the destination point of a quarter-mile walk up granite steps past various scenic overlooks, balconies, and gazebos, which offer a delightful, ever-widening view of Seal Harbor and its islands.

17

A garden can mean different things to different people. This cutting garden at Emmaus, Pennsylvania, celebrates the act of growing while providing a public place to share with others the bounty of their crop of lilies.

continued to learn that the best gardenmaking is a form of art—a creative act that comes from the marriage of the designer's hands, heart, and mind. You use your entire body when you haul, dig, move earth, or even plant, weed, or prune. You challenge your intellect when you design layouts or planting plans, or figure out construction details for a deck, wall, or water feature. But most important, you use your heart —your intuition, aesthetic sensibility, and feelings—to guide the process from start to finish. Few other occupations unite these disparate aspects of the self as effectively as garden design.

I want to teach you the art of making a garden by creating a place in your backyard landscape that emanates from deep within you, that expresses your feelings in each square inch of land that you possess. Through animating your intellectual, physical, and spiritual sides, I will challenge you to become passionate about your garden, from the first glimmering of a design idea to the clipping of the last rose of summer.

WHAT IS A GARDEN?

To most people, a garden is that portion of their yards that has been planted, tended, or landscaped. It may be a small vegetable patch, a bright flower border, or a carefully land-scaped outdoor room. In this book, a garden means far more than just a planted place. It is a touchstone; a repository of memories that forms a place of joy in your life. A garden exists not only as part of your backyard landscape, but as a site that resides in your imagination, a collection of personally satisfying images that can be expressed upon your land.

A garden is as much a state of mind as it is an actual place. It exists because you discover a place of beauty that feels set apart in space and time. For instance, when you've trekked for hours, finally reaching the hut on the mountain's peak, the view across those distant hills feels like a panoramic garden. Or, when you skip pebbles across the surface of a pond, its ripples begin to form an abstract landscape of glass. In such moments, we see the world as a garden, and this sight enriches our souls.

I have found, through years of practice, that people garden in order to make something grow; to interact with nature; to share, to find sanctuary, to heal, to honor the earth, to leave a mark. Through gardening, we feel whole as we make our personal work of art upon our land.

THE ACT OF GROWING

Growing a plant is one of the most basic pleasures of having a garden: starting with a seed or seedling, nurturing it to maintain its health or increase its size or yield; harvesting it as a full-grown, handsome specimen of its kind; or allowing it to grow to maturity and enjoying its blossoms, its scent, taste, color, texture, and form.

We also can find delight in combining plants that bloom at the same time or have related flower colors, textures, and shapes that play off one another in anticipated—or accidental— ways. The act of growing plants can be a most sophisticated form of art.

RECKONING WITH NATURE

For many of us, a garden is also one of the few places to experience the demands of the natural world. However formally it is laid out, however unnatural its features may appear, the garden is still the place where we must reckon with our limitations in controlling the forces of nature. On a larger scale, we find ourselves helpless in the face of windstorms that knock down ancient trees or floods that devastate acres of farmland. On a smaller scale, we fight our daily battles with poison ivy or with slugs and woodchucks. If we are sensitive to the needs of our natural world, then we will be successful gardeners.

A PLACE TO SHARE

A garden is a place to share with others. It is a social space for discourse, for tête-à-têtes, for children's games, for tea parties, for anniversary celebrations and weddings, for straw hats flapping in summer breezes, and ice sculptures in winter. A garden can also be a place of colors and quartets, lanterns and fireflies.

A Refuge

A garden can also be a place of refuge—a sanctuary from the everyday world. After a long day's work, we race through the garden gate, leaving behind daily stresses and strains, to tend to our garden's (and our own) needs: watering its flowers, cutting its grass, breathing in its fragrances, all the while contemplating and dreaming. When we lose ourselves in the care of a garden we cherish spending time alone.

A Place of Healing

A garden is a place of pleasurable images. It is an arena of delight where images of pain, anger, or sadness may be banished. It can act as a healing place, where we can substitute soothing images for disturbing ones.

A friend of mine, badly abused as a child, meditates every morning, conjuring up an image of a favorite beach near his childhood home. In his imagination, he places himself up against a dune and envisions the waves of the sea rolling in. This landscape image helps him feel "emotionally held" and gives him a positive point of departure that sustains him through his day and helps him through his life.

In fact, research has shown that hospital patients who can see a tree outside their window heal many times faster than patients without a view of a natural object. Imagine the healing that is possible were a garden outside each window! Indeed, there may be no more positive image in our lives than a garden.

Paying Homage to the Earth

Making a garden is our most direct way of ritually paying homage to the earth. When you bury your hands in dirt, you unconsciously reanimate the earth: every spring, as you sow your seeds, you symbolically reactivate the energies of the land. As you tend the plants through the summer, you care for the earth; as you harvest the crops, you reap the earth's bounty; and as you mulch the beds in autumn, you put the earth to sleep for the cold winter months.

Leaving Our Mark

Gardens are one form we have of leaving our mark upon the earth. Every tree we plant, every building we erect, has the potential to honor the earth in a similar spirit to that of our ancestors. A garden wall can define a personal space. A sculpture may celebrate an idea or symbolize something natural, something personal, something of deep meaning that resonates across a landscape. A natural rock outcropping might remind us of the layers of earth's history. A sign at the entrance to a garden that reads Quiet Zone suggests sanctuary and contemplation. These markers are conscious ways of revering the earth and our place within it. The more markings we create, the more meaning our garden will have—not only for us, but for those who will follow.

The Garden as a Work of Art

Your garden has the potential to be a personal artistic vision—your own three-dimensional work of art. Just as you communicate your thoughts, feelings, and dreams in a style of house—through the decor, colors, and window treatments you choose—so do you describe your self when you create a garden.

Your garden is the expression of your inner needs, and is not subject to fashion or popular style. It feels timeless yet mutable; archetypal yet idiosyncratic. No two gardens are ever alike. Each suggests individual personality and emotions as three-dimensional form. Each resonates with the sense of joy that we feel when making a haven, a mirror of our character, experiences, and dreams within the vastness of the world.

Your garden, like life, is constantly evolving. Your work there is never done; there is always another seed to plant, furrow to sow, field to harvest, blossom to pluck. In cultivating your garden, you cultivate your soul; in feeding your soul, you can give back more gracefully to this larger garden that we all inhabit.

Joanna Reed of Malvern, Pennsylvania, has continued to work in her seventeen-acre garden and create crewelwork floral designs despite advanced arthritis. As my garden master used to say, "One art means all arts"—if you understand the principles in creating one form of art, you will understand something about all forms of art.

Medersa ben Youssef, Marrakesh, Morocco.

An Image of Paradise

EACH CULTURE ENDOWS its gardens with a distinctive design sensibility based on many things: a blend of geographic, climatic, horticultural, geologic, religious, and aesthetic influences that result in landscape designs that are undeniably of that region. Yet gardens look different from one another, arranged according to individual ideas of what a transcendent world might look and feel like. The Emperor Jahangir of Kashmir, Monet in France, and Prince Toshihito of Japan all had a dream of paradise when they made Shalimar, Giverny, and Katsura, respectively. Each is a personal expression—a mixture of the poetic, philosophical, psychological, and spiritual needs made manifest in three-dimensional form.

Looking back through history, we can identify four fundamentally different images of gardens as paradise. Each provides a distinct vision of how a garden relates to the earth: by ascending from it—a transcendent paradise; by taming it— an ordered paradise; by harmonizing with it—a natural paradise; by collecting aspects of it—a planted paradise. Each of these images represents a different approach to the aesthetics and general layout of a garden. Which of the four represents your own vision?

The transcendent paradise.

Early gardens were designed to set out religious ideals in three dimensions. Islamic courtyard gardens, for instance, were designed according to precepts set forth in the Koran, the Muslim sacred text. Gardens were meant to be representations of paradise, laid out in four parts, enclosed by thick walls, and filled with "rivers of honey" and flowers and trees to provide the "spreading shade" needed to make a cool oasis in the desert climates of the Islamic world. In Europe, garths—medieval cloister gardens—aimed to suggest the design of the heavens in their quadripartite layout and details. Early Japanese "paradise gardens" were designed for the Buddhist deity Amida to celebrate a land of purity and goodness in the form of art and gardens. Kyoto's famous Saiho-ji, commonly known as the Moss Temple, was originally built around this theme.

Villa Balbianello, Lenno, Italy.

The ordered paradise.

The secular gardens of Italy and France sought to suggest a different image of paradise: that of the control of the human being over natural forces. Paradise was sought in the regularized ordering of the design elements: orthogonal lines, vast perspectives, symmetrical plantings, channeled water features, and axial layouts that took their cues from architecture more than from nature.

Villa Melzi, Bellagio, Italy.

The natural paradise.

English landscape gardens and their many derivatives evoked the natural paradise, based upon principles of order that harmonized with, but were distinct from, nature. Their curvilinear lines, framed perspectives, small garden pavilions placed at intervals along a circuit walk, all suggested that a person's relation to nature was not dominant but equal (if not subordinate) to it. The sensitive designer sought to work with the "genius of the place" to play up natural features and to create picturesque journeys through garden settings that called to mind bucolic images.

Castle Drogo, Drewsteignton, England.

The planted paradise.

Here, the plant dominates other aspects of landscape design. Botanical gardens and arboreta flourished in the nineteenth century, creating a cult of the specimen plant—the cultivar, clone, hybrid, or cross. From the early twentieth century, the design of the English perennial border was raised to a high art. Many American gardens today are based on these images: the collector's paradise, with one of each new introduction carefully set out and marked; or the perennial paradise, with its swaths of seasonal color, its "white garden" or its "gray garden" foliage, each enclosed in a separate high brick wall.

As children, we were
unafraid to explore the
world through our bodies,
running free, hiding
beneath bushes, climbing
trees. As adults, we often
rely on the memory of
these experiences,
exploring the world
through our minds.

CHAPTER II
ARCHETYPAL PLACES
THE FIRST GARDENS OF OUR LIVES

WHEN I WAS A CHILD, the world seemed filled with secret places. My family's home boasted a wide lawn, vegetable and flower beds, a swing set, and a playhouse. However, it wasn't these "official" play areas that my brothers, sisters, friends, and I most delighted in, but those our parents hadn't built and didn't own: the vast woods around our house, the cow pasture and meadows beyond, the pond in our neighbor's backyard, the apple orchard down the lane. These "wild" terrains possessed an enchantment and mystery far more compelling than the tamer worlds our parents had created for our pleasure.

They were, in fact, our real gardens. We would wander from our special "Indian tree" in the woods to a log bridge over the brook that fed the pond. In an old orchard, we'd each climb our own apple tree, staking claims and fighting over who

got the highest one. Then we'd hide under the white pines at the edge of our property, on the lookout for trespassers like the milkman or the diaperman. In May, we'd suck the nectar from the blooms on towering lilac bushes; in June, bury our heads in massive peony blossoms; and in August, raid the grape arbor, puckering at the tartness and spitting out the purple skins. Our best times were spent outside, in our neighborhood's natural and constructed landscapes, which, under the influence of our youthful imaginations, assumed a magic they would retain for the rest of our lives.

A garden wasn't just a planted enclosure in those days, but a place for discovery and enchanted dreams. Jungle gyms, pillow forts, tree houses, and *Alice's Adventures in Wonderland* all possessed a similar quality for us, places that allowed us to play in our imagination. A box was a cave; a rock, a ship; a door-mat, a magic carpet. We held tea parties under our dining room tables and made miniature jungles for our army men under the shrubs. Best of all were the quiet times, when I'd make a special dreaming place for myself under my bed or hidden away in the attic eaves. These were my very own contemplative places—secret, magical, animate realms that formed my first experience of the feeling of being in a garden.

We each carry personal memories of beloved places from our past. Each place carries associations of our emotional state while in a particular setting, which still affects us: where we feel comfortable, where we choose to sit, to walk, to dwell. These emotional landscapes, then, become cherished symbols that denote a particular special place in our lives, and influence our vision of beauty and meaning in a garden.

Whether you grew up in the country or in the city, a small town or a tract development; whether you experienced a happy childhood or a painful one, whether you were vivacious or shy, rich or poor, you found magic places in your backyard, alleyway, bedroom, attic, basement, park, or street that made up the landscape of your early life. Over the years, I have asked many kinds of people about their daydreaming places from childhood. The answers I receive are wondrously rich in detail and remarkably constant in content. I found that adults remember vividly their childhood contemplative places, and long for such spaces in their contemporary lives. These images from our early lives carry strong physical, psychological, and spiritual meaning forever.

It was not until I became a mother that I began to understand the origins of these longings. Watching my own children explore the meaning and magic of space, I came to understand that there is a developmental process of spatial exploration that we all go through—seven distinct archetypal vantage points from which we experience the joyfulness of space at a very early age. These developmental stages can be likened to natural images: the sea, the cave, the harbor, the promontory, the island, the mountain, and the sky.

YOUR FIRST LANDSCAPE

The body of your mother was your first and perhaps most indelible landscape. The good feelings engendered by inhabiting places inside and outside of a large, protective form become our primary associations of security, warmth, comfort, and protection.

As we grow and learn to explore the world outside our mother's body, we begin to link our first feelings to the landscape around us, viewing it almost as an animate being. No matter how old we are, we never lose entirely these primal feelings toward the earth. Instead, they float beneath the surface of our adult lives, revived by images of natural beauty—when we stand in awe at the immensity of Niagara Falls or sit silently while watching a tiny spring bubble up out of the ground. In such moments we see nature again as childlike creatures, open, fresh, curious, reverent. We feel again the power of Mother Earth as a living spirit, and bring this understanding to the designs we make upon her surface.

Through the child's physical experience of place, a psychological concept of the world is created: the sense of withinness, inside to outside, enclosure, being at the edge, outness, upness, and beyondness; all are learned prenatally, then as an infant, small child, adolescent, and finally, an adult. When we experience a place in later life that recalls these early feelings, we know it as an image of paradise.

In your journal, write your reactions to the archetypal spaces that I describe below. As you read, let memories and images flood your mind. Record these associations, and note the qualities of the spaces that you remember as compelling. You will be surprised at the details you recall and the stories that they tell. These places form the deepest core of your inward garden.

THE SEA: WITHINNESS

Inside each of us may lie a latent longing for the sea, deriving perhaps from the security of our immersion as embryos in the liquid world within our mother's womb. We re-

THE SEA

Our earliest memory of a contemplative place may be the "sea" inside a warm womb, where, as tiny embryos, we felt immersed, surrounded by softness and peaceful solitude. When we swim in a pool, submerge ourselves in a spring shower or a sauna, or find ourselves surrounded by the soft boughs of a pine forest, we remember the feeling of the first sea of our lives. A Minnesota pond.

create this sensation throughout our lives—by soaking in a hot bath, scuba diving beneath the surface of the sea, standing under a misty morning shower, or luxuriating in a steambath or sauna.

Many of us love this feeling of being blanketed. In the natural landscape, we'll seek the middle of a deep forest or lie engulfed by a vast field of wheat. Atmospheric effects immerse us: a pea soup fog, a snowstorm, a torrential rain shower, or sand- or windstorm all allow the elements to swirl around us, engulfing us within their greater power. In immersion, we find contact with a simple, completely inward world that reminds us of our very first experience of space.

THE CAVE: INSIDE TO OUTSIDE

We often love cavelike spaces, close-fitting little vantages upon the world. This may derive from our experience of space just prior to and just after being born. From the caves inside and outside of the body, we can come to feel secure in tight, small places that fit our form and enjoy a small oculus that opens out onto the world. Our earliest architecture is structured on the model of a comforting cave: the cradle, the crib, and the perambulator all form cavities that fit close around small bodies.

From then on, we tend to seek out places to snuggle within; we collect caves. Nooks and crannies, igloos, berths, burrows, and hollows feel like our elemental home. Our house or apartment feels like a cave in relation to the neighborhood around it. The bedroom, study, nook, or attic within the house, or the pergola, playhouse, or porch outside of it can be perceived as caves of different sorts. More evocative still is the cave our bed becomes when we nestle deep under soft eiderdowns at night. Or, embraced by our lover's enclosing arms, we are held tight, like a child, in a snug cave.

THE HARBOR—ENCLOSURE WITH A VIEW

As little children strong enough to hold up our heads, we may have found security and vantage from a new locale: our parents' laps. In this *harbor,* we enjoyed a protected 180-degree view onto the world, backed up by their bodies and held in by their enclosing arms.

The harbor is an anchorage, an enclosed refuge that is found wherever an area protects one part of the world from the rest. In landscape terms, a valley, a copse, or a glade all offer a "circle of safety" from which to view the outside world. A cloister, court, plaza, or square are architectural equivalents of the wing chair, booth, playpen, or fenced-in yard that formed the harbors of our childhood landscapes. Enclosures—hedges, walls, fences, buildings, or arcades—are felt as "enclosing arms," and give us the security to perceive ourselves as the weighted center of any landscape in which we sit. By feeling securely enclosed, we feel as though we are the center of the world. One important way that we find our place in the world is by discovering harbors in which we can relax and feel safe.

THE PROMONTORY—AT THE VERY EDGE

After learning to crawl and then to walk, we became a kind of promontory in the landscape of our childhood by pushing our small bodies to the edge of our known world. Most of us felt exhilarated by this daring vantage from which we could scan the world, yet secure in the knowledge that we were connected still to the mainland represented by our parents and caretakers.

Promontories abound in natural and constructed environments. Cliffs, bluffs, canyons, spits, capes, or headlands are types of promontories, as are balconies, balustrades, belvederes, and catwalks. When we stand at the very edge of something, we often feel both thrilled by and afraid of the 270-degree expanse around us. That is why the parapet or turned-up edge, low railing, or wall that protects the periphery of a building is often vital to our sense of security while standing at the brink.

THE ISLAND—AWAYNESS

As we grow older, many of us long for isolated retreats. We seek more independence from our care-givers and imagine

THE CAVE

The cave is a sanctuary of our gardens. With a little opening onto the outside world, it is often a form-fitting place where we can retreat when we want to be alone. The Garden House, Devon, England.

THE HARBOR

A harbor is an enclosure with "arms" that define a realm of refuge and a large view out. This U-shaped exedra—a room for conversation furnished with benches—creates a perfect place for viewing a gilded sculpture of Pan, the Greek god of shepherds. Augustus Saint-Gaudens's Garden, Cornish, New Hampshire.

THE PROMONTORY

When we stand or sit at the edge of a landscape, as on a balcony, belvedere, or cliff, we are on a promontory—an exhilarating vantage point that feels as if it is perched out over the world. View of Lake Como, Villa Melzi, Bellagio, Italy.

THE ISLAND

An island is like a promontory, except cut loose to become a landscape all its own. With a 360-degree view of the world and a vision of the heavens above, one feels like an island when floating on the sea or lying in the center of a meadow. Saiho-ji Temple, Kyoto, Japan.

THE MOUNTAIN

To be atop a mountain is to occupy a high vantage where the familiar landscape lies far below. Chasma Shahi, Srinagar, Kashmir.

THE SKY

In the sky, our minds leave the known landscape far below and feel free to enter the boundless realm above us. Sunset over Lake Dal, Srinagar, Kashmir.

traveling beyond the limits of our known world.

Islands can represent safe and secret havens and symbolize total "awayness" from the world. To inhabit an island is to feel oneself as the center of a circle, surrounded by a horizon line that seems endless. The islander feels in control of this 360-degree vantage—knowing immediately, viscerally, when someone or something appears to violate its purity. Here, we feel free to contemplate the sky, the clouds, and the heavenly vault above, while backed up by all the earth. At night, we become tiny islands upon another island—Earth—while pretending to inhabit the starry isles that make up the universe.

Islands abound in the landscape: a large specimen tree surrounded by lawn, a platform in the middle of a forest, a picnic blanket in a field, a house in a yard, all feel like habitable islands. When some of us encounter such a spot, we long to lie upon it and face the sky, floating alone upon an undifferentiated sea.

THE MOUNTAIN—UPNESS

As adolescence approaches, we realize that the mountain, like the island, can be a source of solitude. High, remote places become significant hideouts from a world filled with heightened emotions and turbulent feelings. Turrets, cupolas, widow's walks, treetops, towers, all possess mountainlike qualities.

To adults, ascending a mountain may symbolize the quest for wisdom and the attainment of a state of enlightenment and inner peace. We become a mountain upon a mountain, resting squarely at the summit with a grand panoramic view to the profane world below and the sacred one above: to the sky.

THE SKY—BEYONDNESS

From early childhood, we dream of flying, of becoming lighter than air, defying gravity, soaring above the earth. We swing, ride horses, ski, bike, fly kites, jump with parachutes, glide, become astronauts, hoping somehow to transform from physical entities into pure spirit. A great blue vault over the earth, the landscape of the sky has come to symbolize a celestial paradise, an ideal of a transcendent world that has inspired different cultures to create its images in the form of gardens.

Both sea and sky can represent something fluid alongside the solidity of the archetypal landforms that are our vantages upon our world. Perhaps from the sky we are reborn and become once again immersed in the sea. The life cycle may be an endless spiral.

THE ARCHETYPAL LANDSCAPE

What does all this have to do with gardens? When we remember the many precious places in our lives, we mentally construct a garden of images. These memories feel tangible—nearly three-dimensional—and emotionally charged. In our mind's eye, we place ourselves into each different childhood setting and relive our feelings of delight, awe, romance, melancholy, joy. Perhaps these places become touchstones for spatial experiences thereafter. We measure each new setting against those of our past. In this sense, these early places of spatial exploration become archetypal.

Space is like air: it flows all around us without definition. A space becomes a place only when we find a spot within it to inhabit. The archetypes suggest seven different habitable vantage points that give us a place to be within otherwise boundless space. There are two ways that we can reside within these seven points of space: through our own bodies or through our minds. Thus, when we walk down any street, we "read" the landscape around us as a series of contemplative vantage points, picking out a cavelike nook here, a mountainlike spire there; a harborlike enclosure here, an islandlike terrace there. As we walk by, we fleetingly imagine ourselves in each one, noting its presence as a place of security and quiescence in a busy world.

The archetypes also link our feelings, memories, and associations to a particular spatial form. You may experience the same surge of joy looking out from your skyscraper office window that you felt in your tree house. You take the same delight in drinking tea in your garden's pergola as you did when you ate cookies beneath a special rhododendron bush. And you may respond to one archetypal space above all others. (I am a promontory person, for instance; my husband loves harbors.) Knowing this, you can begin to understand why a particular landscape thrills you—because it is mountainous, or by the sea, or forested, for instance; or why you rented your apartment or bought your house—you liked being up high, down low, you liked its coziness, or its panoramic views. When you explore the archetypal places of your life, you find their emotional and physical traces throughout your world. The seven archetypes allow us the security to reflect on our selves and our place in the infinite.

How does this apply to your inward garden? Look closely at your site and understand the archetypal feelings that may be recalled there. Your land may be entirely forested (the sea), tiered in levels up from the house (the cave), enclosed by trees to form a glade (the harbor), out at the edge of a ravine (the promontory), open and grassy (the island), high on the top of a hill (the mountain), or located by a reflective body of water (the sky). Some sites are rich in archetypes, while others are barren. A newly cleared site or a small city lot may not suggest any archetypes at all. This presents you with an opportunity to decide which of these vantages you'd like and where you might best design and incorporate them for yourself.

One of my friends is an avid first-time gardener. We discussed my theory about spatial archetypes, and she found that while she responded to each one, she was most drawn to harbors and promontories. The problem was that her yard was small, open, and had no prospect but the back of her neighbor's apartment house. What was this gardener to do?

My first suggestion was that she enclose her yard with a fence to give it a harboring quality. This fence could be taller and more sheltering where her terrace was located (near the house) and lower to the back of the site. I then proposed that she plant trees in front of her neighbor's house in a soft curve that would act as a backdrop for something that she might want

to view—an arbor, a water feature, another bench. The addition of fencing and trees, judiciously placed, would give my friend the sense of prospect and refuge that she had always sought.

Another way that the archetypes might be applied to your site is for you to imagine how you might change your yard to reflect those spaces that you most respond to. My husband and I, for instance, chose our property because its varied landscape caught our imagination. We liked the quirky hunting lodge of a house, built by an architect in the Arts and Crafts style in 1926. It feels like a dark cave from within, with an inglenook, leaded glass, and a wall of Palladian windows that face south. Any changes we make to the house must allow light to penetrate the thick stucco walls in equally special and interesting ways.

Our half-acre of land houses other archetypes. The whole site sits up on a promontory from which we can see the seven miles over intervening hills to Boston's tallest buildings, the Hancock and the Prudential, which jut like twin towers above a low privet hedge. We also have "mountains": two fifteen-foot glacial stones that define one edge of our property. Enclosed by hemlock hedges, our site feels like a harbor as you enter. Sitting under a swath of oak and hickory tree trunks at one corner of the yard, you feel as though you're immersed in a sea of leafy shade and coolness. Lying on a chaise longue upon our lawn, you feel like an island, looking up at the vast sky above.

Different from most properties I have come across, our site features each of the seven archetypes; most parcels of land are neither so sizable nor so varied. But, whether the smallest lightwell embedded in the city or the grandest estate extending over hundreds of acres, a site will suggest one or more archetypes in the mind of its user, whose responsibility it becomes to both preserve and enhance these features as the basis for a garden's design.

Walk your land and note all its archetypal places and how they make you feel. Imagine where you might introduce new archetypes and take note of their location. Knowing the

Landscape architect Fletcher Steele designed this classically inspired garden throne for his client Miss Mabel Choate's Afternoon Garden.

archetypes will give you the confidence you need to begin the process of building your inward garden.

A shy but determined acquaintance of mine tried in vain to design a terrace for his small, wooded backyard. He had measured his site, read many how-to books, and drew plans that never felt quite right. I encouraged him to begin to think about the places that were important to him as a child. He realized that he was always drawn to nooks and crannies for hiding, usually located at the edge of a grand expanse of open space. Somewhere on his site, he thought, he could find the spot to build himself a harbor.

He decided to throw out all plans and just walk his yard, sitting in different locations to see how each felt, to find out just where he wanted to be. He found a spot, off in the corner, where the combination of canopy, view, and light felt right—a place he had never previously considered. He then built his terrace there—his own adult daydreaming place that mirrored his images from childhood.

This patient man found a place in his yard that perfectly matched an image in his heart. He constructed his inward garden by trusting himself, his inward feelings, and his outward site. To make a space for yourself in this world, you must start by understanding the importance of archetypal dreaming places in your life, and then reinterpreting them in your own backyard.

Doug Gosling, creator of the garden at the Occidental Arts and Ecology Center in Occidental, California, mingles organically grown vegetables and ornamental and edible flowers together to wonderful effect.

CHAPTER III
ANALYZING YOUR INWARD AND OUTWARD SITES

THE SOUL NEVER THINKS
WITHOUT A MENTAL PICTURE.
—*ARISTOTLE*

YOU HOLD WITHIN YOU, from earliest childhood, a garden of images that no one else possesses. Your land is also unique. It contains special features and engenders particular associations that make it different from all other land around it.

To make a garden that has meaning and magic in your life, you need to take stock of all the things that make both you and your land special. Once revealed, these qualities will help you know just how to design your garden.

Your inward and outward sites are your two greatest sources of inspiration for creating a work of garden art. They provide the concepts that will then suggest the mood and the look of the garden that you wish to create. They suggest mental pictures that link specific feelings to a particular form and serve as a guide throughout the design process.

YOUR INWARD SITE

My first meeting with new clients is spent learning about their lives and their land. First, I observe signs of their personality in their manner of speaking and dressing, their style of decorating, their taste in art and music, and the way they

Landscape architect
Fletcher Steele
planted this dell of
Petasites, *a
perennial herb that
forms a dense,
waist-high thicket
of rhubarblike
leaves that can grow
to three feet across.*

interact with others: their partners, children, neighbors, pets. I ask specific questions, designed to resurrect memories and preferences, which then provide me with ideas for their garden's design. A good designer must be somewhat like a therapist: trained to be aware of subtleties of nuance and meaning, and unafraid to ask probing questions. However, these questions are posed to learn about a particular set of associations—the positive images of pure pleasure that a place can bring into our lives: joy, contentment, delight, contemplative solitude. A designer uses this personal information to craft a garden that includes elements that hold positive emotional meaning from a client's life.

In this book, you are both client and designer. Following is an inventory of ideas and images that may help you uncover the sources of inspiration that lie deep within.

Filled with duckweed, this bog garden looks completely natural, but a few clues suggest otherwise. The large leaves of the gunnera plant are cultivated additions, as are the broadleaf plantings, huge trees, and lawn that grace its surrounds.

IMAGES

Your inward site is composed of the images that derive from the impressions and experiences that affect you in a positive way every day of your life. These may be grand episodes (a trip across the country, the birth of a child, the creation of a work of art) or small events (a candlelit dinner; a long, hot bath; a walk in the forest). Immediately after one of these experiences, you can recall it with great clarity, and re-create your emotions and senses of the moment. But soon, the details recede and you are left with an *image*—an impression that you hold in your memory bank.

An image can be defined as a mental picture that you form when a particular sight, sound, smell, taste, or touch from your storehouse of memories is awakened, often reminding you of something you have experienced before.

An image can provide a source of inspiration for the designs you make on your land. For instance, an event (your walk in the forest) gradually becomes an image (forest) that holds particular qualities (deepness, dappledness, coolness) together with related feelings (contentment, awareness, serenity) that resonate within it. The image, then, relates your feelings to a particular form through the qualities that the form possesses. If you want a garden of serenity, then, it could have the qualities you associate with forest: deepness, darkness, and coolness. This doesn't mean that you must build a literal forest in your backyard, but that those forest qualities are important to gaining the feeling that you seek for your garden. Knowing the sources of inspiration—the images—that make up your inward garden will enable you to identify the qualities you long for on your outward site.

What images do you possess that might affect the design of your inward garden? Let's find out. Childhood places, travel, books, the arts, training, and family all act as sources of inspiration for your garden's design. Each image translated into a garden element has the potential to represent a scene, a site, a smell, a moment, a gestalt, a gesture, an event that has brought you pleasure. You must begin by examining your life.

LANDSCAPE AND VISUAL IMAGERY—IDENTIFYING THE FEATURES OF YOUR INWARD SITE

Like your childhood daydreaming places, the landscapes you have known throughout your life leave strong impressions and can create inspirational images for your garden's design. The gardens that you played in, the regions in which you traveled, went camping, hiking, cross-country skiing, scuba or skydiving, all have placed you in a special proximity to landforms and landscapes that you have loved. You may never have actually experienced a particular location but have seen it portrayed in books, photographs, or magazines; such a site can become a dreamscape that holds potent meaning for you.

Some of us were lucky to grow up surrounded by gardens that provide us with distinct images for our own designs. Canadian plantswoman Susan Ryley's garden, photographed for books and magazines around the world, is located in Victoria, British Columbia, where she grows hundreds of plants in a horticulturally perfect climate. "I learned what I know about plants by example, from my parents' garden and from others'," she remarks. Having grown up in a famous Victoria garden with rhododendrons, azaleas, primulas, roses, lilies, and an alpine garden, Ms. Ryley learned about plants almost by osmosis. When she bought her own home, she began to plant the things her parents had grown. But soon she found that her tastes were beginning to change: "Once, my mother took me to a very old woman's garden in which she grew all the wonderful old-fashioned, lovely things—pinks, campanulas, lilies, and with climbers everywhere: old roses, creamy-yellow clematis, and potato vine. My garden was a desert in comparison, so plain and neat. So now, thanks to her, my garden has become wilder, with plants in profusion, softness everywhere. I take in things that I see, I try out things, and I read all the time."

It will help you to remember in detail the gardens that you have experienced in your life. Sketch out the aspects of their layout, plantings, and materials that most appealed to you. Record their qualities—how did they make you feel? Visit

An allée of paper birch, planted by the sculptor himself at the turn of the century, graces a sunny field at Augustus Saint-Gaudens's garden in Cornish, New Hampshire. On his 150-acre site, known as Aspet, Saint-Gaudens fused his reverence for classical design with his love of this dramatic New England landscape, with its views across fields and forests to Mt. Ascutney and the Green Mountains range.

Autumn colors in the northeastern U.S. countryside bring out the "leaf peepers" in October. This artificial waterfall and pool in a New York garden mixes native and exotic plantings to give the effect of a natural stream in the woods, an image that is enhanced by the brilliant hues of the oak and hickory forest "captured" in the background.

friends' gardens for ideas whenever possible and browse through books and magazines for images.

Next, think about the range of landscapes that you have loved throughout your life, the images you associate with them, and the qualities you would like to incorporate. These landscape images can suggest design features for different parts of your garden. The story of some recent clients provides a good example.

My clients immigrated to the United States from Eastern Europe many years ago. They recently bought a house in a forested area near the university where they teach. Both admired rock gardens, and wanted me to create one on part of their property. During our initial meeting, I questioned them about many issues, including their childhood daydreaming places, and landforms and landscapes that they loved. I learned that although born in the same country, the husband was raised in the mountains; the wife grew up in the plains.

Then we toured their site. Stone walls with large boulders edged their property on one side. Here was the very material I needed to make a garden. Yet the husband, worried that these striated, oversized stones would overpower the site, asked that I import smaller rounded stones. A week after our meeting, just as I was about to begin working on their garden plan, I received two postcards from the couple. On one was written, "We send you two postcards—two different sides of us!" The husband sent an Ansel Adams photograph titled *Surf and Rocks,* taken along the Monterey coast of California—a scene of powerful vertical stones rising out of the sea. His wife mailed me a Matisse painting of a riverscape with trees arching over a serene body of water. My clients sent these images in the hope of conveying the feelings and forms that they had been unable to put into words during our interview.

They couldn't have expressed them better. Contrary to his spoken concerns, this man wanted a truly powerful landscape, with huge rocks reminiscent of his childhood mountain home. His wife, previously voicing little opinion about the garden, held a strong image within—she sought a soft, verdant place that matched her memories of the plains. Thanks to these postcards, I knew how to design their garden. In the following few months, I built a foreground composition of craggy, vertical rocks, with a background "pool" of moss and cherry trees lining its far edge. Some of my clients' inward garden of landscape images now exist in three dimensions upon their outward site.

Since that experience, I continue to ask clients to collect images that express their feelings about gardens. You should do the same. Gradually fill a notebook with a loose collage of thumbnail sketches, pictures from magazines, postcards from beautiful places, travel photographs, garden illustrations—and keep it close at hand during the design process. Some images may come from actual places, others may be enthralling imaginary sites from literature, music, art, film, or art of your own making. Keep track of any verbal references that might suggest garden qualities: lines of poetry, lyrics, literary passages. Reread your favorite children's books for their descriptions of enchanted places, or for their richly detailed illustrations—clients have mentioned being influenced by the magical landscapes described in certain fairy tales, by scenes from *Winnie-the-Pooh* or *Tom Sawyer,* and by Beatrix Potter's delightful drawings. When you know the qualities of the garden that you hope to design, then you have taken the first big step toward building it.

SENSORY IMAGES—ESTABLISHING A MOOD

A good garden design establishes a mood by calling up sensory memories that arouse feelings in a visitor. Being in a wonderful garden or natural landscape can be like listening to a favorite piece of music—you are surrounded by sensations that, taken together, create a particular mood that feels just right at the moment you experience it. You are immersed in a space and a time of heightened sensory awareness, where certain emotions seem tuned to a particular play of light, a repeating cadence, a fragrance, or a song. A garden, like a piece of music, is designed to stir us in a viscerally compelling way.

Scientists have discovered, as Marcel Proust and his *petite madeleine* taught us long ago, that tastes, smells, and visual impressions from our past can be revived through stimulation of certain parts of the brain. We each have the capacity to recall the stuff of our experiences and to use it creatively, as the basis for our garden designs.

The problem is remembering. Sensory memories are hard to recall intellectually. Instead, we must reawaken them by visiting places where we immerse ourselves anew in light qualities, colors, sounds, and smells that we have loved from our past, or with which we have just become acquainted. Visit natural places, parklands, and gardens that you find attractive and walk through them with your five senses heightened. Try practicing a kind of "walking meditation" as you observe the beauty around you. As you do, follow a few simple rules: (1) Go by yourself or with an intimate friend and observe in silence. You see more clearly when your voice is quiet. (2) Open your heart to the beauty and meaning around you, as my garden master instructed me in my first year of apprenticeship.

A daisy flower, perhaps of the Compositae family, seeking to survive in the harsh conditions of Zion National Park.

Don't approach the landscape intellectually. (3) Revisit the place or places frequently, at different times of day, in different seasons, and in different weather conditions. Learn what a space can teach you over time. (4) Note your reactions, the images that come to mind, and the qualities and details that you find special. By becoming aware of your sensory memories—those that include the qualities of light, colors, sounds, smells, and plants that you have known and loved—you will re-create them in your garden, adding a personal richness that brings you joy. Let's examine each one.

The Quality of Light. Light illuminates the landscape around us. We receive our sense of sight from light, which floods our brain with information about the world, constantly moving as it is absorbed, reflected, or refracted by molecules in its path. Objects become luminous, iridescent, vivid, dazzling, glistening, radiant, aglow with light. Depending on the intensity and location of its source, light brightens, highlights, silhouettes, floods, dapples, or bathes all elements suffused by its beams.

Light shapes the design of our gardens in many critical ways. First, the amount of light determines the types of plants that can thrive in a particular space: we can't grow sunflowers in dense shade; we can't grow moss in bright sunlight. So, unless we alter the light conditions on a site, we need to recognize the quality and quantity of light in any given space. Second, we choose to inhabit light and shade under different conditions. On a hot summer's day, we seek to sit in a shady spot, not in bright sun; on a blustery spring afternoon, we choose to sit in bright sun, not in full shade. Third, our ability to see the plantings and objects in our landscape is affected by our relationship to the light. Whether light comes from a source behind or in front of an object, whether it is seen through mist, rain, snow, or a clear haze affects the way in which we perceive our garden spaces and the objects within them.

The quality of light also determines the state of our emotions in a space. Think about the three basic types of light and how you react to each of them. *Full sun* can give you the

Delphinium, daisies, bee balm, sedums, and perovskia mix wonderfully with conifer trees and grasses in this Colorado garden. The choice of low-growing perennials and ground covers links foreground to background.

A stand of ferns with moss-laden tree trunks marks a place of intense shade, where the sun may penetrate only occasionally as shafts of light. Such a place, deep in the Canadian wilderness, reminds us of Longfellow's famous lines, "This is the forest primeval. The murmuring pines and the hemlocks . . . / Stand like Druids of old."

The flowers of a Japanese Iris—
Iris ensata—*stand tall in a*
strong shaft of afternoon sun.

sealike feeling of complete immersion in space. Your eyes compress to slivers against the glare, your pupils contract to close down the amount of light entering your retina, and your body temperature warms in response to the sun's radiation. Depending on many factors—the intensity, the exertion required, the presence of companions, the scale of the space—in full sun you can feel exhilarated or parched as the plant and animal life around you might be.

In *deep shade,* you also experience a kind of immersion in space, but now in cool, dark shadows. Once your eyes have adjusted to the darkness, you see with clarity only the area directly in front of you. Although the pupils have expanded to bring light into the retinas, you cannot see that which is not illuminated with peripheral vision.

In places where light fails to penetrate, a particular pared-down ecosystem occurs; verdant groundcovers and mosses hug the ground, while a towering canopy of conifers or deciduous trees block out the growth of middle-story shrubs. Such shade

produces a pristine environment, muted, subtle in color, and often fresh in atmosphere.

Dappled sunlight provides a different experience of the space it illuminates. Since it is created by penetrating a tree canopy from above, it imbues the ground plane below with a shimmering, translucent quality, highlighting objects caught in its rays and picking out the myriad shades of green and changing patterns of shadows cast across the forest floor. You see most clearly in this mixture of bright sun and deep shadow: your pupils expand to let in light, and its bright ambient quality heightens and provides contrast for the textures and colors all around you.

Imagine how objects look in different types of light—when light is cast from behind and an object is in silhouette; when light is cast from the front and an object is in highlight; how light looks at different seasons, and at different times of the day—winter sunsets, summer late afternoons, dry fall mornings, spring at dawn. Remember how light penetrates different

The yellows of yarrow, lilies, and coreopsis combine wonderfully with the white of lilies, phlox, and delphinium in this carefully composed perennial border in a Maine garden. Notice how these two bright colors occupy the sunny center of this design, changing to deeper pinks and reds as one moves to the shadier edges.

atmospheric conditions; in mist, through clouds, as rainbows, as moonlight. Noting qualities of light and working with its effects will help you to fashion the mood of your garden.

Colors. Most of my clients hold strong color preferences. Some refuse to have yellows or mauves or pinks in their plantings; others want a wild mixture of bright hues; still others want only different shades of green.

What colors do you prefer? Bright casts or deep ones, earth tones or primary colors? A limited palette of the shades of one color, or a cacophony mixing together every color in the rainbow? Which of the many overtones of green appeal to you: light- and dark-green, yellow-, gray-, and blue-green? Note your color preferences so that the plantings you design may come to match your internal image.

Your perception of color depends on the quality of light with which you perceive it. In full sun, the color of an object tends to wash out, so that sunny locations need strong colors in order to be seen clearly. In full shade, we cannot see any color well but white, which stands out brilliantly in a dark and muted environment. Colors are best perceived in dappled light, in early mornings, and on cloudy or rainy days.

Color also affects your own mood and the mood expressed in your garden. A common perception is that red, orange, yellow, and brown hues feel warm, while blues, greens, and grays are thought to feel cold. (To achieve the same sensation of warmth, a pale-blue room requires a higher thermostat setting than one painted in pale orange.) Red, orange, and yellow hues are thought to induce excitement, cheerfulness, stimulation, and aggression; while blues and greens are thought to exude security, calm, and peace; and browns, grays, and blacks are thought to induce sadness, depression, and melancholy. These are not hard and fast rules, however; color preferences may vary depending on one's age, culture, mood, or mental health. Colors affect the perception of size as well. White or other cool colors make a space appear larger than when painted in dark or warm colors. Black and very dark-hued colors have a shrinking effect.

Bluebells have self-seeded throughout a wood, highlighting the bright pink of this rhododendron as well as the spring green of native ferns.

Combinations of colors can also affect a viewer's emotional state. Researchers have found that when you view a pleasurable color after one that you dislike, it produces more pleasure than when viewed by itself alone. Imagine how you would relish a bright border full of your favorite blue perennials after walking past a dun-colored mulch pile! This state, known as affective contrast enhancement, is a basic principle of all design.

Sounds. It is important not to forget that you hold an auditory memory as well as a visual one: you can "hear"—in your mind—sounds that you have heard in the past. In a garden, most noises emanate from a few basic sources: birds and animals, wind, and water. The former, of course, provide a huge repertoire of possible sounds. Each species of bird has its own song, and with the addition of berrying and fruiting plants, you can attract a chorus of singers into your garden. You can entice bullfrogs, crickets, and peepers to a wetland or boggy garden. You can even go so far as to enclose sheep, horses, or cows in an adjacent field, enjoyed for their baas, neighs, and moos.

More natural sound effects may be achieved by sensitive manipulation of the elements in your garden. Wind—as it strikes, washes past, or whistles through trees and vegetation—provides a continuous background noise that can soothe or

The strict formality of this tiled garden at the Hotel Mamounia in Marrakesh, Morocco, is made dynamic when rose petals float on the waters in its fountain. The Persian poet Rumi saw each natural element as a manifestation of God's presence when he wrote, "Whatever animal or plant they behold, they contemplate the gardens of divine beauty."

scare depending upon its force. The clucking and swishing of bamboo culms in a slight breeze cools those who hear it. Water, in the form of rain, can fall heavily or gently on different surfaces. A stream, waterfall, or fountain can gurgle, ripple, babble, trill, or splash along a channel. Moments of silence, too, have their place. Examine your memory for sounds you've known and hope to re-create in your garden.

Smells. Smells permeate a garden. From the dank odor of fresh dirt and rank stench of composted fertilizers to the hay-scented pungency of freshly mown grass and the perfumed fragrance of climbing roses, we are exposed to smells that range from earthy to sublime. As we add different spatial qualities and new plantings to our garden, we increase the number and variety of aromas that our noses can distinguish.

As gardeners become increasingly sophisticated in their use of plant material, many are developing "scented gardens." These are composed of annual and perennial plantings with wonderful fragrances—roses, nicotiana, pinks, lily-of-the-valley, peonies, and lilies, to name a few.

Plants. Certain plants evoke special memories. Think of the favorite trees, shrubs, and flowers that you have loved from your childhood, your travels, or other important moments in your life. Write them down. Plants—especially flowers—wield a nostalgic power for us all, flooding us with sensual, aesthetic, and emotional reactions from our past.

Special characteristics of certain plants make us love them: the tactility of a lamb's ear; the ruffled dewiness of a lady's mantle; the towering brilliance of a sunflower. The seasons are evoked by certain plants: the unfurling of fern fronds in early spring, the simple daisy with its plucking ritual of "He loves me, he loves me not" in summer, the pale blue aster that signals the cool weather of fall, and the bright red berries of winter-berry against the snows of winter are just a few of the many seasonal plant associations I enjoy.

Some flowers have direct associations with travels in our lives. For me, bergenia is Lake Como; jasmine suggests Marrakesh; the delphinium is forever England; and the lotus,

Kashmir. Just imagining a chrysanthemum, I can taste the tart leaves that garnished my favorite foods in Japan.

Each one of us must compose our list of favorite plants. As gardeners we should ask ourselves, What plantings stimulate my senses and evoke memories so that my garden will blossom with meaning? The question should evoke a long and satisfying response.

Fern fronds unfurl beside a pink rhododendron, signifying the fleeting joys of spring.

PERSONAL AESTHETICS

Every day of your life, you make fundamental aesthetic choices in response to something in your environment. Look at two different living rooms, for instance. One will have pristine white walls and spare, modern furniture, with a few selected pictures and objects carefully placed. Another will feature a patterned wallpaper, antique furniture, and Oriental rugs, with family photos, pictures, and knickknacks scattered across every surface. Each room reflects the very personal aesthetic vision of its creator. In a similar fashion, your garden should reflect your preferred way of organizing space and arranging objects within it. Noting your reactions to the choices below will help you "see" your garden's design, based upon the personal aesthetic that you—consciously or unconsciously—have evolved over the years.

Geometric Order vs. Natural Order. Some of us respond to an orderly existence in which everything has its place and is accounted for. We look for clarity of line, layout, and viewpoint. Ordering our world according to geometric principles helps us feel secure and in control of our lives. Straight lines, symmetrical arrangements, axial paths, ninety-degree angles, all provide an order to our gardens that makes us feel good.

Others prefer a less orderly existence that instead feels rich, diverse, and spontaneous. This may mean a looser, seemingly random garden design based on natural principles of order rather than architectural ideals. If this is our tendency, then our designs will be made up of curved lines, asymmetrical arrangements of space, meandering paths, and accidents of design, rather than what we may feel as predictable and controlling patterns on the land.

Unity vs. Variety. Unity means a wholeness, simplicity, uniformity, and indivisibility that may be your life's goal. In a garden, unity suggests a total, sweeping concept, a simple planting palette, a uniform treatment of materials, and a layout of spaces linked together as an indivisible whole.

Variety, by contrast, suggests a multiformity, a complexity, a nonuniformity, and a divisibility that may better match your character. In a garden, multiformity comprises a total concept

The brilliant magenta color of this loose clump of valerian (Centranthus ruber) peeks out over the formality of the knot garden at Bodysgallen Hall in Wales. Contrasting natural with geometric order, or unity with variety, enhances the qualities of each.

This New England front garden is enclosed by an orderly white picket fence inside which a host of well-loved objects—birdhouses, flower boxes, trellises, and birdbaths—flourish in a wonderful jumble of colorful, textural plants.

that includes many different forms and styles, a complex and varied planting palette, a diverse and nonuniform treatment of materials, and a layout of spaces set out as a series of divisible units, possibly unrelated one to the next.

Spatial Combinations. Some of us like to combine different types of spatial layouts in one garden. My mother, for instance, tends to be an orderly soul, and so has laid out her main landscaped space—her herb garden—as a fenced square with symmetrical raised beds that sits below the house. But other, smaller gardens along the street side of her house are enclosed as a set of three garden rooms, each designed around some different asymmetric arrangement. The contemplative garden features a walk ornamented with hostas and ferns that snakes through a pachysandra bed to a bench backed up by mountain laurels. Next to it and parallel to the house lies a long, skinny lily garden, punctuated by stone animal statues placed here and there along a straight walk. This leads to her front garden, where a crabapple tree juts out from a porch and acts as an asymmetric centerpiece for the perennial beds around it. While the herb garden, with its full-sun display of color and texture, may be the most photogenic of the group, I find her smaller, naturalistic gardens the most charming.

Sometimes a person's character is revealed in the layout of his or her garden; sometimes it is the character that he or she longs to have. A friend of mine lives a simple, orderly, meditative existence with enough time and space for reflection, and few distractions but her work. Her garden, though, reflects a different side of her nature: a cottage garden packed with flowers of every size, shape, color, and texture. In contrast to hers, my life seems frenetic, with children, animals, a husband, myriad friends, neighbors, school activities, and a variety of different jobs and projects that fill my days. While my house may reflect the cacophony of my life, my back garden suggests a different ideal: wide-open, soothing spaces, some naturalistic, some geometric without undue clutter, and with a long view out onto the world. Perhaps we wish our gardens to reflect our ideal rather than our real natures; our dream state rather than the everyday reality of our lives.

The Character of
the Gardener

Mariii Lockwood and daughter Azzurra Merlino pick cherry tomatoes in their edible garden. Formerly their front lawn, the garden now feeds both family and friends.

PICTURE YOURSELF IN A GARDEN. Place yourself within it. What activity are you engaged in? Gathering bright blossoms for vases? Planting billowing masses of perennials? Staking delphiniums? Harvesting vegetables?

Or are you gazing out to a distant view from a rose-scented arbor? Snoozing in a hammock? Strolling along a shady path? Listening to the trickle of a waterfall?

What kind of gardener are you? If you are a **dirt gardener**, you are a gardener of the hands; a fierce worker who devotes many a waking moment to the quest for the exact spot to put a favorite delphinium or the best organic deterrent for the Japanese beetle. You feel most comfortable contemplating your garden world close-up—down to the petals, the stamen, and the worms. You worry about plant groupings, effects of frost on early peas, and what kind of tiller to buy. And your work is never done, except for the short period of time after the garden is put to rest for the season and before the first seed catalogue arrives in the mail. You are a gardener who uses an ornamental bench to stack pots or display annuals rather than—heaven forbid—as a seat. Your garden should be chock-full of plants and you should be in the thick of them.

If you are a **mind gardener**, your preferred role may be to snip the most exquisite rose, to experience the fragrance of the peony, or delight in the setting of the stone, rather than get down and dirty pulling weeds. Knowing this means that you may be most happy owning a garden that is elegantly simple and easy to maintain, or hiring others to manage the improprieties of garden weeds, deadheading, and pruning. If you are a pure mind gardener, you may be perfectly content to never actually finish planting your garden, because you can so vividly imagine what it will become. For you, every undug hole is filled with exotic species, each unsightly view soars as distant vista. You may not require an actual garden because you already have a fully developed paradise in your soul.

Most of us are a mixture of both kinds—what my husband calls "dirty-minded gardeners." We see a garden as a place that—when successful—requires the union of mind and dirt: art and science expressed as design and horticulture. Even though our own talents may tend toward one arena or the other, to be successful gardenmakers we must know something of both. The Japanese garden master knows how to set a stone or pluck a pine, having been through an arduous period of apprenticeship. The English perennial gardener of vast white, blue, or gray borders must know the myriad cultural requirements of each plant, yet have a vision of the aesthetics of the whole composition.

The mind gardener seeks out places to contemplate the landscape. This garden viewing house at Knightshayes Court in Devon, England, overlooks a greensward in the foreground, a belt of four-hundred-year-old specimen trees in the middleground, and a flock of sheep grazing in the background.

The Outward Site

After the initial interview that helps reveal the qualities of my clients' inward site, I then study the outward site to determine the qualities of the land on which their garden will sit. Together we walk the property, stopping here and there to discuss its existing layout, plantings, and features, and address the problems it imposes and the possibilities it suggests. I also take note of any associations that the land triggers in both of us. This inventory of site information, associations, and images will provide the foundation for designing an artful, meaningful garden that fits your land.

Your piece of land is your sacred realm on this earth. As its owner, you are its self-appointed trustee for a tiny but critical moment of our planet's two-billion-year life span. You can take many different attitudes toward your site: choosing to preserve what is, to build upon it without particular forethought or plan, or to transform it into a sanctuary of beauty and meaning—a sacred realm upon a sacred earth.

When you treat your site as sacred, you uphold its unique qualities and celebrate those attributes that set it apart as special. Only when you understand it well should you take the bold but important step of altering your land according to your dreams.

Special Features

Every member of a family has one or more special places on a property. The archetypal vantages identified earlier are one kind of special feature on a site. A child may treasure a particularly scrubby bush because it bears a white berry in the fall. Your spouse may have strong feelings about a certain view, a particular tree, or a potential sitting place that you had never considered before. Even the family dog may have found a ritual sleeping place on your site. Each individual's viewpoint must be considered with care before you undertake to make changes on your land.

Your property possesses a unique set of features. When people walk onto your land, what do they exclaim over? What do you take pride in showing them? Being fully aware of these special places will mean that you take care to incorporate them or leave them unaltered when you work out your garden design.

Your site and its features provide major clues to thinking about the design of your garden and its own set of problems and opportunities. Knowing what they are will reveal its practical limits (too much shade, poor drainage, infertile soils) as well as its hidden potentialities (picturesque vistas, specimen trees, a meandering stream), places where design can clarify its character, build new connections, or develop deeper meanings.

Recently, a client requested a design for a path that would lead from the sidewalk up a hill under a massive copper beech tree to her large turn-of-the-century stone-and-shingle house set high above the street. The problems created by the steep grade and by the shallow root system and deep shade of the hundred-year-old tree were offset by the creative opportunities offered by its stately branching structure and gray trunk, and the superbly crafted materials and massing of the house. My challenge was to make a walkway that brought opportunities and constraints into harmony with each other. The solution was simple: to make a set of steps of oversized, gray-granite natural stepping-stones that wound up the slope in a handsome S-curve, bringing materials, colors, and textures into union.

Walk through your yard and ask yourself what elements you like or dislike, and why. Then ask each family member the same questions. Summarize the whole group's reactions on a single sheet of paper, and refer to it often as you read on. Asking each family member for an opinion early will help you know the "value" to place on a site's special features.

Patterns on the Land

When you begin looking closely at your environment, you may find its diversity bewildering, complex, or even disorderly. Upon study, you'll find that there is a pattern and order to your land, based on the recurring features and phenomena of your regional landscape. Each property is a living, changing community of plants and animals that represents a continuity with the larger landscape of its region.

The open, rolling hills of central Devon are marked by hedges as far as the eye can see. These enclosures provided a means of defining the different leaseholds of tenant farmers as well as keeping grazing animals out of planted fields.

Understanding these patterns on the land—its landscape features, geological patterns, topography, soils, climate, vegetation, and artificial features—all may help you design with, rather than against, nature. As you read, think about the patterns on your land and record your thoughts in your journal.

A landscape is composed of the landforms of a region in the aggregate: the hills, valleys, plains, rivers, or streams that make up the particular geography of a place. Your site is a piece of a larger landscape that you may sense directly, as long views across fields or mountains, or as cityscapes; or indirectly, as elevation changes within your property.

Sometimes, as in a flat urban setting surrounded by tall buildings, your site seems to bear no relationship to a natural landscape at all. Yet this is precisely where, for psychological and emotional reasons, you crave a garden that looks like a microcosm of the natural world. For centuries, urban gardeners have found the need for establishing natural order in their cities, from the Chinese gardens at Soochow, to the Japanese *tsuboniwa* (courtyard gardens) in Kyoto, to the Manhattan pocket parks. As you will see in chapter 6, you can take your ideas from nature, no matter where you live.

What are the issues that you need to address on your outward site? Existing landform, geology, soils, climate, vegetation, and structures affect the layout of your garden and need to be studied and inventoried before any design work can take place.

Building on Beautiful Sites

I FIND IT VERY DIFFICULT TO DESIGN a garden for a very beautiful site. Perhaps this is because my definition of a garden is so broad—if the site is beautiful, then it must already **be** a garden! I find that there are two approaches to building on beautiful sites: the light touch, where the garden feels like a natural extension of the landscape; and the heavy-handed approach, where the garden stands out as completely distinct from its surrounds. Take a forest site, for example. You could choose to make a simple path around your site, following existing animal trails and leading to small glades and clearings, cleaning up what was there before you, and using indigenous plants that would grow there anyway. Or, you could carve a garden out of the forest, as Leo Tolstoy did in Yasnaya Polyana, his estate in south central Russia. He used allées, circular clearings, etoile patterns, and other formal devices to link orchards, plantations, groves, and ponds on his three-thousand-acre estate. He made his whole site a garden by means of ornamental features, all set deep in the middle of a forest.

Another beautiful site is the Vale of Kashmir in the north of India. Its gardens rest on the edge of the lovely Lake Dal, surrounded on all sides by various mountain ranges, including the Himalayas, to the north. When I first arrived, I asked myself, "How can a garden possibly compete with such a beautiful landscape?" I found that each of the four famous gardens, still extant from the Moghul era (c. 1500–1750), stands out as having a power and beauty that rival its surrounds. Using the axiality and symmetry of the Islamic garden, the Moghul emperors and their powerful courtiers applied this ancient form, based upon enclosed desert oases, to the terraced foothills of the mountains, creating a powerful formal order that slices through the breathtaking beauty of this dreamlike valley.

The Villa Serbelloni garden in Bellagio sits high upon a promontory overlooking a breathtaking scene: a formal terraced garden that faces a field of cypress, cherry, and olive trees and beyond to Lake Como and the mountainous terrain of northern Italy.

Landform. Landform gives a basic unity to a garden. Just as the shape of the ground is the foundation of all landscape, so too is landform the basis of most of the great gardens of the world. The Italian garden evolved from the need to terrace down hillsides; the English park accentuated softly curving land with compositions of gentle hills crowned with monuments and temples; the Japanese garden is an abstracted and miniaturized version of the islands and mountains that form the backbone of that country.

What is it about the form of the land that makes us feel good? It forms the body of your garden; the enclosing arms, the breasts, the waist, the neck of your landscape. Take time to nestle in it, to stand atop it, to roll down it—to feel the power of the humps and hollows, the uplands and lowlands and the flats that form your land.

Your relationship with the slope of your land depends upon your vantage. A property can pitch in one of three ways: it can incline upwards from your point of view; slope downhill, away from your point of view; or remain flat. An uphill slope is a still life, a close-in landscape for reflection. A downhill slope is a vast landscape painting, one over which you have a wide panorama or—if the vista is not aesthetically pleasing—that you must block out.

The feeling you get from an uphill slope is an intimate one, where you study your land and its features close-up. Facing an uphill grade, you feel enclosed within a landscape, as if looking out from a cave. There are various ways to deal with this condition: you can make terraces that run in parallel lines up the hill; you can design an artistic composition of rocks and plantings that seem to fall down the slope to your vantage point; you can make a waterfall that forms the focal point of this intimate view; or run steps that meander up the hill to a higher vantage point above.

Designing a garden around a downhill slope may prove to be more difficult. Since your vantage point is out and over your land as it falls away from you, it feels promontory-like. Your choices depend in large part on whether you have a long

view out of your property to something wonderful beyond. If so, then incorporating the distant scene into your garden's landscape (a design technique called *shakkei,* or "borrowing the landscape") will serve you well. If you frame your view with tall trees and a hedge line, you will have abstracted the background landscape and have "borrowed" it by relating it to the foreground.

Without a distant view from the high vantage that you enjoy, a downhill slope makes gardening difficult because you have less visual and physical access to your land as it falls away down the hill. Designers through history have solved this problem in one of two ways. One is by terracing the downhill slope, making tiers or large steps that relate to the house above and give the owner some usable space in an otherwise unusable yard. The other solution is to plant your hillside as a field that your eye grazes over as it looks out and over your land. Both are aesthetically pleasing solutions and stop erosion on steep sites, but are lost to your viewpoint if your house is located above.

Flat sites allow you unlimited possibilities for design. You can lay out nearly any type of garden: intricate parterres, herb gardens, orchards, or grassy glades without any topographic distractions in your way. Ironically, though, you'll find that the flatter the site, the more the need for something that gives a vertical dimension to an otherwise horizontal stretch of earth, such as a wall, a hedge, or a set of softly undulating artificial hills.

The best time to study the topography of your site is in winter, when only the skeletons of plants distract from viewing the bones of your site. At this time of year, you can envision the big, sweeping moves that you want to make in your garden, the structural changes that will give it power and substance.

Geologic Formations. Geologic formations on your land can form the basis for your garden design. If you are lucky enough to own a rock, have a view of a butte, or live on a piece of the red desert, geology will dictate, in large part, the form of your garden. Your site's geology may not be evident if it is overlain by a thick layer of vegetation. In New England, where I live, many rocks break through the surface of the ground and are

When set firmly into the ground, a rock acts as a solid mass against which this cutleaf Japanese maple seems to dance. Nothing is more satisfying than placing rocks into a landscape. Set them so that they stand out as focal points, yet feel as if they have always been part of the garden.

You can tell a lot about conditions on your land—the quality of its soils, the amount of sunlight received, and its relative wetness or dryness—when you examine its existing plantings. These autumn leaves found along the Pacific Crest trail in Washington state tell us that the area is both moist and shady.

either part of a deep bedrock layer or leftover glacial debris from the Ice Age, in the form of drumlins and eskers. If you study the geology of your region, you may find some interesting information that could affect the design of your garden.

Our garden is oriented around a particular geologic feature: a fifteen-foot-high ledge that travels for forty feet along our property line before returning underground. The rock is a rose granite that is covered with lichens and has a large striation that runs diagonally between the tallest peak and its adjacent neighbor a few feet below. The effect is that of twin peaks, which we have emphasized by building a small rocky pool at their base. We have made a trickling rill by running water down the crack between the rocks, and have drilled a tiny hole below the peak of the lower rock through which water seeps as

though from a secret spring. Both are powered by a small recirculating pump. Our garden revolves around these rocks, for we use them both as focal point and backdrop, and enjoy the trickling sound of a "natural" waterfall in the process.

Soils. Soil is the medium by which gardeners grow plants. This pulverized mantle of the earth is formed from rock and vegetable remains, and by the action of weather and organisms. Your ability to excavate, drain, and support structures is dependent upon the type and structure of your soil.

Organic topsoil is essential for the living community. Of critical importance are its content of humus, its relative acidity, the presence of available nutrients, and its drainage capacity. Knowing the makeup of your soil and improving its deficiencies will produce the optimum growing medium for the plants that are best suited to your locale. Simple-to-use soil testing kits are available at most garden centers, or you can send samples to your local agricultural school or botanical society for testing.

Climate. We all must bow to our region's climate—that ocean of air that is constantly changing its temperature, humidity, precipitation, cloudiness, wind speed and direction, sun path, and purity. Yet, as gardeners, we must work with it, locating our garden elements in microclimates that best suit them.

Research has shown that people like to sit in the sun, and will move their chairs to follow it. This means that a terrace, patio, or balustrade should be placed so that the sun strikes it when people will most likely want to sit there. But it might also be good to have a terrace in dappled shade for the days when the temperature rises over 80°F, the upper edge of our comfort zone. Placing a tall deciduous tree to the south and west of your terrace will offer appropriate shade during the hottest times of the day in the summer months.

Most vegetables grow best in full sun. Locating the spot where your squash will get its requisite six hours of sun allows you to reap a successful harvest in your first year. Discovering where the favorable and unfavorable winds come from can also help determine where to screen or not to screen. Being aware of the times of day, during which season, and from what direction the sun is best avoided or invited is a helpful clue to properly locating the elements of your garden. Climate data for your region can be collected from the U. S. Weather Bureau or learned by keeping informal notes for the year before you make final plans for your garden.

Much of this you will learn by studying your property carefully throughout the year. To understand the way in which light strikes different parts of a garden, you need to evaluate it based upon your slope, degree of shading, and orientation to the sun in terms of season, latitude, and hour of the day—a complex equation. Easier than analysis is simply observing your site under different conditions for a full year. Keep a "sun diary," noting the amount of sunlight received in different parts of the site at different seasons and times of the day. Observe

your site at night, noting where the moon rises and sets, how moonlight is cast and where. Wake early and write down the conditions of your garden at dawn. Watch for special light qualities on your property and jot them down.

All this information will prove invaluable when it comes to creating your garden. You'll know the light conditions of all parts of your site and will find plants that fit their requirements. You'll know where you want to sit at what season of the year and at what time of the day. You'll know the magic moments of light in your garden. And, if you hire a professional designer to help you, you'll be able to share this information, ensuring that these conditions are understood and adhered to throughout the design process.

Vegetation. When I walk onto a client's site, the first thing I do is look at the existing vegetation for clues about soils, orientation, and hydrologic conditions. I can learn in a glance which plants do and don't seem healthy, and can begin to surmise the reasons for their success or failure. From all this information, I can make assumptions about which plants to use when I make a new garden in the space.

The surface of your land is a plantscape that can help indicate the conditions under which new plantings will grow. Different plant species live together in a habitat and thrive only under a particular set of climatic, soil, and water conditions. Oak and hickory trees, for instance, grow together on warm, dry land; red maple, hemlock, and willow like wet ground that is poorly drained. A natural stand of red cedar indicates poor soil, while spruce and fir thrive in cold, moist conditions. Pitch pine and scrub oak prefer dry land with excellent drainage.

As a designer, I take my clues from the land and try to work with the conditions that it offers. When I see a patch of trillium, for instance, I know that I am dealing with an area that enjoys dappled light, acid soil, and winter wind protection. Thus, I know that the conditions are right for a host of other wildflowers that thrive under similar conditions: bluebells, Solomon's seal, bloodroot, mayapple, and creeping dogwood. Assuming that my client is happy with such soft-hued, early-spring-blooming plants in this location, I have learned from the existing vegetation what image would work here—a shady wildflower garden, for instance—and could proceed with my design accordingly.

Sometimes, though, you will have to make drastic changes to the existing conditions of your site to uphold a particular image. If you want a bright perennial border and have no other open, sunny spots in which to make it, then I would have to cut down trees, improve the soil, and dig out new beds for these sun-loving flowering plants to grow in.

Often you have to remove previous owners' plantings before you can begin to plant your own. Their image does not match with yours: where they had maintained ball-shaped yew hedges, you may prefer a loose row of large-leafed rhododendron. But sometimes existing plantings work wonderfully with your own ideas for your site. On our street side, we own a stretch of high hemlock hedging that screens our side yard from view on a busy street. The story goes that a neighbor in the landscape business bought and planted our hedge and those of all our neighbors, for he wanted a soft wall that would offer uniformity to the streetscape and privacy to the individual property owners. We love this aspect of our site. Whatever we do within that hedge will enhance the effect that our farsighted neighbor wanted for us more than twenty years ago.

Structures. Unless you are constructing your garden on a previously unbuilt site, your property includes certain structures: your house or apartment building; outbuildings such as a garage, garden shed or tool house; and roads and paths. Knowing where these are located, how they are used, and what changes may be made to them in the future will help you know how to locate other elements of your garden.

Our garage, for example, is a small two-car structure built in the 1920s. My long-term dream is to make it my writing and design studio. This would mean that a driveway would not need to extend directly to it, freeing us to construct a stone courtyard that would link our back door with the new studio space. With this renovation, the garage would change from a forlorn structure perched at the edge of our property to a centerpiece of our landscape design—a pavilion surrounded on all sides by beautiful gardens. To its west would be the cobbled court that would capture the strong rays of the sun in summer evenings; to the north, the view of our waterfall; to the east, the sunrise and the big view to Boston with a picture window to frame it all; and to the south would be the vegetable garden and rose beds that I hope to build next year. Sometimes a small change in the use of a structure can make your whole plan come alive.

Note the location of your existing structures and think about their relationship with your garden space. Can you easily move from inside to outside, or are there major physical obstructions blocking your way? What about shadows that are cast by the structures onto your garden—what time of the day and what season of the year do they cause a problem? Does the driveway cause an interruption to the flow of garden spaces? Can it be redesigned? Look closely at each structure and think about its place and position within your garden.

SOURCES OF INSPIRATION

Now that you have found sources of inspiration in both your inward and outward sites, your work is not done. There may be mismatches between inward images and outward reality. Whether you can make an area to grow things, a place of refuge, and a geometric paradise full of bright colors and sweet scents depends in large part upon whether your hilly, north-facing, heavily treed, clay-soiled site can support these images. But don't despair—how often does outward reality perfectly match our inward dreams?

The qualities we long for and those we live with can only fit together when transformed, by design, into a new reality composed of both aspects. One way to marry the inward to the outward is to acquire more information and richer images about designing gardens. Our task now is to expand our vocabulary of resonant images by studying the basic building blocks of a garden—its primary elements.

This Colorado gardener is turning the constraints of his site—its rocks—to advantage as the foundation of his garden.

An ancient apple tree anchors a corner of the garden of the Occidental Arts and Ecology Center and frames its gardener as he pauses in his daily harvest.

Types of Builders

THINK ABOUT YOUR ATTITUDE TOWARD ALTERING your land to suit your inward garden ideals. Are you a preservationist, a workhand, or an artist?

The Preservationist.

If you are a preservationist, the very thought of pulling a weed repels you, cutting down a tree seems impossible, and bulldozing a site is out of the question. Land is sacred only in its unadulterated, unadorned state. Holding this extreme position, how then do you build a garden?

One way is to work with the elements you have, refining

or augmenting what you know and love. If your land has a stand of white pines, carefully control the growth of other trees to simplify the design and make an elegant, soft grove. If your site is full of fall asters and goldenrod, add more varieties of the same plants, some soft grasses, and some Joe Pye weed to boot. Also, you could build yourself a garden that melds with your regional landscape, such as a prairie garden in Illinois, a spring wildflower garden in New England, or a cactus garden in the Southwest. Or, you could simply place a rustic bench in a favorite corner of your yard, and use it often. Just because you are a preservationist doesn't mean that you can't create a garden.

The Workhand.

If you are a workhand, you love to change the elements on your site. You aren't afraid of hurting what exists, you remain undeterred by technical problems, and live for the moment when you get outside with your workboots on, ready to reconstruct the world. You love nothing better than earthmoving and getting down and dirty to push big chunks of soil around. Often you work without a plan, using whatever materials are at hand to build whatever comes into your head. This attitude does not always produce a harmonious design.

But it can produce hand-crafted, delightfully quirky forms on your property. We all have seen the results: walls built of colorful tiles, flowerbeds edged with beer bottles, teahouses of roots and sticks crafted with loving care and rough-hewn grace. Workhands get things done. They work their land until they get it right, then they work it some more. A somewhat re-served friend who owns a small city lot renovated her house herself, and built her own perimeter fence, a dovecote, grape arbor, terrace, and planting beds. When you walk through her front gate, you enter her personal, hand-crafted world, and take delight in knowing—through her deeds—a little more about who she really is. Workhands treat their site with commonsense delight, eager to get out and build.

The Artist.

If you are an artist, you approach your site without precepts or preconditions. Your idea is to allow the land to "speak" to you, to tell you what to place upon it and how to alter its character. A site is both the backdrop for your garden—the canvas—and the idea behind the conceptual ideal. What you end up doing to your garden is as unpredictable as you are.

You work easily with images and ideas and make big moves in your landscape for purely aesthetic reasons. You use plants for their form and shape rather than for their flowers, designing miniature mountains, topiary animals, or a sweep of perennials that paints a picture in your landscape. You hope others will understand your work. But if they don't, it won't bother you for long, because you are on to the next idea, or the next site.

Artist-builders will often try out an idea, reject it, and, in a split second, move on to a new concept, leaving the residue behind. With so many ideas flooding their heads, artists usually have ten projects going at once. Being mind gardeners, they leave most of these projects half-finished; they can just imagine how it will all turn out. An artist's yard, then, is more like an outdoor studio than a garden, a place to display the results of creativity.

Just as with gardener types, most of us are a combination of two or more of these types of builders on the land. I am both artist and preservationist. I have no trouble dreaming up what to do on our land, but I am loath to remove the smallest sapling in order to bring about my design. Luckily, my husband is both artist and workhand. He critiques my ideas and adds some of his own, but has no trouble clearing, bashing, or reordering features that I'm afraid to remove. He is never happier than when he's tearing out sumac, grading a slope, or excavating a terrace. We make a good team.

When you realize what type of builder you are, you will make design decisions that feel right to you; ones that reflect your level of participation in the building process and the degree of change that you can tolerate on your land.

The seven primary elements of a garden—the grove, hut, enclosure, threshold, meadow, mount, and spring—each derive directly from archetypal vantage points that we find in nature and the constructed world around us. A garden is really an ornamental form of nature.

Chapter IV

The Primary Elements of a Garden

A GARDEN IS AN ORNAMENTAL FORM of the natural landscape. Whether symmetrical or asymmetrical, tiny or huge, urban or rural, a garden is really a cleaned-up, organized version of the elements that we find every day in nature. Therefore, we can look to the natural landscape to provide us with a set of resonant images—the primary elements of garden design.

The feelings that we hold for our gardens' features may come directly from our feelings for nature. We remember the sensation of walking through a flowery meadow, swimming in a rocky pool, wandering in a deep forest. These experiences in nature become images that are felt through our bodies, our minds, and our souls. By recalling these images, we can better design our gardens.

Without such an image, you can't design a garden. To design is to transform—taking one place and making it into something else, into more than what it once was. To be able to transform something means that you must be able to see beyond the existing scenario to something quite new: to an image that appears in your mind's eye. It is in this leap from reality to imagination that the design process becomes magical, when the designer turns from methodical engineer to mystical artist. One secret to becoming a good designer is to acquire a

"Trees come close to our lives. They are rooted in our richest feelings and our sweetest memories," wrote Henry Van Dyke about broadleaf trees. Each of the burls along the trunk of this Cornish tree developed as a hard woody growth of a flattened hemispherical form. Burls are prized for the beauty of their graining and are used for furniture veneers; the growth makes this someone's cosmic tree.

wide-ranging and expanding repertoire of images that resonate both within yourself and in others.

This chapter looks at seven fundamental images of garden design—the grove, the hut, the realm, the threshold, the meadow, the mount, and the spring—and examines their historical, psychological, and aesthetic meaning for a landscape. Each different primary element is derived from one of the seven spatial archetypes that we discussed in chapter 2. Just as a garden is an ornamental version of a natural landscape, so too are the primary elements ornamental versions of the archetypes.

Keep your journal handy and record your reactions to these images and design ideas. My hope is that, having taken the building blocks apart and examined each one carefully, you will be better able to put them back together as a composition of resonant images that will reverberate in your mind as you design.

I. COSMIC TREES AND SACRED GROVES

A tree may be the single most basic element of a garden. The most prominent and long-lived of your plants, it determines the scale and growth conditions for all other vegetation in your backyard landscape, by acting both as canopy and backdrop. A single specimen tree can completely change the microclimate of your yard over a very short time. Nothing in the world of gardening requires more courage or foresight than planting a shade tree or a grovelike grouping of saplings that will long outlive you and even your offspring. How do you choose which species to plant? How do you know where to place it? Thinking about your feelings toward trees and the form they can take in the landscape may suggest how and where to place them in your garden.

COSMIC TREES

Trees provide a leafy canopy, acting as a ceiling over our gardens and the natural world around us. A towering tree by itself or in a group as bosk, grove, or forest suggests the extent of Mother Nature's influence upon the earth: linking the forces of the earth, through its root system, to the forces of the sky, through its canopy. Architecturally, a tree is like a column, a tensile structure that holds up the ceiling of branches that define the upper limits of our human-scaled world. Without trees, we are exposed without reprieve to the baking heat or icy cold emanating from the vault of the heavens above. With trees, we feel surrounded by and immersed in the "vasty deep" of bowers that bestow shade, coolness, and protection onto an otherwise wide-open world.

A specimen—an individual tree planted for its distinguishing ornamental or symbolic qualities—stands as a representative of other members of its kind. Besides the practical purposes of providing shade against harsh sunlight; a barrier to counter strong winds; beauty through branching structure, flowering habits, and bark textures; and nutrition through bearing of fruits and nuts, a specimen tree can become a touchstone for a higher spirit, ascending above and watching over our daily lives like a benevolent god. Think about a specimen as being a *cosmic tree,* a common mythical motif found in religions throughout the world. It symbolizes immortality: the trunk provides a means of ascent to heaven, or represents the symbolic central axis of the world. Anyone who has seen the two-thousand-year-old redwood trees in California's Muir Woods towering 350 feet in the air knows how very cosmic a tree can feel.

Many ancient cults believed that trees housed spirits. Shinto worshipers in Japan bound ancient trees with *shimenawa* (rice straw) to show that *kami* (gods) lived within. Ancient Egyptians believed that a tree represented the soul. For us more temporal beings, trees feel cosmic mostly because during our childhood they provided enchanted dreaming places. We climbed them, made forts under them, imagined flying from their topmost branches. Even as adults, many of us unconsciously seek out or plant a cosmic tree wherever we live, no matter what our age, grounding us to the earth while our imaginations soar.

A young man attending one of my lectures told me that he had lived in four houses in his life, and each one had a

Your choice of cosmic tree may change depending on the seasons. This ginkgo specimen stands out in the fall as its fan-shaped leaves turn bright yellow. Native to eastern China, Ginkgo biloba *stands as the sole representative of the genus* Ginkgo *and has been preserved as a temple tree, as it is very rare to find it in the wild. Above it towers the beautiful red pine,* Pinus densiflora, *another cosmic tree within this cultivated forest grove in Japan.*

sweetgum tree in its backyard. When he went out looking for a house recently, he bought it because it too had a sweetgum, down by the train tracks. He admitted that he climbs his favorite tree daily to watch the trains go by.

Write the names of the cosmic trees from your past. Can your favorite trees survive in your present climate? If so, is there a place to grow a specimen on your property? Next, record the location of all special trees that already grow on your property. Can you think of some way to set them off as special?

FORESTS AND GROVES

Forests offer another set of childhood memories and images. Whether we remember a bamboo grove, a rain-forest jungle, or a deciduous or conifer forest, most of us have strong associations with trees growing naturally in communities. Depending on climatic conditions, these tree groupings may be a collection of individuals of just one or a few species, as in temperate regions, or mixed with many other species of trees and shrubs, as in tropical rain forests. In our youthful fantasies, we envision a forest not as the scrubby wilderness it often is, but instead as a pristine, dewy, verdant grove. It is this vision that we bring to our grown-up gardenmaking: the metaphor of the sacred grove.

Think back to your favorite groves and the feelings that they evoked in you. My memories suggest a range of different places and emotions—the sunny glades in which I'd bask in the mixed-hardwood forest behind our Illinois house; the path I'd take in hushed reverence through the cathedral pine forest in Connecticut; the wild stomping of Austrian dancers at an evening *waldfest* (forest festival) set deep in the Steiermark woods; the cooling swish and clop of a bamboo grove in Kyoto; the protective mantle of snow settled heavily on the hemlock trees next to our present house. These feelings can be re-created in your garden with the judicious placement of just a few trees together as a grove.

A bamboo grove provides a strong, earthquake-proof webbing of roots underfoot, a verdant tent of cool leaves overhead, tasty bamboo shoots to eat, and strong culms that can be used for a myriad of practical and artistic purposes. Known as an invasive plant that is difficult to contain, bamboo is worth using for its elegant architectural form and for its leaves, which hold on through all four seasons, only to fall in the spring as the new growth pushes out.

A grove may be the oldest of garden features—found even in the times of primitive forest dwellers. Ancient Greeks used a grove to promote a meditative mood; the Platonists conducted sessions under the umbrella of a plantation of olive trees; the Aristotelians taught while walking through a formal planting of trees; Romans met for conversations in the Sacred Grove of Apollo on the Palatine.

Forests and groves are composed typically of three parts: a stand of trees that make up their expanse, paths that cut through them, and clearings—spaces or rooms cleared of wood and brush that let in light and air. Understanding the design of each element and its transformation from forest to garden grove allows us to know how and where to plant trees in our landscapes.

First, you must decide whether you want an effect that feels ordered or natural. Ordered versions include orchards and *boschi*—domesticated groves that were designed to fit the size constraints of a garden. For example, the eighteenth-century Villa Carlotta at Cadenabbia on Italy's Lake Como employs the device of a *bosco* of clipped ilex. This acts both as an evergreen screen from a heavily traveled road and as an intimate and mysterious path that leads to an azalea garden beyond. The French employed a similar device called a *bosquet*—an ornamental grove traversed by walkways of curvilinear patterns or geometric shapes. André Le Nôtre's vision for Versailles included a geometrized forest with clearings in which various ornamental and architectural surprises were placed. Trees from neighboring forests were transplanted by the thousands in formal patterns in keeping with Louis XIV's delight in maintaining control over nature. Within the *bosquet*, one found *salles de verdure* (green rooms) and *cabinets de verdure* (smaller subenclosures: "small green rooms"), each surrounded by clipped hedges. Other openings in the forest were bounded by trees and shaped into ellipses, circles, and star patterns. We too, if aiming for a formal effect, can plant our trees and shrubs in a grid pattern that enhances the architecture and clarifies the extent of the elements in our gardens. Mazes, parterres, and

A double hedge of hemlocks keeps the garden at Naumkeag in Stockbridge, Massachusetts, well separated from the adjacent drive. At the terminus of the grassy hill lies a circular glade of red Japanese maples that forms a stopping point for the eyes and a boundary for a path, flanked on the right by a Chinese-inspired pavilion.

This allée of live oak trees with azaleas planted at their feet forms an enticing entrance to a Mississippi plantation. English essayist William Hazlitt wrote, "Give me a clear blue sky over my head, and the green turf beneath my feet, a winding road before me, and a three hours' march to dinner—and then to thinking!"

80

formal garden rooms all require that you employ a strict geometrical organization when laying out your garden space.

Magic words describe places where light enters a natural forest. The word *glade* makes us think of a place where rays of light manage to penetrate through thick stands of trees to light up beds of moss or pools of fern—sylvan havens where small creatures live safely together. The word *clearing* conjures up a different image: a larger, more open, light-filled area of a forest where—as the great midwestern landscape architect Jens Jensen said—one can "clear the mind." If your land contains a small woodland or scrubby border, think about creating a glade or clearing within it, flanked by a bench and a small pool, or covered in haircap moss or soft grasses.

You can also use newly planted shrubs or trees to create an ornamental ring of trees as a place for reading or picnicking, as a fort for children, or as a focal point for the eye to rest upon. Mammoth redwood trees grow naturally in such round patterns, called "fairy circles." An ornamental rendition of this can be found in San Francisco's Izaak Walton Park. A cow lie—a ring of shade trees set at the crest of a hill to form a cool, grassy resting area for grazing animals in England—is another circular space created in a landscape and another idea for your garden. Such round garden rooms offer an unexpected contrast to other geometric forms, and stand out delightfully in an informal setting.

A forest path can be a trail as meandering and indistinct as a set of animal tracks or a lane as formal as an *allée* (alleyway). This French word describes a colonnade of trees lined up on either side of a path, a form derived perhaps from the wind-breaks found on open land throughout the world. Whether straight or serpentine, or planted as pollarded, clipped, or pleached trees, an allée resembles a long tunnel that opens out onto a long vista, a house, or a garden room. Leo Tolstoy tamed his forest landscape at Yasnaya Polyana by creating allées and *preshpekt*—avenues that link one place with another. Birch, linden, maple, hazelnut, honeysuckle, and shrub rose allées crisscross the thousand acres that make up his beloved ancestral home today. Although you may garden upon a mere quarter of an acre, you can plant in allées to give a formal, tunnel-like experience in your garden. Planting trees or bushes in regular formation along front entry walks and driveways can foreshadow the geometrical organization of the house and enhance the feeling of anticipation in getting there. I will discuss in more detail the design of pathways in the next chapter.

Ordering your property according to natural principles creates a looser, more irregular sensibility. The garden at Saiho-ji Temple in Kyoto, Japan, suggests an effect that seems both natural and pristine at the same time. Beneath a leafy canopy, a winding path of tamped earth circles a clay-bottomed pond and its rocky islands, all made soft by a floor of forty-four varieties of moss. Light dapples the shade of cryptomerias, Japanese maples, and a large stand of bamboo. Only trunks of trees are visible above the velvet ground cover, with no middle-story shrub layer to muddle one's impressions of this dewy four-acre sanctuary.

Another natural effect is achieved in a woodland garden, which is an attempt to re-create the mix of species that is normally found in the wild and is often designed with a winding stream and a meandering path, as would occur naturally in a forest. Usually carved into an already existing woodland, these gardens are enhanced by careful introduction of native and exotic species. A good example is found in Sir John's Wood at Knightshayes Court near Tiverton in Devon, England. With so much of our own country covered with forest, such woodland gardens are appropriate to sylvan regions and provide wonderful imagery from which to draw.

Even a few straggly trees or a scrubby tangle at the edge of your property can act as a grove such as I have described. With some thoughtful cleaning up, the addition of specimen trees, a meandering path, and a clearing—however small in scale—you can re-create the feeling of a forest in your own backyard.

WILDERNESS

Perhaps the most informal means of organizing a garden grove is to think of it as a "wilderness." In seventeenth- and eighteenth-century Europe, the term designated a wooded area with winding paths running through it. In reaction to the increasingly open gardens of the period, the wilderness supplied the sense of enclosure and mystery in which a garden visitor might undertake a spiritual sojourn and experience the thrill of being lost in a vast forest. Timothy Nourse recommended in his *Campania Foelix* (1700) that a wilderness should contain "up and down Little private Alleys or Walks of Beech . . . Let this . . . Wilderness be Natural-Artificial; that is, let all things be dispos'd with that cunning as to deceive us into a belief of a real Wilderness or Thicket, and yet to be furnished with all the Varieties of Nature." Even the formality of Versailles gave way to a sort of wilderness in the Grand Trianon's Jardin des Sources, a dense planting of fruit trees shading a series of irregularly shaped water channels running amid the grass.

I think of a garden wilderness as being an untamed area of a property, left in its natural state with paths cut through it. A favorite such place is at a cottage by a pond on Martha's Vineyard in Massachusetts—really nothing more than a thicket of scraggly scrub oaks that form a diminutive forest rising out of swaths of huckleberry and wild blueberry that ring a clearing at the back of the house. A little track winds through the stand to the salty blue expanse of water and sky beyond. Although composed by natural forces, this "garden" is one of the most beautiful places I have seen.

Another favorite wilderness garden is a large tract of land owned by a wealthy, bedridden woman. Although she can no longer walk out to see it, she keeps its trails and glades clear for others to enjoy. Somewhere deep in the middle of this woodland acreage, you come upon a mammoth clay pot—a Greek amphora—that seems to rise straight out of the ground. How it came to be there, its owner only knows—it seems a miracle.

A simple mown path beckons as it winds gracefully through this meadow garden in Cornwall, England. In springtime, the orchard is filled with a carpet of flowering bulbs, whose withering foliage is concealed by field grass.

II. The Hut

Is there anyone who doesn't long for a little hut perched far, far away from the madding crowd? The primitive hut is the cave of our gardens: the direct translation of the fort, the snuggery, or the nook of our childhood games. This little elemental home—an arbor, gazebo, pergola, or trellis structure—allows us to find a quiet shelter in our gardens, a place from which we view our landscape set as far out into nature as our property allows. We can garner new images for our garden architecture by thinking about the design of huts from around the world.

The primitive hut was the origin for most forms of building in the world. As architecture developed in many complex directions, garden architecture remained essentially hutlike in its features: minimal sheltering, diminutive size, and simple construction. Our desire for a hut in our garden may well suggest a longing to return to our roots, a hearkening back to an idealized, simpler past.

The earliest huts were built by nomadic tribes who needed a temporary shelter, lean-to, or portable home, or a set of informal houses as they traveled in search of food. A hut's design was dependent upon the physical characteristics of the places it occupied and the materials at hand. Think of the wide range of huts found around the world: the tepee, the kiva, the tent, the igloo, to name a few. All employed the simplest of materials: branches for Madagascan huts, trellising for the walls of Mongolian yurts, grass for Ethiopian huts, wood for Lapp log huts, skins for Bedouin tents, and of course hard-packed snow for the exterior of Inuit igloos. Our own huts might best be built of materials that are local, readily available, and simply hewn and adorned.

As nomads turned to agriculture, their wanderings ceased and they came to live in more permanent settlements and houses. Here, the primitive hut found its place inside the walls of a garden, occasionally designed as a miniature version of a large home, or built to carry a particular design feature of the house into the garden landscape. More often, though, a hut was

This viewing room at the Saiho-ji Temple looks out upon a verdant landscape of forty-four varieties of moss that carpet the banks of the Kokoro Pond. A roofed viewing platform, raised two feet above the ground, allows visitors a protected, promontory-like vantage over the garden.

This little hut is one of a series of way stations along the roji, *or "dewy path," that constitutes a tea garden. The teahouse itself is designed to shut out a direct view to the garden outside. Using* shoji *(rice-paper screens) and slatted openings in walls to allow muted light in, it bestows the proper contemplative mood for the taking of tea.*

set in a naturalistic place outside the formal garden realm to suggest a wilder, freer, more uncivilized area in which the owner could act without regard for societal norms and expectations. Marie Antoinette built her Hameau outside the formal gardens at Versailles for this purpose—a garden stage set that included a thatched farmhouse, cow shed, dairies, and kitchen garden, all built in a deliberately rustic and primitive style, a grandiose example of an idea that could be applied to our own smaller properties.

Three types of huts provide shelter, security, and vantage as we ponder our backyard landscapes: the house, the garden hut, and the bench. The house acts as a hut—albeit on a large scale—at the center of the garden. The garden hut often is placed at the edge of the garden realm. The bench is an un-roofed hut set out to take advantage of views.

THE HOUSE AS HUT

Although perhaps not immediately apparent, a house is a kind of well-built, sophisticated hut. Like the archetypal cave, both a house and a hut provide enclosure within and vantage without. Inside a house, certain rooms—with their special windows, eaves, cupolas, turrets, or porches—suggest the feeling of a hut or little house that sits in, on top of, or at the edge of the garden outside its walls.

Examine your own house from this perspective. Where are your favorite places to sit and gaze out? Where do you feel cozy yet engaged with the world outside? Where do you have both a corner and a view? In our house there are three such places. From the couch in our living room, we view the wildflower garden through a large leaded-glass window that enframes and divides the view into myriad facets. From our dining room, we look out upon a series of gateways through enclosures that step down a steep hillside. From our screened porch that sits out over the side yard, we feel surrounded by a forest of high oak trees while being cooled by summer breezes.

How a house is designed to open up to or close off from the landscape and its light is a matter of importance to a garden's design. Two hutlike structures built in traditional Japanese style—the *chado* (teahouse) and the *shoin* (temple building)—illustrate elegant solutions that relate garden to house in very different ways.

The *chado* was built to wall off its inhabitants from the outside world. Constructed of rustic materials in the *sukiya* style in the seventeenth century, teahouses were built to provide an intimate and tranquil setting for the serving of powdered green tea to a few select guests. There they would partake in a ritual devoted to the contemplation of aesthetic objects set upon an altarlike niche—the *tokonoma*—and to the discussion of art and philosophy. Participants entered these elegant but simple huts from a tea garden, stooping through a small wooden door that was slid shut upon entry, eliminating all view of the garden. Light entered these structures through *shoji* (rice-paper screens), allowing a muted, softened glow within the three-mat (6' x 9')

The moon-viewing window of this small waiting pavilion at the Saiho-ji Temple garden in Kyoto frames a view of the Kokoro Pond. Shoji slide into the wall on a wooden track, allowing a variety of viewing possibilities and lighting conditions within this little teahouse.

Tolstoy, a vegetarian, took most of his meals from the fresh fields, forests, gardens, and orchards of his three-thousand-acre estate near Tula, Russia. This porch, with its whimsical carvings and vines, was often filled with people, including Tolstoy's wife, eight children, and many visitors.

or four-and-one-half-mat (9' x 9') interiors.

The *shoin*—a post-and-beam temple building of the fifteenth century—was built to open up to the south, where an abstract garden was laid out for contemplation by resident monks. Wooden screens called *amado* could be opened up to allow a full view of these tennis-court-sized gardens. A roofed veranda, the *engawa,* created an airy and elevated viewing position, and provided a transition point between inside temple and outside garden space. With the onset of bad weather, the *amado* could be shut across the length of the structure; otherwise the *shoin* seemed like a large pavilion, perfectly scaled to match its adjoining garden space.

The artistry of these examples lies in the deliberate connection or disconnection of their architecture with the adjacent garden, a relationship as much psychological as physical. Opening up a wall with windows, door, or screens will pull a garden space into the room—an advantage in terms of light and viewpoint, as long as there is no visual disjunction between styles of house and garden. If outside and inside are very different—for instance, a traditional herb garden adjacent to a spare, modern room—then you may want to close down views to the outside.

Depending on climate, customs, and function, houses are built with varying degrees of closure. Modern glazing, insulation, and heating techniques give the contemporary designer greater freedom than ever before to choose the way a house relates to a garden—something to keep in mind throughout the design process.

Other traditions suggest a different way to approach your house as hut. The English cottage, for instance—with vines, roses, and perennials drenching its walls—derives its charm from the unity between building and garden. The planted vertical landscape that seems to cover all hint of structure reduces the prominence of the house and gives a softly overgrown, ruin-esque quality to the cottage garden and its setting.

Country-style gardens like my mother's suggest a still different technique to marry a house with its landscape. Artist that she is, she brings her farmhouse into her garden space and garden space into her farmhouse by "painting" both spaces with bright, cheerful colors that are repeated all around her property. Bright blue shutters are painted the same color as her many birdhouses, which link visually with the sapphire-hued catmint, delphinium, and Jacob's ladder in her herb garden. Collections of brightly painted signs, baskets filled with flowers, stained trellises, and topiary animals make ebullient what is otherwise a rather staid New Hampshire farmhouse. Relating inside to outside, with attention to light, closure, views, color, and details, can all enhance the hutlike feeling of your house as it sits in its garden setting.

GARDEN HUTS

Garden huts can take many forms. Pergolas, gateways, arbors, trellises, gazebos, and pavilions all suggest the primitive hut as modified for the modern garden. Knowing something about the origins of garden huts can suggest ideas for your own backyard structures.

The proliferation of stick-and-twig furniture, gateways, and pergolas may suggest a modern-day nostalgia for the primitive hut. Huts of boughs made typical bridal chambers in ancient Mesopotamia and among the Blackfoot Indians. In a traditional Jewish custom, young couples were married under a canopy of boughs, perhaps a more formal version of the trysting places in nature where the couple might first have found intimacy.

Trellising, too, is an ancient garden art, going back to Roman times. By the fourteenth and fifteenth centuries, "carpenter's work" in increasingly elaborate forms became a distinctive feature of gardens. According to Crescentiis, a writer of the day, "in the most suitable places, one must make trellis work and tunnels in the shape of houses, tents or pavilions." He suggested that even more ornate trellising be constructed in noblemen's gardens, recommending a "palace with rooms and towers made uniquely from trees, where the lord and his lady . . . may go in fine dry weather." He wrote that trees should be

An arbor is a series of lined-up gateways that create a frame for a distant view. Here, at Monticello, Thomas Jefferson's home near Charlottesville, Virginia, the simplest of black locust saplings are lashed together to hold bean plants, an effective garden hut that can be constructed in a weekend.

planted several years in advance where walls were to be, and trained and clipped to form roofs and walls. What a joy to see such structures built in our contemporary gardens!

Arbors were often constructed as shelters for looking out on the surrounding countryside. Some were small rectangular buildings placed at the corners of gardens, while others were ornate and permanent fixtures of the landscape. Montacute in Somerset, England, possessed such garden shelters. These arbors were seen as garden extensions of the principal building, linked to it and emphasizing the common architectural style of the whole, much as guardrooms and gatehouses do.

Other garden architecture was extremely elaborate. In 1581, a banqueting house was built at Whitehall, England, for the entertainment of the French ambassador. It was 322 feet in circumference, with a canvas roof like a tent or marquee painted to suggest clouds. Constructed of holly and ivy, it was decorated with hanging baskets filled with bay, rue, "and all manner of strange flowers garnished with spangles of gold." Such "huts" were less functional than fanciful—follies in the landscape. A more modern *jeu d'esprit* is the "Saracen's tent" built by landscape architect Fletcher Steele for the Allen residence in 1939. Evoking a festive Arabian tent in shape, but made out of a stiff mesh (the sort used for purses of the period), this hut is topped with metal flags and big enough for just an intimate two. Overlooking a formal wading pool, Steele's tent suggested faraway lands and seductive allurements in the middle of Buffalo, New York.

New kinds of garden architecture emerged in the eighteenth century, in the era of the great English landscape gardens. Hermitages—complete with monks and nuns, grottoes oozing with slime, and picturesque cottages housing shepherd families—were built at Stowe and Stourhead along a circuit walk that traversed a lake. An eighteenth-century French aristocrat, François Nicolas Henri Racine de Monville, created a *jardin anglo-chinois* at Chambourcy near Paris. Follies in an odd assortment of architectural styles—Classical, Oriental, Gothic, Egyptian—are strewn throughout its hundred acres, leading to Monville's strange four-story house—La Colonne Detruite—which indeed looks like a broken column. Jutting provocatively upward from its hilly perch, it acts as a vertical focal point, sending a visitor's line of sight—and thus, his or her spirits—soaring upward.

THE GARDEN BENCH

Most of us don't have the means to construct magnificent garden pavilions, gazebos, or ruined towers. We can, however, choose benches in place of huts—ones that match our garden's style while providing a place to rest. These may come in all kinds, shapes, and materials. Birch, twig, redwood, iron, wicker; English, Adirondack, Country Chippendale; porch swings, gliders, chaise longues; all are available to the hut-maker of today.

How and where do you best incorporate a bench into your garden? Consider two aspects carefully: the back against

A twig bench represents a rustic design for a garden seat, one that might be placed in a woodland setting or at the outermost edge of your property.

91

Each of us seeks out a corner of our yard for daydreaming. This roofed chaise longue at Naumkeag in the Berkshires acts like both cave and harbor as it sits upon a promontory-like stone terrace overlooking Stone Mountain in the distance.

which the bench rests, and the view onto which it faces.

Every bench, no matter how secure an area it sits within, feels more inviting if it backs up against an enclosed corner of the yard, or is nestled against a tree trunk, hedge, wall, or shrub that acts as a niche or harbor in the landscape. From this hutlike location, even without a strict roof overhead, you feel secure to gaze out over the chosen view that will capture your imagina-

tion and give the bench its purpose. I often construct a small terrace of flat fieldstone or cut stone upon which the bench can sit, as a foundation and clearly demarcated place within the landscape. To see a bench sitting firmly backed, clearly marked, and with a point of focus onto which it faces, is to long to occupy it: the sign of good design.

When a bench is placed close to a house or piece of

A do-it-yourselfer's dream arbor: off-the-shelf trellising is nailed to a simple wooden frame, on which hangs honeysuckle vine, a birdhouse, and a twig garden ornament.

A bench is like a hut only when it feels "backed up." Leaning against this cypress tree while relaxing on this classical stone bench, one gets a grand view down and across a formal garden to an olive grove and beyond to the two arms of Lake Como.

architecture, its design should relate to the design of its constructed neighbor. A white house looks best with a white bench in the dooryard; an Arts and Crafts structure might call for unpainted, pegged furniture both inside and out. But the farther away from the house you go, the less architecturally related the bench needs to be. Leo Tolstoy's favorite stopping place, located a good half-mile's walk from his white stucco house, was a simple birch-log bench set in a small clearing in a deep fir forest. Closer to his residence, he placed more formal park benches, painted green and set along the allées that related outbuildings to the family's house.

Then there is the matter of the purpose of the bench within the garden. Depending on the type of gardener, the bench is more focal point than viewing position. The mind gardener, in occupying the bench, makes it a vantage point—and from it, he or she understands the design of the whole space. Usually set at a dappled corner of perennial plantings, against a billowy-shrubbed border, or up against a massive tree trunk, the bench becomes the viewpoint from which one's eye takes in the whole space and its individual parts, moving from one focal point to another, all around the garden.

For the dirt gardener, the bench, holding containers spilling with blossoms, overhung with a trellis of clematis, or backed up by a short span of attractive fencing, is often the main focal point itself—the object around which the design of the whole garden is centered. It becomes a point of desire—a miniature planted place of repose within the larger garden realm.

A bench within a garden is like a garden within the world: a place that can satisfy our need for relaxation, for refuge, for introspection and intimacy, and for reckoning with nature. After a long day's rototilling, weeding, staking, pruning, or deadheading, for instance, there is nothing more rewarding than taking your ease upon a cozy seat, with long, cool drink in hand, and contemplating your labors from afar. What delight to talk through the day's events with a friend, a companion, or a small child seated close in the crook of your garden bench

surrounded by flowers you cultivated from seed. A bench in a garden is a place for the contemplative gardener, allowing us the time and space to reflect upon those moments of grace which restore us to our own best selves.

III. ENCLOSURES AND SACRED REALMS

Certain places hold a nearly spiritual importance in your everyday life. A particular restaurant, a booth in a certain bar, the family retreat, a beloved mountain peak, a summer campground, all hold significance beyond others of their sort: they are distinctly special in an otherwise mundane world. Viewed from an outsider's standpoint, your places may seem trifling and insignificant, but to you they hold a meaning that is hard to put into words. And when one of these places changes, closes down, is renovated, or is lost, something magic goes out of your life.

I call such places "sacred realms." They are sacred in that they are personally compelling, secure, and set apart—psychically and often physically—from the everyday "profane" world of normal life all around us. Like harbors, they are realms because they are enclosed places, domains, territories, or arenas that act as discreet, safe havens in our lives. We can count on them to make us feel secure and content within their walls.

Sacred realms feel like contemplative worlds—designed or natural—in which we can wander, sit, and muse without fear or stress. They are spaces where the secular world recedes for a moment and the celestial enters; places where we remember who we really are. A sacred realm may be big or small, one large area or a series of small ones linked to make one continuous setting. A sacred realm may be a sanctuary in a stressful city; or a tranquil section of a populated region; or even a whole country, as we remember back upon our experiences there. But the sacred realm that resides closest to home is our garden.

ENCLOSURES

As an ornamental version of nature, a garden often requires an enclosure to set it apart from its surrounds. So

Hedges can be used both as a unifying design element and a space separator. They are grown as small saplings, planted close together, and pruned to force new growth and to make the hedge mass uniform. Many kinds of plants can be used for hedging material, including flowering bushes such as shrub roses, forsythia, or lilacs, as well as broadleaf and needleleaf plants. Mixed hedges create an interesting effect; choose plants that have the same rate of growth and similar tolerance for shearing, and prune them as one large mass.

interlinked are gardens to their boundaries that, in many cultures, the word *garden* actually derives from the word for enclosure.

Niwa, the word for garden in Japanese, means "an enclosure purified for the worship of the gods." At the Shinto sanctuary called Ise Inner Shrine, one can view an original *niwa*—a sanctified gravel-spread area enclosed by a wooden wall and three fences. Here, every twenty years the entire shrine complex is renewed, rebuilt to essentially the same plan as was established in the seventh century. Two adjacent sites are used alternately in the rebuilding of the inner shrine. Only after the area of white stones is occupied by the new shrine buildings and the enclosures are erected is the renewed space considered sacred.

In Persia, as early as the sixth century B.C., a garden was considered to be intimately connected to its architecture, surrounded by it either in the form of a porch or portico attached to a palace or a pavilion, acting as a shelter from the intense summer heat. Thus, the Persians called their gardens *pairidaeza*—*pairi* meaning "around" and *daeza* meaning "wall": "walled garden." *Pairidaeza* were enclosed, private retreats from the noisy, dusty world outside their walls. These gardens formed inward-looking spaces considered the center of the family's world—*pairidaeza* on earth—and were used as places of pleasure. There, lovers enjoyed solitude, the despairing found solace, and the wealthy provided hospitality in an atmosphere of sensory delight: pavilions surrounded by orchards of fruit trees, the scent of fragrant flowers, and the sound of birds singing in the shade trees that, along with a fountain, cooled the air in the garden.

Hortus conclusus, a medieval garden term, means "enclosed garden"—a secret garden set within a larger garden space. In practice the *hortus conclusus* was often a rose garden with fountains, walks, and arbors, all surrounded by a hedge or wall.

Each of these enclosures—the *niwa, pairidaeza,* and *hortus conclusus*—were sacred realms marked by a boundary of various materials, sizes, and degrees of openness.

A garden's enclosure can take many forms. A forest can demarcate a field, a wall surround a compound, a fence define a yard, a hedge mark a garden room. Some enclosures can be twelve feet high, some merely a few inches—as low as a mowing strip to provide a clean edge to a garden bed. Some enclosures are impenetrable, made of mud-and-wattle, concrete, brick, or stone. Others are screens that allow you to view through to a distant landscape. And some enclosures act as backdrops to garden elements, while others are the elements themselves—such as a perennial border that acts both as a wall and a focal point in a garden space.

WALLS AND GARDEN ROOMS

Many Americans are notoriously afraid to enclose their yards. Perhaps it is our notion of the democratic front lawn that everyone in the neighborhood can see, and which suggests the owner's friendliness and accessibility to the outside world, that creates this fear. Many communities even have front-yard fence restrictions, ensuring that space remains essentially underutilized because of its openness to view. As space becomes a premium, population increases, and properties become smaller, the unenclosed front yard will soon go the way of more and more backyards in this country: it too will become enclosed.

People prefer enclosure for most activities. They enjoy using their yards privately, without being observed by neighbors, and they need enclosure to keep pets in and unwanted visitors out. When I suggest constructing an enclosure to people, their first reaction usually is, "But won't it make my yard seem smaller?" No, it won't. One of the delightful paradoxes of building enclosures is that the more you enclose, the bigger a space feels, and the more valuable every piece of that space becomes. Think of the difference between a tennis-court-sized space that is all lawn with scrubland at its perimeter, and two yew-hedged garden "rooms" next to each other that occupy the same amount of space. Because the garden rooms are defined by clear edges, they have eight clearly articulated walls instead of four undefined boundaries, eight distinct corners instead of four indistinct ones, and two central open

This beautiful see-through fence is composed of vertical frets of finely split bamboo that are bound with coconut palm roping. This type of bamboo fencing, used at the Yabunouchi School of Tea in Kyoto, is called teppo-gaki, *or "rifle-barrel" fencing. By providing both enclosure and visual access, such a fence makes different areas of a garden feel both separate and related.*

rectangles instead of one large, amorphous space. Indeed, the subdivisions can go on and on within the yew-hedged rooms: you could add boxwood edging, benches, a fountain, statues, and trees in one, and a box-hedged maze in the other, making two completely different spaces side by side. Simply by subdividing and enclosing one large space, your garden seems bigger, more diverse, and enticingly mysterious. You are unable to grasp the whole with one glance.

A fence is not an enclosure until it actually *en-closes* something; until it turns a corner in the landscape. The corner of a fence, after all, is the area to which people most often gravitate. I've placed sculptures, fountains, arbors, benches, and even a secret child's seat in corners—the more corners the better!

A fence is a critical part of the architecture of your property—that's why it costs so much to erect. When you construct one, make sure that it relates visually to your house, either in color, material, or particular details. Chances are, you've seen a ponderosa-style stockade fence in front of an ornate Victorian house. The two are visually jarring; a mixed metaphor. But the white picket fence bordering the front of a white colonial house feels neat and trim—the two seem to complete one another. If the picket turns into a white board fence along the side and backyard, that too feels appropriate. As we'll see in the next section, a fence screens in different ways, depending upon its use as a device for marking or for creating privacy.

SCREENS

You don't have to make garden rooms to incorporate subdivisions into your garden space. Screens—see-through fencing—can subdivide space and make it feel larger. The Japanese, with their tiny lots and intricate gardens, have known this for centuries. They employ two major types of fencing in their gardens: *shahei-gaki,* fencing to enclose and block views; and *sukashi-gaki,* fencing that you can see through and that subdivides space. The first may take the form of tall bamboo fencing of myriad delightful sizes and degrees of blockage. Of the hundred or so kinds of bamboo fences, some of the most popular derive from Zen temple enclosures: the *daitokuji* fence, the *ginkakuji* fence, the *ryoanji* fence, and others. Our own stockade and board fences are western forms of *shahei-gaki* fencing.

The second type—*sukashi-gaki*—is used for a different purpose. A psychological barrier as much as a physical one, this type of enclosure demarcates space as you see through or over it. Screening takes three forms. The first type is a tall fence that allows viewing but no movement through a space. These are often openwork enclosures made of lattice, woven bamboo, or thin boards. The second type is a low fence that you can see over but not walk through, such as a picket fence, a boxwood hedge, or a border of lavender. The third type of see-through enclosure is a screen that is attached to the house. This *sodegaki* ("sleeve fence") looks like the sleeve that hangs down from the body of a kimono and has a similar metaphorical purpose: to extend the architecture further out into the garden, and offer privacy from the casual viewer.

A hedge and fence come together to form the northeast corner of Katsura Imperial Villa in Kyoto, demonstrating how one plant material can be employed to make an enclosure. Here, living bamboo saplings are bent double and lashed together to form a perimeter boundary that defines the edge of a bamboo grove. A handsome cut bamboo fence is created from larger-diameter culms and twigs, stripped of their leaves and sewn together.

99

An elegant planting of astilbe, lilies, daylilies, purple meadow rue, and cleome shows the border as it defines the edge of a garden path.
Combining perennials so that they bloom together in an artful way, providing a continuous display of color throughout a season, is a high art.
A border, besides being a beautiful focal point, also acts as an enclosure in your garden.

BEDS AND BORDERS

Although we plant our shrub beds and perennial borders as colorful focal points of our gardens, they also serve as enclosures. More ornamental than a standard fence, the border acts as a space definer, just as a wall or a screen does. Usually placed as an eight- to twelve-foot-deep bed at the perimeter of a property, against a wall, or in front of a hedge, a perennial border is often a brightly colored ornamental enclosure that surrounds a lawn. Taller flowers—delphinium, summer-blooming phlox, iris—are placed in the back of the bed, and billow softly down to ground-hugging plants—forget-me-nots, primrose, sweet woodruff, and rock-cress—at the grassy edge.

When you think of a border as being an enclosure, it helps you to define how you want the border to look. Do you want to create a strict hedgelike planting or a billowing, curvaceous one? A symmetrical arrangement with tall plants in the middle and short plants to either side? Reds at the edges and hot pinks in the center? Do you want to limit your plants to white flowers or plant a carefully conceived floral carpet? And how far do you want the border to encroach into the garden space: strictly edged with a space of grass to set off the plantings, or, as in the case of many cottage gardens, an unending border that soon overruns the entire garden? Each answer comes from your own sense of taste and the needs of your design. Understanding that your border is both an enclosure and a decorative element in your landscape allows you to design it with greater clarity of intent.

EDGINGS

Not only are walls, screens, beds, and borders important to the design of a sacred realm, but so too are the smallest-scaled enclosures of all—the edgings. Edgings define the territory of a realm. They complete the statement, the line, the volume, that you are trying to achieve.

Imagine a cobble-edged perennial border with blossoms tumbling over it. The overall effect feels soft and romantic, but tailored. The clarity of the line of the bed sets off the billowing plantings. Now imagine the same perennial border without a defined edging—no clearly outlined difference between bed and walkway, border and grass. The effect in this case feels blurry, unkempt, imprecise.

Even a deep and carefully dug edge to a border allows us to enjoy the difference between what grows inside the margin and what grows outside of it. With attention to its edgings, we perceive the extent of a bed's boundaries and sense its relation to the total design.

Americans are gradually becoming more conscious of the need for enclosure, a concept prevalent in other, often older cultures, who for centuries have lived in close proximity to each other. The rapid urbanization of the past century has helped to change our attitude. We are seeking to enclose our sacred realms, thereby bestowing greater value upon the small spaces that we are lucky enough to possess and create as gardens.

Raised beds allow a neat-looking yet fertile ground for growing herbs and vegetables together in this Nova Scotia garden. The wooden edging enables you to lay a gravel path between beds; for a softer look, you could plant grass paths instead.

A threshold designed by English architect Edwin Lutyens forms a landing for pausing along this set of stone steps, as well as a gateway through which one enters a sunken walled perennial garden.

IV. ON THE THRESHOLD

We can't—and shouldn't—totally remove ourselves from the outside world, even in our gardens. All enclosures inevitably need to be penetrated—by gateways and thresholds. If the enclosure is a harbor in our lives, then the threshold is a promontory—the place between the sacred realm and the profane world, the gateway to your garden's soul.

I have long been fascinated by thresholds. As a little girl, on May Day I'd sneak up to my neighbors' doorsteps and leave baskets of freshly picked nosegays to celebrate the coming of spring. As a lovestruck adolescent, I'd walk by a certain front stoop, watching and waiting for my beloved to appear. As a young garden apprentice in Japan, I'd leave my shoes outside on a masonry sill, and ascend in stocking feet to the smooth coolness of my six-mat tatami room in the Zen Buddhist nunnery where I lived. Today, I arrange an array of relics around my front threshold: clay pots filled with flowers, concrete lions and rabbits, trelliswork with cascading wisteria vines, and a bronze Austrian bell—all to suggest the whimsy of the family within.

Whether we're journeying through gardens or through life, we cross thresholds: stopping places where we take stock of what has been, and what will become. To *thresh* in its earliest form meant to tread or trample. A threshold, then, is literally a piece of timber or stone below the bottom of a door that we tread over when we enter a space. *Threshold* has several figura-

The character of this brick path changes as it reaches this vine-laden stone gateway. The formality of the boxwood garden gives way to an informal wild garden, signaled by the threshold of gravel underfoot and the abrupt turn to the left through a tunnel-like planting of shrubs and trees.

tive meanings as well: an entrance or beginning, the border or limit of a region, and the starting point of any undertaking or journey. Thresholds are places poised in the present, the "nowness" between past and future. They are contemplative intervals, pauses that at the same time suggest boundary and passage. Like a promontory, the threshold suggests the edge condition between one realm and the next.

I think of a threshold as a two-dimensional line in space that marks the border between two different regions or realms: outside and inside, room and hall, house and garden, sacred and profane. The garden is, of course, the inner, the sacred, "the richer realm," as writer Alice Brown noted. Though often only an imaginary division, a threshold is traditionally crossed, stepped over, or traversed. Crossing a threshold uninvited is tantamount to trespassing; one of its purposes is to make clear the bounds of one's possessions, privacy, or personal space.

What does this have to do with gardens? Thresholds organize otherwise undifferentiated space, where one realm meets another: the primrose path and the hosta garden, the herb garden and the orchard, the fenced-in front garden and the street, the meadow and the forest. Thresholds allow us to make sense of the differences that separate the world of the garden from the world outside.

The entrance to India's Taj Mahal is a dramatic example. Outside its gatehouse and red sandstone walls lies the bustling urban sprawl of Agra, while inside can be found a raised marble reflecting pool in all its serenity. Crossing its threshold is like being lost in a desert and coming upon an oasis. At the entrance to this garden, you pause and gape unbelievingly at the riches within. Here you understand the gestalt of the space. You see that this place is not a mirage.

So, a threshold is a savoring place. Without it, we move unimpeded from one extreme to another, bumping up against experiential and spatial dissonances without cease. With it we have a point of graceful anticipation and delight, a spot in which to slow down and move onward with dignity rather than with haste.

Diagram the thresholds that you already have or want to build in your own garden. Three kinds of thresholds can be found in a garden setting: the gateway, the terrace, and the bridge.

THE GATEWAY

A gateway is the opening that entices you to enter a garden. It can sit at the edge of your property, beckoning you to step in, or within your garden, summoning you to discover whatever lies beyond. Going through a gateway—as constructed as a gatehouse or as accidental as a pair of trees—signals the beginning of a spatial adventure.

Adding a gateway at the entrance to your property or between one area and another adds clarity and character to your grounds. Depending on the design of the house and its place in the landscape, the gate may be rustic or formal, two- or three-dimensional, imposing or unassuming. A gateway can be a portal, designed as a small outdoor room with benches facing one another. Roses or wisteria, hydrangea or clematis vines might climb over its frame. Pots spilling with flowers might grace its path, and its threshold might be elevated slightly to gain a better view of the garden within. From this vantage, you see the house enshrined through the gateposts and take a moment to consider its details. If you're a guest, you can adjust your hat, put on lipstick, or think of your greeting; if you're the owner, you can ponder and admire the world you have created.

From a gateway, a visitor gets a first glimpse of your character as portrayed by your house and front garden. Go out to the front yard and look dispassionately at it. What description are you giving to your friends, the mail carrier, new acquaintances? Ask yourself: Who do I want to be to the world outside? How should I portray myself? Am I a house covered up with overgrown yews? Am I a cottage set in a wild tangle of flowers? A castle set high on a hill? At what point do I reveal this? Slowly and meanderingly? In one fell swoop? Through design, you have the opportunity to display and control this information.

A threshold stone provides a subtle stopping place at a gateway in this tea garden in Kyoto. The nobedan (plank stone) acts as a ramp where visitors can look up as they approach the waiting pavilion in the background.

Jacques Majorelle, son of painter Louis Majorelle, built this sapphire-blue villa in his Jardin Majorelle in Marrakesh, Morocco. The terrace is both promontory and threshold, perching out over a reflecting pool and water channels. Adjacent to it curves an agave, its color and shape an appropriate planting display against such a dramatic piece of architecture.

THE TERRACE

The terrace is a viewing platform: a patio, porch, or deck that acts as a promontory and threshold in your backyard landscape. As a pausing place between inside and outside, a terrace is a pool of space that is both part of the house and part of its landscape, straddling both. It can act as an extra-large threshold or, with a prospect, can become a place to view your formal garden, swimming pool, or distant prospect.

One form of a terrace is the doorstep—a small threshold that moves you from house to landscape and back again. When attached to the house, the doorstep can be a small outdoor room, such as a porch, portal, porte cochere, anteroom, foyer, portico, or vestibule. The doorstep holds the potential for bringing aspects of both house and garden into play. A cottage gardener might grow pillar roses or trumpet or honeysuckle vines up and over the front door, stuffing plants at the base of the front steps and setting them in pots, both inside and outside the door.

Sometimes a terrace can be a tiny threshold that is a momentary pause, rather than a roomlike interval of space. In a Japanese tea garden, for instance, stepping-stones—foot-size flat rocks that keep your shoes from getting muddy—form the path. Every once in a while, in a seemingly random pattern, a larger stone interrupts the path's flow. Here you can place two feet, pause, and look up. This pausing stone within the garden space becomes a subtle viewing position, a place to let you know where you're going next on the journey to the teahouse. Further along the path, you might cross a piece of curbing near the teahouse that forms a sill over which the stepping-stones are set, signaling the realm of the artificial over the natural. This kind of threshold divides a small space into increments, and thereby distends it, making it feel much larger.

You don't need to make a Japanese garden to use this idea in your backyard landscape. You can locate pausing places constructed of cobbles, bricks, stone, or wood where your visitors can merely stop to enjoy a view or where they can sit down on a terrace just large enough for one bench, or a small

This terrace acts like a dock floating upon a grassy sea: sitting on it, one feels anchored to the house, while enjoying a distant view.

A log, a board, or a short plank of granite is all you need to create a bridge that spans two shores across a little garden stream. Like a tunnel, a bridge is a perpetual threshold that keeps the stroller poised between one place and another.

table and chairs, a sitting rock, or a hammock. You can design stone balustrades that seem to project out over a bluff, or raised wooden platforms that float over a field, or pine-needle niches that soften a path. In small but important ways, these surprise thresholds increase your enjoyment of your landscape creation.

THE BRIDGE

A bridge is an extended pause between one realm and the next. This perpetual threshold feels like a space and time in itself; a passageway of drawn-out, heightened emotions. When strolling across Claude Monet's Japanese bridge at Giverny, for instance, you wish never to reach the opposite shore, so delightful is the feeling of being suspended over his famous water-lily pond. On a catwalk or in a tunnel, a long corridor or colonnade, you feel caught in a similar state of suspended animation—moving along endlessly until you "see the light at the end of the tunnel," and enter a different realm.

A Japanese tea garden employs a long cut-granite stone called a *nobedan* as a bridgelike threshold. This planklike slab enables you to change your gait from stepping carefully from stone to stone, to striding boldly across the garden. Often set parallel to a nearby building or placed diagonally across the mossy ground, the *nobedan*'s size and shape allows you to raise your eyes from the path for a while as you walk along its planed-stone surface, and to take in the space around you. As with other corridorlike spaces in a garden, this one links one area to another, yet provides its own particular spatial experience along the way.

INVISIBLE THRESHOLDS

Sometimes a well-marked threshold is undesirable. An invisible threshold allows a place to remain secret, existing side by side with the known world, but hidden from outside view. The walled garden described in Frances Hodgson Burnett's *The Secret Garden* illustrates this point. A lonely child discovers an ancient door secreted in a vine-covered wall. Within lies a neglected secret garden, separated from the adult world by a

thin veneer of brick but representing a world of play, good health, and friendship. No grand threshold this, but only a doorframe and high walls, making a special world for a lonely child to plant and play within.

Even the barest of thresholds can suggest the median between one extreme of emotion and another. Urban planner Kevin Lynch found that "many people, if asked to describe the ideal house of their fantasy, will sketch one from whose front door one steps onto a lively urban promenade, while at the rear there is only silent countryside." If a single door divides excitement and serenity, he says, the pleasures are sharpened on either side by the thought of what lies beyond. Imagine such disparate images in your garden; imagine the significance of its thresholds! In the end, it is from your own gateway, terrace, or bridge that the soul of your garden becomes most apparent.

An invisible threshold.

V. The Meadow

I recently asked an outdoorsman to describe his favorite landscape. Without hesitation he replied that once, when hiking high in the Sierra Nevadas, he came upon a glacial lake that had filled in with silt. Over time, this lake had turned into a meadow filled with wildflowers in shades of blue, pink, white, and yellow. His reaction? To throw himself headlong into the middle of this upland field and lie surrounded by blossoms, scents, and the blue sky overhead. Holding the image of a meadow in our minds helps us as we design the floor of our backyard landscapes. Related to the archetypal island, this fifth primary element forms the pool of space that surrounds us when occupying the center of a broad expanse—when we feel as though we are a floating island upon the world.

Think of all the meadows you have loved. An expanse of prairie grasses mixed with Queen Anne's lace and black-eyed Susans forming wave patterns in the wind . . . a clipped lawn strewn with miniature white daisies . . . a bed of dewy moss. Have you ever experienced a bank of spring-green ferns just opening in a forest glen or an expanse of desert in full bloom after a rainstorm? Among our favorite places are those where a soft, verdant ground cover blankets an open landscape: a field, a glade, or a light-filled garden room.

A meadow plays an important role in our backyard gardens, providing a horizontal area that, like water, can offer a calm, still background for adjacent plantings or become a dynamic, vibrant visual element of its own. A simple example is the difference between using wall-to-wall and Oriental carpeting in your living room. A wall-to-wall carpet, if not designed with a strong color or pattern, will tend to act as a muted background against which other elements—furniture, pictures, and detailing—stand out. An Oriental carpet, with its rich colors and patterns, is a feature as important as the couch, the piano, or the fireplace. Your garden's meadow can be a soft, uniform background or a varied visual field that adds a pattern all of its own.

Where do you want to be when you find yourself in a meadow? We tend to seek out the center of such a field, where we picnic, tryst, or contemplate the heavens. In the middle of a lawn, we set out a chaise longue, a hammock, or a little terrace for tea table and chairs, each placed as floating islands on a sea of grass. We put focal points in the center of a space—statues, specimen trees, or obelisks—each, perhaps, a surrogate for the self in a meadow.

Think of all the expanses of open space in your backyard. Some of these may be planted in lawn, others seeded in field grass; some covered in gravel or asphalt, while others are left undeveloped as tangled undergrowth. Now imagine planting each space differently, as a kind of meadow, making the ground plane flowery, feathery, velvety, plushy, silky, verdant, or downy; qualities that are gentle on the eye as well as to the touch.

Following are three different images of meadows that we can use to help design the horizontal stretches of our gardens. The flowery mead, the greensward, and the dell each feel like a different kind of growing carpet in the landscapes that we create.

The Flowery Mead

A meadow that is interplanted with flowers may be called a "flowery mead." An old-English term for a meadow, its earliest known reference occurs in the *Decameron,* written in the mid-thirteen hundreds by Giovanni Boccaccio. He wrote of a meadow dubbed the "Valley of the Ladies," and called it a secret "flowery mede." The meadow sits in a perfectly circular valley surrounded by hills of similar size, which "are regular series of terraces . . . like the tiers of an amphitheatre." Beneath some trees on the plain lies a "continuous lawn of tiny blades of grass interspersed with flowers, many of them purple in colour." A later passage describes a woman in the middle of the garden, which is "dotted all over with possibly a thousand different kinds of gaily-coloured flowers" and in the center of the lawn, "a fountain of pure white marble, covered with marvellous bas-reliefs." This image describes a classic flowery mead, enclosed by walls and featuring flower beds and expanses of grass.

This meadow of Flanders Field Poppy (Papaver rhoeas) at the Hog's Back in Guildford, England, shows the delight of the flowery mead. Some of us prefer such a uniformly colorful effect in our gardens; others like a wildly varied tangle.

Daffodils are easy-care perennials that can be planted in groups of ten or more for best effect.

Persian gardens also employed flowery meadows as a design element, although to somewhat different effect. Created as strict quadripartite compositions with walls, these gardens featured flowering plants scattered so that the visitor could enjoy the individual characteristics of each species and wander through intermixed colors, textures, scents, and heights. As symbols of paradise, each flower had an image and a meaning: the narcissus was the likeness of man's spiritual eye, which has not yet been fully developed; the rose was the most perfect manifestation of divine beauty and majesty on earth. According to the Persian poet Ghalib, "The eye of the narcissus was given the power of seeing to look at the rose and the grass."

Persian and Moghul floral carpets brought the pleasures of summer into the house throughout the year by featuring meads within a formal courtyard setting full of brightly colored flowers, carefully rendered in wool. Moghul rugs display a bounty of flowers, including hollyhock, wallflowers, cyclamen, and larkspur among their Oriental planes, date palms, mulberries, and cypress trees, each an important poetic image for its knowledgeable owner.

Today's flowery meads can also be found in the formal perennial beds that replace the lawn in many European gardens, or in the more informal drifts of naturalized daffodils, snowdrops, crocuses, and other early bulbs that bloom in the first weeks of spring. A meadowlike effect can be sustained in a large or small space by interplanting wildflowers—such as the invasive loosestrife, wild geraniums, iris, sweet peas, wild rose, and poppies—among the early-blooming bulbs and grasses. After a few seasons, daisies, black-eyed Susan, Queen Anne's lace, and chicory weed will appear on their own. If you mow the meadow infrequently, as little as once or twice a summer, you will preserve this wildflower effect. Birds, butterflies, bees, and many forms of wildlife will soon be attracted to your own very flowery mead.

Constructing parterres of ornate patterns or formal floral displays on the ground plane is another way to create a flowery mead in your own backyard. Often made of bands of low

You can use different species of grass to define the different areas of your garden. Carefully tended turf at Knightshayes Court in Tiverton, England, gives way to field grass in the distance. Where the two meet sits a "haha," a sunken fence that keeps grazing sheep from straying.

hedge such as boxwood grown next to turf, colored gravel, or flowers, parterres were studies in designing the garden floor with strict geometric patterns. These became most popular during the seventeenth century in France, where *parterres debroderie* ("embroidered parterres") were grown. *Parterres à l'anglaise,* done "in the English manner," were often of plain grass with a statue in the center. A flower garden usually placed in the area adjoining the house, a parterre acts like a miniature maze and mead in one, designed for the delight of the mind's eye.

GREENSWARDS

Greensward is another word for lawn, an English term for an expanse of grass in parks and large gardens. It suggests a more ornamental image of the meadow, pasture, or field that we try to capture when we seed our backyards with this verdant groundcover, as we spend countless hours and dollars weeding and grooming our lawn to perfection.

Why is grass so important to us? Studies done by ecologist Dr. John H. Falk suggest that humans display an innate preference for grass. He surmises that our love for grass originated with our earliest savanna-dwelling ancestors, the hunters and gatherers whose habitat was the grasslands of East Africa.

Albertus Magnus (c. 1200–1280) may have provided the earliest known instructions for making a grassy lawn in *De vegetabilibus,* written around 1260. "Nothing refreshes the sight so much as fine short grass. One must clear the space destined for a pleasure garden of all roots . . . The ground must then be covered with turves cut from good [meadow] grass, and beaten down with wooden mallets, and stamped down well with the feet until they are hardly able to be seen. Then little by little the grass pushes through like fine hair, and covers the surface like a fine cloth."

Medieval gardens featured turf seats—raised banks for sitting that were covered in grass. These soft, albeit damp, perches were placed at the side of a grassy lawn, around a tree, or along a wall. Albertus Magnus discusses this feature:

"Between the beds and the grass a raised turf section must be set up, filled with delightful flowers, and nearly in the centre, suitable for sitting on, where the senses may be refreshed and where one may rest with pleasure." Turf seats would be held up with boards, like raised flower beds, or with woven wattle or bricks. Contemporary illustrations portray seats with flowers— chamomile, strawberries, violets, daisies—growing in the grass. Herbs, vegetables, flowers, and especially roses were also grown nearby in raised beds.

Dartington Hall in Devon, England, goes one step beyond the seat—to turf "bleachers," deep enough for picnicking on, that spill down a steep hillside to what is said to be a jousting court at its base. Bowling greens were also popular in English gardens, especially in the late nineteenth century, where perfectly groomed rectangles of grass were grown in most estates of the day. Parks of every culture were dependent on grass as a tough and resilient ground cover for strolling,

English daisies (Bellis perennis) *self-seed in a lawn.*

This ornamental dell at Allerton Park, Illinois, is composed of two plant materials: "Naked Ladies" (Lycoris squamigera)—a hardy bulb that blooms in mid-summer—which grows out of a bed of pachysandra, an evergreen ground cover that welcomes shade.

116

playing games upon, and even, occasionally, sheep-grazing.

Be creative when you think about using lawn in your garden. You can use different varieties and lengths of grass to define spaces and make paths. You can lay out a perfectly circular lawn that can be felt as a "pool" of space, surrounded by perennial beds, shrubs, or forest. In your grass you can sow seeds of clover, a plant that attracts bees but stays green when drought browns out other grasses. And you can allow your front yard, normally the domain of the lawn, to become wild, in the form of a grass or wildflower meadow. You may also wish to bring ornamental sedges, grasses, and reeds into your garden beds, joining the millions of other gardeners in growing these striking plants in billowing masses, reminding us of childhood wheat fields, or salt marshes, or our ancestors' savannas and veldts.

DELLS

A dell may be defined as a small, secluded hollow or valley usually covered with trees, turf, or ground cover, often of a single species. The image of a place of aesthetic unity is appealing: of extended beds of grasses or moss, ivy or vinca, ferns or foamflower. Bluebells paint the forest floor in spring, just as the new leaves break forth. Heather gardens, with their patchwork textures of tiny leaves, diminutive flowers, and billowing mounds, act as soft hills and valleys in the landscape. Stands of spring-green ferns such as maidenhair, its fronds forming arcs on fine black stems, seem to moisten and brighten the forest floor beneath a high canopy of leafy green. Others, like the royal fern, prefer their feet wet in a boggy place. Even water lilies or lotus floating on a pond are a kind of dell, growing in a dense mat in shallow ponds with little current. What planting you place to create a dell will depend in large part on the particular ecosystem in evidence there: if you have a dry spot with full sun, you could plant a dell of anemones, alyssum, daylilies, asters, or thyme; if you have a constantly wet area in semi-shady conditions, then you could plant a dell of myrtle, trillium, primroses, liriope, or hosta; if it is moist but in

deep shade, then you could plant a dell of baneberry, bunchberry, hepatica, hosta, or many varieties of ferns.

To design your meadow, you need to know the conditions of your site, but you also must decide whether you prefer unity or variety. Choosing unity—allowing one species of plant to sweep through a singular large open space—will give your garden the simplicity you may hope to achieve. Choosing variety—intermixing species in a lovely tangle throughout your open space—will provide liveliness and interest throughout the growing season. Each type of meadow acts as a pool of space in your garden, handled as a calm, still background or a vibrantly patterned landscape carpet.

VI. SACRED MOUNTS

Like many people, I am drawn to high places. I long to sit in peace atop a tower or pagoda, a balcony or a mountain peak, rejoicing in this realm far above the world. "Being is experienced essentially as verticality," according to perceptual psychologist Rudolf Arnheim. Spatial orientation is perceived through our relation to the vertical. In other words, our vision takes to the upright, both in the physical plane and in our mind's eye. There are two ways to experience a sacred mount: to journey up it or to occupy it in one's mind.

Nearly every culture has acknowledged the holiness of height. Primitive people made marks on their landscape by raising artificial hills or rearranging stones, as at the Seven Barrows in Wiltshire, England. Mesopotamians built the ziggurat as a holy mountain, a home for the gods, and as an observatory to study astronomy. Borobudur, a Buddhist shrine in Java composed in mandala form, represents the spiritual journey from birth through death and upward to the realm of the void, beyond thought or form. The Mississippian tribe produced a hundred-foot-high sacred mound for ceremonial burial rites at Cahokia, Illinois, achieving a sense of the eternal through abstract geometry and exaggerated scale.

Smaller-scaled mounts were a popular feature of medieval gardens. Called "toot-hills" in England, mounts were lookouts

You can find the highest point in your backyard and enhance it, or create a mount for yourself that is up a bit from your garden. From this arched earthen bridge at Katsura Rikyu Imperial Villa in Kyoto, you can orient yourself in the garden, looking back on where you came from and ahead to where you intend to go.

for observing the approaches to a property. The Elizabethans built banquet halls on the tops of hills to get the free flow of air and to dispel evil "humours." Such places provided a stand for watching stag-hunting, horse racing, or hawking in progress. Round or square in plan, few mounts survive in England today except in the gardens of Oxford and Cambridge colleges.

The idea of enjoying a view outward from a garden didn't take hold until the late Renaissance. Plans of the Villa Medici from the late seventeenth century show a round mount encircled by tall trees and approached through a densely planted forest. Describing the ascent, thickly shaded with ilex and leading to a small pavilion, historian Christopher Thacker wrote, "While climbing the steps, the visitor is prevented from seeing far to left or right, and so the spectacular view at the top, out over the city of Rome, is all the more enjoyable . . . In the whole world of gardens, I know of no more beautiful 'surprise.' "

You don't need to reach for the skies so grandly, though, to produce a heavenly effect; the English created other, slightly more modest examples of vertical landscape design. In 1629, at Cobham Hall in Kent, John Parkinson wrote of a large lime tree whose branches had been trained to form three arbors, one above the other, joined by a staircase and floorboards on each level. This was, Parkinson concluded, "the goodliest spectacle mine eyes ever beheld for one tree to carry." Today, one such elaborate tree house survives at the seventeenth-century Pitchford Hall in Shropshire.

The Chinese also understood the place of the vertical in the predominantly horizontal world of their gardens, collecting shi-feng rocks for the construction of artificial "mountains" or placing solitary stones of odd shapes alone in special pavilions or on marble plinths. The Japanese prefer less unwieldy objects, placing their granites and schists in groupings of three, five, or seven. The tallest rock in a Japanese garden often symbolizes Mount Meru, long considered by Buddhists to be the mythical center of the universe.

These design traditions continue today, though perhaps

Coming upon these standing stones in a forest garden in Northeast Harbor, Maine, you feel as though they are miniature mountains, set tall for your mind to climb. Natural stones should be set to suggest that they have always been there.

with less obvious intent. We unconsciously organize space, as the ancients did, by placing either ourselves or other objects in it to gain access to the sacred power of the high place, the vertical point in the landscape. Whenever possible, we situate our homes on the heights, creating cupolas, widow's walks, and turrets for the best possible vantage on the world. We festoon our gardens with tree houses, pergolas, lookouts, overlooks, and decks, adorning them with sculptures, fountains, topiaries, stone lanterns, vertical rocks, and obelisks to rivet our attention, sending our gaze heavenward. In my backyard, for instance, a huge boulder acts as a climbing place for children, a focal point for plantings, and an overlook onto the grounds and landscape beyond.

What if you lack such a high vantage? A clever professor of mine, without the money to buy a waterfront lot on Martha's Vineyard, nevertheless desired the view. So, with the help of his family, he erected a wooden tower that peeks out over the scrub oaks and black pines of his inland site, with room for an intimate three at the top. Another gardener friend created an artificial hill on her flat Illinois landscape and designed a snaky path to its summit, where she erected a Chinese pavilion to sit under, her reward for a hard day's work.

Your property undoubtedly offers its own opportunities to garner the power of the sacred mount. What important vertical features exist at present? Where could you imagine placing a vertical element to help organize your landscape? Whether a view of distant mountains, a lookout over trees, or a singular vertical object, a high place liberates us from corporeal limitations, the gravity of the earth, and our quotidian lives. It is from such pinnacles that we are able to discover within ourselves the potential for enlightenment, to gain a clear and unobstructed view of the world.

This stone precipice at Naumkeag, really a group of large boulders carefully composed to look like one magnificent rock, may have been created as a viewing position for Berkshire sunsets.

121

Water will always take the form of its container, as it does in this simple pool at the Bloedel Reserve Garden on Bainbridge Island in Washington state. As a mirror for the sky above, it provides a fascinating point of contemplation, no matter how still or turbulent it might be. A stand of sheltering cedar trees encloses the site.

VII. Water Rites

Water is the essential element of life, the most common and most powerful substance on earth, carving mountains into canyons and wearing stone to sand. It covers 71 percent of the earth's surface, filling rivers, lakes, ponds, and the air we breathe. As embryos, we are composed almost entirely of water; by old age, the proportion is still 65 percent. "Water precedes all forms and upholds all creation," says theologian Mircea Eliade. "Every contact with water implies regeneration."

The spring is to the garden what the sky is to the landscape: an azure expanse of constant but ever-changing energy and light. Both are composed of water molecules that reflect light from the sun, creating shimmering illuminations that deflect in response to the movement of wind as cloud formations above and wave patterns below. Sitting on a west-facing beach at sunset, you can directly experience the transcendent power of these two sources of energy and light: the rays of the sun double as reflections in the sea, while every organic thing recedes to flatness as silhouette. Other parts of the landscape seem static and rooted to the earth next to the dynamic splendor of the sky and the spring. And just as the sky is the source of water that falls upon the earth in the form of precipitation, so the spring is the source of water running within the earth in the form of underground streams and aquifers. Just as the sky contains all the elements of the spring, so the spring reflects all the elements of the sky: the smallest puddle can contain the heavens.

Through history, many cults and rites were connected with springs, streams, and rivers. Particular watercourses were thought to house a sacred presence. Springs—especially hot or salt springs—emanated mysteriously from the subterranean streams that run beneath the earth and allowed a continuous flow of potable water to regions without sufficient supply. Spirits with divine or prophetic powers—oracles, nymphs, and gods—were thought to reside in or near springs. Sanctuaries, churches, temples, enclosures, and altars were built beside them and sacrifices and "ordeals" performed as rites to them, suggesting our ancestors' ambivalent feelings of fear and attraction to water.

It is hardly surprising that water has long been a central element of landscape design, from the earliest gardens in the irrigated Mesopotamian valley to the water walls in the pocket parks of contemporary cities. Today, we excavate pools and ponds, lining them with clay, butyl rubber, or concrete. We divert streams, construct waterfalls, and install fountains. All are designs that depend as much on water's physical properties as on your individual taste. The latter is, of course, specific to every gardener. Let us here explore some of the former.

—*Water refrains from taking a form of its own but instead fills out any offered to it.* We experience water's essential forms in two very different ways: as a contained element (a pool) and as a flowing element (a channel).

Water provides an ever-changing natural focus in a garden. It also acts as both humidifier and noise filter, especially in pocket parks such as the elegant Paley Park in Manhattan.

The Water Runnel, created as a link between upper and lower fountains at Naumkeag, shows how a walking path and a water channel can take the same form.

Shalimar Bagh, the "Abode of Love," is a Moghul garden set high in the foothills of the Kashmir Himalayas. A central watercourse fed by mountain streams falls down the terraced mountainside, forming the garden's aesthetically pleasing structure through alternating turbulence and stillness, slowing to a near eddy in Shalimar's wide pools and accelerating to a rush in its narrower channels. Thrones placed just over, far above, or directly on the water evoke the contemplative state that was surely the architect's intention. In creating our own gardens, we must always remember that water will only go where, in what form, and at what speed we tell it to.

—*Water reflects when still.* We feel invited to ponder a pool's silent depths and contemplate its glassy surface, aware that even a single raindrop or the softest of breezes will send ripples cascading to its outer edge. The darker the pool's color, the deeper it will seem; the mood of the visitor may darken or deepen accordingly.

An ornamental reservoir—a *bassin*—acts as a reflecting pool at André Le Nôtre's first great garden at Vaux-le-Vicomte in Seine-et-Marne, France. Constructed between 1656 and 1661 for Nicolas Fouquet, Louis XIV's minister of finance, the chateau's grounds also boasted a moat, pools, cascades, a grotto, an allée of water fountains, and a great canal more than three thousand feet long. But the biggest surprise was the square *bassin,* called the Grand Miroir d'Eau, which reflected the entire facade of the chateau from a great distance. Calculated perfectly by Le Nôtre, the angle of reflection of the chateau equaled the angle of incidence of the viewer. Used to reflect a statue, an ornament, a weeping tree, even the sky, a still pool in our backyard gardens has the power to enchant.

—*Water always seeks its lowest level.* In so doing, it creates the rivers and streams that delight our senses with complex patterns, unpredictable rhythms, velvety softness, and murmuring sounds. Watching water spill down a mountain slope or meander through a sunny meadow is one of life's simplest, most eloquent pleasures.

The Rill garden at Coleton Fishacres, in Kingswear, Devon, England, is a channeled streambed built in a combe—a deep, narrow valley along the flanks of a hill. Designed by Oswald Milne for Mr. Rupert and Lady D'Oyly Carte in the 1920s, the rill emerges from a grotto to flow through a thin canal of silver stone into a bright perennial garden. From there, it wanders down through the landscape, ever seeking its lowest level, creeping along the valley floor in ponds and rivulets before disappearing over the cliffs into a harbor in the English Channel. The footpaths that crisscross the stream transform

This Japanese chozubachi *(water basin) is placed along a tea garden path for ritual cleansing of the hands and mouth before taking tea. Even a scoopful of water can capture the glint of the sky, enlivening your garden.*

Studying a natural watercourse, such as this Oregon rivulet rushing over rocks through a field of wild lupine, gives us an understanding of how to better design our own backyard water features. Observe the way water erodes and deposits along its banks as it moves along a streambed. Note the position of stones and plants in its wake, and design your own water features according to natural principles.

what was merely a storm-water runoff into a fluid focal point of the surrounding gardens and an inspiration for the designer who would use the laws of gravity to create charming watercourses at home.

—*The character of a fall of water is determined by the edge over which it spills.* Do you want a smooth or aerated sheet of water falling into your garden? Will it flow in threads or tiers? Here are some tips: a wide mouth will produce a thin expanse of water; a narrow mouth, a denser column. The longer the drop, the louder the sound at fall's end. The more obstacles in the water's path, the more it will riffle. A stone at the base of a waterfall will produce more of a splash than will water falling directly onto water.

A particularly interesting example of water's strength, speed, and energy can be seen in Lawrence Halprin's Lovejoy Fountain, a public watercourse in Portland, Oregon. Halprin created it as a series of natural falls, concrete cliffs, and chasms upon which viewers can perch or stand, or from which they can dangle their feet into the gushing flow.

—*Water seeks to travel in a straight line.* Water will both erode and build up streambeds through this process, wearing away a channel until it hits a noneroding surface, depositing the refuse on the opposite shore.

The designers of traditional Japanese stroll gardens took care that their ponds or streambeds be honest representations of natural waterways, using rocks to maintain the banks of a stream that would otherwise suffer erosion, or reproducing the buildup of sand that occurs in the lee of a small island. When creating our own gardens, we can hardly use a better model than nature.

—*Water flows in patterns of waves and currents around objects in its path.* Japanese *karesansui,* or dry landscape gardens of the fourteenth and fifteenth centuries, featured such naturalistic watercourses without the actual movement of water. The

Spray jets propel water up into the air, both softening and animating the Untermeyer Fountain in Central Park's Conservatory Garden.

decorative patterns made by raking gravel or sand suggested oceans, rivers, islands, and eddies in a landscape built to encourage enlightenment through intense concentration on the abstracted waters and landforms of these small temple gardens. A good example is found at the famous Ryoan-ji in Kyoto.

—*Water pressure can direct a flow against gravity.* This principle can be seen in anything from a geyser or a water fountain to a spouting whale, and can be put to dramatic or amusing effect. Italian designers of the Renaissance loved to create *giochi d'acqua* (water jokes). *Automata* (trick fountains) generated by concealed pipes surprised and delighted strollers caught unawares. The Villa Medici at Castello, Tuscany, boasted hydraulic wonders that showered onlookers with water manipulated by a gardener said to be "two hundred paces away."

We all want water to animate our garden designs. If only a tiny pool, a birdbath, a stone basin, spray jet, or wall fountain, water brings a tiny trickle of constant delight into our designs. Even a mirror surrounded by boxwood or a lavender bed will capture the movement of the clouds overhead, a wonderful substitute for actual liquid if the latter is too difficult to install.

If you want to create a natural water feature such as a pond, a waterfall, or a rivulet, you will have to do some research. Although there are many books on the market that will tell you how to design a water garden—and it is vital to understand the technical issues involved—there is no substitute for studying natural watercourses closely. This is what Japanese gardeners traditionally have done; they went to the source of garden ideals—to Mother Nature herself. There, they observed and sketched waterfalls, rivers, ponds, and streambeds, and noticed the formation of islands, fields, and hillscapes. They then returned to their townscapes and abstracted what they saw, being careful to maintain the structure but weed out the extraneous details. They noted, for instance, that in a fast-moving stream, soil is eroded at its banks until a rock is revealed, behind which a meander forms. They observed that in a wide streambed, a stone around which water divides will form a small beach of eroded material in its wake. These are small details, but important aids in making design decisions as you build your watercourse. By observing the way water moves in nature, you will ensure that your garden's spring feels as though it flowed straight out of the ground.

"Meditation and water," wrote Herman Melville, "are wedded forever." This miraculous silver liquid, the creator and sustainer of life itself, can transform an ordinary garden landscape into a spiritually rejuvenating refuge, a shimmering oasis of aesthetic beauty and peaceful contemplation. The only limits lie in our imagination.

A black glass reflecting pool covered by a thin veneer of water pulls the sky directly into Naumkeag's Afternoon Garden, where owner Mabel Choate took tea. Melville wrote in Moby Dick, *"Yes, as everyone knows, meditation and water are wedded forever . . ."*

A good garden journey is taken by foot (a stroll journey) and through the eyes and heart (a mind journey). Here, at Naumkeag in western Massachusetts, a lane underscores the beauty of the Berkshire mountainscape beyond.

Chapter V
Garden Composition
Stroll Journeys and Mind Journeys

To become a coherent whole, a garden needs to be composed—arranged in an aesthetically pleasing way. Just as dissonant sounds need to be melodically related to become music, so different elements need to be artistically related to become a garden. Although nature and serendipity will certainly influence your garden's composition, your role as designer is paramount. You choose the materials and you place them on the land in a way that makes them feel harmonious, both to another viewer and to yourself.

This may sound like a daunting task, but it is not. Aesthetic composition is something that you do unconsciously every single day, whenever you set the table, make your bed, arrange pillows on a sofa, hang pictures on the wall. When you give a dinner party, you "compose" all the elements that go into making it special—choosing a theme, forming the guest list, preparing the menu, arranging the flowers, designing the table settings, and orchestrating the flow of the party itself. When you give a presentation to a client, you compose your ideas in a manner that most effectively explains them. When you decorate a room, you arrange all the furniture, rugs, curtains, artwork, and knicknacks into a "composition" that most comfortably expresses who you are.

The Roman poet Horace articulated what many of us feel. "This used to be among my prayers—a piece of land not so very large, which would contain a garden, and near the house a spring of ever-flowing water, and beyond these a bit of wood." This pond was built into the existing ledge and contained by means of a dike, which also acts as a stone walkway.

Using granite curbing, cut bluestone, and cobbles, I designed a stroll journey in the form of a set of garden steps that entice the visitor though this little garden near Boston. Wetting down your path before guests arrive brings a freshness to the air while deepening the textural beauty of the stones.

Indeed, you already know as much about spatial composition as you need to become an effective garden designer. The problem is that you may not trust your aesthetic judgment. In this chapter, I will put words to ideas that may be implicit in your thoughts but have never been expressed before. I will help you take these inward perceptions outside, into your garden, where they may change the way you see the world.

THE METAPHOR OF THE JOURNEY

The single most useful image that I know for composing the elements of a landscape into a coherent and interesting whole is the *journey*. Every time we enter a garden, we make a journey—we travel from one place to another. This is an image that we all understand, for our lives are composed of journeys: we drive to work, wander in the forest, vacation in the country,

take a trip around the world, voyage to the moon. We make a pilgrimage, go on safari, trek in the mountains, or simply amble around the block, journeying in body and spirit through time and space. In a good journey, the psyche is altered, the soul refreshed, the senses reinvigorated. By taking note of the feelings and the forms that journeys have taken in our lives, we will know how to compose such experiences in our gardens.

As I design a garden, I imagine what it would be like to voyage through the landscape I am creating. Where will I begin the journey? Where will I end it? Will my path be bumpy or smooth? Straight or meandering? Will my pace be brisk or leisurely? Will I have many routes through the space or only one? Where will I stop along the way? What will I see and experience? Our implicit knowledge of how it feels to make a journey can inform the designs we make on our land.

TYPES OF JOURNEYS

All journeys are composed of paths and places. Paths are the passageways along which we move, either by foot or in our minds. Places are the stopping points where we pause, vantages from which we contemplate the world.

We experience two kinds of journeys: those that are actual—stroll journeys—and those that are imaginary—mind journeys. A *stroll journey* is a walk along a path where particular events are revealed to pique the senses and evoke thought. A *mind journey* occurs when we come to a place where a scene or object seizes our attention and becomes the focus for contemplation. Your garden is really a composition made up of mind journeys and stroll journeys.

STROLL JOURNEYS

You make a stroll journey whenever you move through space—something you do all day, every day. From the moment you rise and go about your morning rituals, during the day as you go to work, visit the coffee machine, or take a brisk walk on your lunch hour, to the time that you finally return to your bed, you are making small forays through space, stopping here, going there, as a planned journey or a serendipitous one. Each daily outing possesses the same elements as a grand expedition, a safari, a pilgrimage, or a marathon run: the departure and destination points, events along the way, and the path that links them all.

Think back to a favorite journey in your life. Think about its elements, its character, its quality underfoot: highs and lows,

A tea garden is composed of many stepping-stone paths that lead from one event to another. Your departure point often is a small waiting pavilion; your destination point is the teahouse itself. Along the way, you are taken through bamboo gateways and past stone lanterns (ishidoro) to the water basin (chozubachi), where you ritually cleanse hands and mouth. The bound stone (yogoseki) acts as a stop sign, indicating that you may not take a particular route at this time.

To become a coherent whole, a garden needs to be composed—to be arranged in an aesthetically pleasing way. One way to compose your garden is to use a "trimming line" like this Maine garden's informal hedge, which acts as a middleground to the plantings in the foreground and to the woodland in the background. You too can layer your garden space in such a way as to "capture" the area outside an enclosure, thereby making a small landscape seem much larger than it really is.

meanders and straight shots. Now imagine that journey re-created in your garden, whether it is as small as a tiny terrarium or as huge as a grand estate. The metaphor of the journey can organize your garden's design and provide a richness of associations that has universal but also soul-satisfying qualities. Let's look at each of its elements in turn.

THE DEPARTURE POINT

Every journey needs a departure point. A gateway through which you leave one world and enter another, the departure point is really a threshold between two realms: the profane outer world and the inner sanctum of the garden. Your departure point marks the beginning of the garden experience, as either a rickety front gate, a set of French doors that open out onto a terrace, or a mile-long birch-lined drive. It may be imposing and ornate, like the portcullis of a castle, or as ephemeral as a banner draped across two trees.

A departure point must extend a clear invitation for you to enter. A simple open gate, water sprinkled over the threshold, flower petals strewn along the path, or oil lamps lighting the way are all graceful ways of inviting guests to begin their stroll journey through your garden realm.

THE DESTINATION POINT

The destination point is a space of special, nearly magical qualities. It is the place of dreams, of a different size, shape, and quality than that of our everyday lives. It represents a simpler existence than the one we know; the fulfillment of secret longings; the expression of our truest nature. Here, you reach the objective of the garden experience, the point where the stroll journey ends and the mind journey begins. This may often be a hut, gazebo, or arbor because it is a place where you may sit, stop, and contemplate a vista, either within the garden or outside its walls. But your destination can also be any one of the archetypal vantage points or primary elements: a high place on your property, a promontory-like bluff, or even a shady grove, a secret spring, or a mossy island in a bed of grass.

A path edged with old roses offers the visitor a view across a wildflower meadow to the destination point of this journey: a New Hampshire farmhouse perched high up a hill. From the house, one can look out onto the Connecticut River and the rolling Vermont hills beyond.

Where is the destination point in your garden? Where do you like best to be? Perhaps there are several places. Shalimar Garden in Kashmir boasts many separate destination points, thrones housed in pavilions from which the Moghul Emperor Shah Jahan greeted his petitioners, met his courtiers, or watched his harem dance. Saiho-ji Temple in Kyoto holds several teahouses that act as minor destination points, but one major climactic feature: a dry waterfall that seems to cascade in tiers down the side of a mountain—the whole a focal point for meditation. Florida's Bok Tower Garden is crowned with a carillon tower as its major destination point. Visitors move purposefully along the winding gravel paths, seeking the place from which music wafts every half-hour throughout the day.

Sometimes, too many destination points can be confusing, always pushing you on to the next place, never allowing you the satisfaction of just sitting and feeling that you have "arrived." If you choose to have many stopping points, be sure that they are hidden from one another, so that each discrete experience feels whole.

You should express the very different natures of the departure and the destination points in your design. The departure point, often a gateway or walled opening, usually relates to the architecture of the house. The destination point, a long way from the departure point—psychologically, if not in actual distance—may be more rustic and less related to the architectural style of either the house or the rest of the garden.

EVENTS

Events are small landmarks that give pause to the flow of movement along a garden path and evoke thought in their viewer. An event can be as ephemeral as wind rustling through the trees or as momentous as a grand view to a mountain peak hundreds of miles in the distance. In a garden, events can encompass many kinds of small incidents that might occur along a path—a planting of geraniums in a stone urn, a fallen log in a sea of daffodils, a Greek statue placed at the end of a pleached evergreen allée, or a church steeple in a village a few miles distant. The more animate the event, the more our eyes are attracted to it: sheep grazing upon pastureland, koi coming up for breath in a lily pond; such incidents, whether planned or spontaneous, all give life and interest to the gardens we create.

Often, the events we choose to incorporate into our gardens hold personal meaning for us. Ask children to tell you what things they love in your garden and they'll reel off all the events they've noticed and find memorable. My mother's garden, for instance, is full of wonderful incidents that our children love. There is the "magic staircase" that ascends as a bright perennial tunnel to the dooryard garden; the front porch with its wooden swing; animal topiaries. They love the barn birdhouse, the cottage-garden plantings, and their "favorite" garden path that winds in an S-curve to an old blue bench past large-leafed hostas and ferns in a bed of pachysandra. Most special of all is Netherby, their playhouse and often-used destination point, that boasts a picket-fenced "secret garden"

A child's gift to her granny is proudly displayed in this cottage garden.

Petals floating in a Los Angeles garden birdbath. The French poet Mallarmé wrote, "There should be nothing but allusion. The contemplation of objects, the volatile image of dreams which they evoke, these make the song . . . The symbol is formed by the perfect use of this mystery: to select an object and to extract from it, by a series of decipherings, a mood."

with real and painted flowers, one by each grandchild. Objects that are scattered throughout the garden are special events to our children: the stone animal sculptures—the little bears, the arching cat, and the sheep-and-lamb statue; the myriad bird-houses; and certain special flowers such as Johnny-jump-ups, yellow and orange lilies, and catmint, "because the cats get crazy with it." I have learned that, at least from a child's viewpoint, there can never be too many events in a garden.

Sometimes events take on a specific meaning and purpose within an entire garden scheme. The famous garden of Stourhead in Wiltshire, England, now owned by the National Trust, was built in the mid 1700s by Henry Hoare II over a period of thirty years. It hosts a vast landscaped "circuit walk" that was designed as a sequential set of events along a path. These incidents constitute various buildings, monuments, and landscape features, beginning with a grass terrace walk near the house, passing a grotto on one of a chain of ponds and lakes, past temples, and ending in an obelisk.

Literary and classical allusions provide the aesthetic references of the garden's events. The lake suggests Aeneas's vision of Father Tiber sleeping on the riverbank. Along its shores lies the Temple of Flora, and along the walk may be found a panoply of eighteenth-century elements that form other picturesque incidents: a Convent in the Woods, St. Peter's Pump, Alfred's Tower, the Watch Cottage, and a five-arched Palladian bridge with the Stourton church and village in the background, forming "a charming Gaspard picture." Each event placed along the several miles of walking paths pays homage to Mr. Hoare's erudition, his sense of design, and his love of the picturesque, all in his grand "backyard."

Few of us want such esoteric events in our everyday landscapes. The Japanese tea garden suggests a more buildable kind of journey, in which we tread carefully over stepping-stones past one small event after another. Along the way, we are invited to ponder the brilliant blue callicarpa berries, to sit awhile on a rustic waiting bench, to wash our hands and rinse our mouths at a stone water basin surrounded by moisture-loving plants. Traveling through the garden at night, our path is lit by stone lanterns along the way, their lights of oil or candles screened by tiny rice-paper windows inserted into their carved openings. These act as another kind of event: quiet beacons of light that guide us through space.

The Path

The path that links the departure point to the destination point is designed as a continuously changing flow. It moves past events as a river flows past obstacles, swirling around this one, gushing against that one, trickling here, flooding there. The

This Egyptian statue gazes out from the Villa Melzi garden to Lake Como. As visitors, we follow its gaze, illustrating a clever method for capturing the landscape beyond the natural limits of the garden.

A cut stone path leads the eye and the feet to a pivot point—a place of decision for the walker about where to go next—where various stepping stone paths meander.

stroll journey path adapts itself to changing circumstances—to obstacles and events in its wake—yet flows continuously on.

Imagine making a garden journey that feels as if you were canoeing down a river. Glad to leave the mainland, you launch your craft into the swift flow. Your vessel is tippy, but you guide its movement through the current. Each segment of the river seems different: upland here, lowland there, straight stretches, sudden corners, quiet harbors, islands here, jetties there. Suddenly, you hit white water, and paddle fast, fully alert for obstacles that might lie in your path and barely aware of the rapidly shifting landscape around you. But in the wash, you have more leisure to look around and take stock. When you finally tie up your craft in a quiet inlet, you gaze out at where you are, look back to where you've come from, and ahead to where you expect to go. Your body tired, your mind at rest,

you are lulled into reverie. After a short break, you take up your voyage once more.

When I complete a garden design, I always check the flow of my path system by imagining how water would move along it. Wide and straight front walks are like canals, curving paths are meanders in a stream. Steps are waterfalls, and terraces are pools or reservoirs or ponds. Taken together these form a kind of river system: like a stream, the journey snakes along—a winding path; then dams up behind a weir—a threshold; then flows down a series of rills as a waterfall—steps; these fall into a lower pool—a lawn or terrace.

As strollers in a garden we follow lines of least resistance, and we lessen distances by taking shortcuts. We prefer wide, sweeping curves, and need to form pools above and below restricted channels, like corridors or steps. The flow of our paths can be smooth or turbulent, purposeful or meandering. It can be deflected or encouraged by visual attractions, and influenced by levels, openings, or the character of the floor. Like its watery counterparts, a good garden journey suggests the mystery of unknown realms around the next bend.

DESIGNING THE STROLL JOURNEY

As designers, we have the opportunity to choreograph—to control the pace, gait, and direction—of the stroll journey that our visitor takes through our garden. Let me suggest a few design principles that work for the smallest and largest of garden spaces.

MYSTERIOUS MEANDERS

Have you ever seen a trail in the woods that you didn't long to follow? Watch children out for a stroll. They walk along with an easy gait on a wide strolling path, but whenever they spy a turn, they race ahead to see where it leads. They delight in the change of venue, the new orientation, and the magical surprise offered by any twist or turn in an otherwise straight path.

Everyone loves a mystery. A path that takes a sudden turn entices us to see what lies at its bend. We yearn to find the answer to the mystery. When we reach this curve and the landscape doesn't change, we feel disappointed. But if it brings a different landscape, a new view, a piece of sculpture, a dancing tree, a beloved friend, then we are delighted with the experience and it becomes memorable.

ASCENT AND DESCENT

In a stroll journey the experience of ascent is quite different from that of descent. Think about how it feels to climb a tower. Spiraling upward, around and around, we drive ourselves onward with pounding heart and straining breath. Finally, at the top, we eagerly peer out at the view, taking in all that it offers. Once fulfilled, we trip quickly down, noticing little as we descend because we have seen it all before.

Going up something is like entering a sacred realm for the first time. We anticipate what is to come, aware of details around us yet eager to continue forward, to reach the goal. Time goes by very slowly. Going down is like leaving the sacred realm. Our senses are satisfied, and we have seen what we came for. It seems to take us no time at all to retrace our steps and to reenter the secular realm outside. Remembering these differences helps you design your garden's journey.

SPATIAL HIERARCHIES

We all come to crossroads in our lives: places where we see paths diverging, meandering, crossing, or where a clear "high" and "low" road exist for the choosing. How do we decide which path to take? Which route is the right one to follow?

Rhododendron blossoms grace a set of steps that the visitor ascends with ease. On the way up a path, the visitor climbs slowly with senses fully alive to nuance and detail. Descending a path is different—the viewer moves more quickly, eager to reach the destination at the bottom.

As gardeners, we can help our visitors choose which path to take by sending a clear set of signals by means of design. These spatial hierarchies are established and made clear by changing the size, bulk, or material of diverging paths. My front-yard paths provide a good example. The main flagstone walk is wide, easily shoveled for snow, and straight until it reaches the broad doorstep that sits up three steps from its surrounds. To the right, set into planting beds, are several large, irregular flat stones that signal the beginning of a private journey through wildflowers and ferns, a path to be taken by family and close friends only. Opposite this path, across from the front walk, I've placed regular squares of bluestone that wind irregularly through the front lawn and beckon visitors to take this shortcut from driveway to front door. Making clear spatial hierarchies in your house and garden helps signal and mark your intentions for their use.

If you think of the different functions a path can take, then you can quickly imagine its size, shape, direction, and details. I think of the most private, least detectable type of path as a *trace,* a squirrel path barely visible in a forest. At the other end of the hierarchy is the most public walkway—a *promenade,* for two or more people to walk abreast. In between is the *trail*—a narrow, meandering ramble for the solitary walker— and the *walk*—a wider, more direct path that is built for more consistent use. In general, straight paths tend to suggest more public, purposeful stridings, while meandering, mysterious paths mean more private strolls. In diagramming your garden space, you can use these distinctions to figure out where people should go, how they should travel, and what the path should look like underfoot.

Anticipatory Delight

A good rule of thumb for path design is that the longer the stroll, the more intensely we anticipate the delights to come. During a trip to Lake Como, I experienced the marvelous stroll garden of Villa Melzi d'Eril. There, we strode along the lakeside, past wonderful trees and statues, next to a remark-able neoclassical villa, and up the slope through billowing tunnels of azaleas and camellia bushes. Along the way, we found few benches or places to sit, and those that did exist happened too early in the journey for us to want to stop.

After an hour's delightful stroll, however, the bench perched just below the crown of the hill that looked across the misty lake looked very enticing. We sat on the simple bench for nearly an hour, mesmerized by the views up and down the lake. Had the path been shorter or had we stopped sooner, I would not have appreciated the garden as much. The intensity of anticipation gave way to contented exhaustion when my body came to rest and my mind traveled on.

Constancy in Change

A path, according to one dictionary, is "a coherent whole characterized as a collection, sequence, or progression of values or elements varying by minute degrees." This definition expresses an important design principle, which I call the constancy-in-change rule. This means that as you change the quality of one element in your garden composition, another quality should always stay the same: as you move from one area of your garden to another, something—the design of the path, for instance—continues on as before, while you allow the plantings, scale, and light qualities to change.

The easiest way to explain this idea is to suggest what happens to a garden where everything changes and nothing remains constant. For example, an herb garden that stands next to a Japanese garden that opens onto an English flower garden, with no separation between nor shared qualities in common, feels visually jarring. Were some of the white gravel of the Japanese garden used as a path through both the herb and English gardens, then perhaps we could accept their juxtaposition. If each were enclosed with a common wall design, or canopied with the same species of tree, then we would feel these disparate gardens as visually and aesthetically related.

I consult this rule in nearly every aspect of my design work, especially when working with details. Using the

This cut-stone path gains interest from the mounds of pinks (Dianthus sp.) that thrive within its cracks. Setting stones in gravel, stone dust, or soil will allow miniature plants such as moss, pearlwort, or thyme to take root, softening and breaking up the regularity of the stones.

145

This bench is one of several viewing positions in the Pool Garden at Knightshayes Court in Tiverton, England. The crenellated yews create a high "back" and a cut-stone terrace provides a "floor," with yucca plants acting as low "walls."

constancy-in-change rule means that as you change the height of your fence, for example, you hold all other attributes constant, such as the materials, cap details, paint color, and plantings around it. Or, in designing a path, you could change the size of a cut stone, but keep the same material, finish, and spacing. Or you could keep the size constant but change the orientation and spacing. As applied to planting design, you might plant a continuous rose hedge behind a mixed perennial border. Keeping at least one element or quality constant while everything else changes enables you to achieve a feeling of seamlessness in your garden.

When you understand that a garden can be organized as a stroll journey, designing it becomes an intuitive matter. You can tap your own experiences to create a delightfully changing voyage through your backyard. But don't expect to create the perfect strolling experience in the first year you make your garden. It will take time to get the departure and destination points, the events and the path, to feel just right. You'll know you have choreographed a good stroll journey when a child appears at your gate and can't wait to walk—or run—throughout your garden. It is then—when the journey down your garden path feels natural, unforced, free—that you will know you have choreographed a magical pleasure trip: after all, as William Hazlitt wrote, "the soul of a journey is liberty . . ."

MIND JOURNEYS

Just as with stroll journeys, you make mind journeys every waking moment of your life. At dawn, when you gaze out the window from your bed to watch the sunrise, you are making a mind journey. As you wait in your car for a light to change, scanning the road ahead and taking note of the landmarks around you, you are making a mind journey. When you sit on a park bench, observing ducks in a pond, children at play, or simply watching others stroll past, you are making a mind journey. When you relax in a hammock staring up at the sky, watching the shapes the clouds take, you are making a mind journey.

No matter where you are or what you are doing, you are always unconsciously making aesthetic compositions in your imagination—taking mind journeys through the spaces that you inhabit. Like the stroll journey, a mind journey suggests a voyage of the spirit through space; different from the stroll journey, a mind journey engages your mind rather than your feet. Imagine walking into a friend's garden for the first time. You stop at the gate, you look around and take it all in. What happens? Your mind circles around and through the garden, trying to make sense of the space, pausing at the bright places, the colorful spots, the distant views, the benches, and the sculptures. You "read" the garden by journeying through it in your mind. You know that your friend has composed a pleasing picture if your mind "understands" what it is reading as a coherent whole; you sense that the garden is still in process if the total composition feels dissonant or somehow out of kilter.

Your friends read your garden in a similar way. They enter it, stop to look at what you've done, and unconsciously take a journey through it in their minds. Your job as designer is to *compose* this journey, to arrange it so it feels the way you imagine it should feel, to give order to the various elements of your garden so they appear as an aesthetic whole. Just as an artist arranges shapes and colors on a canvas or an architect locates buildings on a site, you too need to compose the elements of your garden so they create a pleasing journey in your—and your visitor's—mind.

This is not as difficult to accomplish as you might think. In this section, I will tell you the three basic components of a good mind journey, and then discuss some compositional principles that will help you arrange the elements of your garden. You'll soon find that you already know everything you need to begin to design your garden; I hope to explain these ideas in terms of your own everyday experience of design.

THE COMPONENTS OF THE MIND JOURNEY

In a garden, park, or any contemplative setting, a satisfying mind journey requires three fundamental elements: a

A frame makes a picture out of what is behind it, in this case a silvery weeping pear tree (Pyrus salicifolia "Pendula").

viewing position—a place that protects and enfolds you so that you can contemplate the view without strain; a *frame* that acts as a kind of boundary or container for your view of the landscape, limiting the vista and framing the image so you can see it as distinct from its surrounds; and the *focus* of contemplation itself—the landscape, scene, objects, or image that you gaze out upon.

Contemplation works like this: As you concentrate on a focal scene, you feel as if you become one with it. After a while, this image loses its literal quality and becomes abstract—you transcend the image and, by extension, the world. After such a reflective experience, you come away refreshed, perhaps more centered, tranquil, and joyful, ready to face the outside world.

The viewing position, the frame, and the focus interact to create a kind of dynamic balance between physical repose and sensory excitement. Your body remains at rest but your mind feels stimulated by the imagery and aesthetic composition of the focus, with your attention "held in" by the boundaries of the frame. You feel simultaneously lulled and lured. If the image is compelling enough, it ensnares your mind's eye, calling you to inhabit a new place. These three simple elements—the viewing position, the frame, and the focus—are fundamental to the design of your garden. Let's examine each more fully.

The Viewing Position. As the destination point from which our minds foray into the landscape, the viewing position is the vantage from which we gaze out. It may be a constructed or a natural place: a gazebo perched over the water, a copse on top of a hill, or a simple clearing in a forest—the archetypal places we find in our landscapes or the primitive huts we make in our gardens.

Gardens can have just one or many different viewing positions. A tiny postage-stamp garden often possesses only one vantage point—the adjacent deck or terrace. Sometimes there are other, less obvious viewing positions to consider when you design the space: any windows, high or low, that face onto the landscape, or doorways that open onto it. Larger gardens often possess multiple vantage points—benches, patios, swings, gateways, porches, cupolas, balustrades, neighbors' windows. Each vantage provides a slightly different view of the garden space: sometimes straight on, sometimes elevated, and, occasionally, from below.

Whenever I design a garden, I examine the site from every viewing position or potential vantage point that I can find, standing or sitting (and sometimes lying) to find out how the garden space looks from each place. You should do the same, studying your site from every angle before, during, and after construction. Once you have determined what vantages exist already, and what viewing positions are needed, then you get to design each one.

If you design them carefully, it seems that you can never have too many viewing positions. Although we own just half an acre, I have made, or planned, at least thirteen areas for viewing. The best vantage—high atop our big rock—is a spot used by children all the time, and by adults when watching the fireworks of three neighboring towns. I put a gift of a rustic bench in a spot backed up by hemlocks for privacy, facing obliquely onto both house and road. During good weather, we

Twin sunken pools at Little Thakeham in Sussex, England, designed by Edwin Lutyens and Gertrude Jekyll, suggest a wonderful technique for moving the mind through space. The foreground pool is filled with water and water plants, the background pool is filled with a bright perennial planting. The careful cut made in the yew hedge—just the width of the pools—pulls the mind's eye even further out, beyond the garden's enclosure into the parkland beyond.

bring a wicker table and chairs out on the lawn, right next to my perennial bed. A hammock rests near the waterfall between two white pines. Our daughters made a little slate terrace under a white pine behind their garden, where they placed their child-sized wire furniture. Our son and his friends have made a web of forts hidden within the ridge that fronts the railroad tracks. My husband and I created a natural arbor, which looks out on our view of Boston, by nailing a beam between two white columns as supports for the tree boughs, and placing an old-fashioned glider underneath. All these—and I have not even started building terraces, outbuildings, pergolas, or gazebos.

The Frame. When you begin to assess the different viewing positions and possibilities in your backyard, you will find that many of the best spots already enjoy framed views onto your garden space. The casement of a window, the posts and beams of a gateway, or the arching branches of a favorite tree can each define a singular view of a landscape. As a metaphoric and spatial boundary, the frame defines the physical limits of an image, isolating that which is contemplative from other experience. Windows, doors, trellises, tree trunks, and eaves are frames that can capture a distant view.

A frame makes a picture out of what is behind it. Think of the difference between a plate-glass window and one with mullions. The plate-glass window offers a sheer, unobstructed view of the world outside. We pretend that the window isn't there; that the outside is inside the room with us. A mullioned window screens the world through a series of small-paned openings. Fragmented into pieces, the view looks both flat and

This viewing position is a destination point of the stroll journey and departure point for the mind journey at the Jardin Majorelle in Marrakesh. It frames a view of a long canal housing water plants and several vociferous bullfrogs, with the garden's villa looking back in the distance.

151

The Moon Gate frames the entrance to Naumkeag's Chinese Garden. The thick wall allows a stop within the arch to take in a view of the Chinese-style court, plantings, and temple beyond.

Thomas Jefferson created a corner in Monticello where two windows frame a view of his vegetable garden. Each fenestrated opening in your house has the potential to provide an eye-stopping framed view to the garden, if you design it carefully. From this vantage, place a focal object or create a garden vignette to take full advantage of the mind's delight in traveling through space.

abstract. We may observe each pane as a separate painting or see them together as a whole.

Even the paint color of your mullioned windows can change your perception of the landscape behind them. Tolstoy painted his window frames in deep earth tones of greens or browns. The effect is to pull you into the landscape outside the windowpane, dissolving the frame and fusing inside with outside. White mullions, by contrast, create a visual separation between inside and outside, rendering the architecture distinct from the garden because our eyes focus on this bright screen of small panes.

A garden such as ours, blessed with a distant or panoramic view, should incorporate the scene by somehow including the view outside of the garden's enclosure in the total composition. The problem in such a garden is to "capture" the background landscape and bring it into the picture plane. Japanese *shakkei* ("borrowed landscape") gardens employ an important element called a trimming line—a low hedge or wall with tree trunks to each side of the background landscape, creating a kind of picture frame that defines and makes the distant view as prominent as the foreground. In our case, we've pruned a privet hedge into a soft curve; behind it peek the two fifty-story

An artist finds his focus at Augustus Saint-Gaudens's garden. The white pine and hemlock hedges act as walls of this garden viewing room, from which one sees Mount Ascutney rising above the fields and forests of the 150-acre property.

154

buildings far off in the distance, framed by the branches of our big white pine.

Gardens without a vast background landscape can use the same framing technique within even the smallest of spaces. Think of a hole cut in an otherwise uniform hedge or fence. Your eyes will rivet onto the small opening and note what lies beyond, and inhabit it if something is there to be inhabited. Framing your garden—using twin birch trees or matching pillars, a moongate or a pergola—will tend to flatten your garden space, but paradoxically give it prominence: people will stop to study it more closely than if it had remained unframed.

When we frame a landscape, we select the extent of the view that visitors can enjoy from each particular vantage point. Through framing, we emphasize certain garden features, relationships, and compositional vignettes, enshrining each one as a different journey to delight the mind's eye. Once comfortably ensconced in a viewing position and looking through a frame, we need an object or image to contemplate—a focal stimulus that encourages the mind to journey through our landscape. It is in the design of the focus that our garden finds its place as a true art form.

The Focus. This is the attraction in your garden that always draws the greatest attention and interest; the place or point upon which all eyes naturally come to rest after scanning your garden setting. A focus can be a singular object (a statue), a grouping (a rock setting), or an entire scene (an herb garden). You may have one central focus or several randomly scattered focal objects or scenes, or foci placed at intervals along a garden path. Look around your own garden and note all the focal points, groupings, or scenes that exist. Each one of these has the potential to become the backbone of your garden's aesthetic composition.

A good mind journey happens only when you set your focal points in your garden in an aesthetically satisfying way—when you place objects in groupings that feel right to the eye, and thus to the soul. The best way for you to hone your aesthetic judgment is to try composing a mind journey for yourself. There is no substitute for the experience of actually doing it. The following exercise aims to give you the confidence to use a designer's eye—your own—for setting objects in space.

SETTING OBJECTS IN SPACE

Choose a set of seven or more disparate objects from your kitchen or pantry, such as a ketchup bottle, a place mat, chopsticks, a bowl, a potted plant. Using your dining room table as a "site," arrange these objects so that they are pleasing to your eye from a singular viewing position. Look at them from different vantages—from a bird's-eye view, from just above, and from down low. When the placement of each object feels right in relation to all the others, ask some friends to critique your composition. Have them move one element to a new location. What happens to the whole?

Now introduce a new object into the exercise. Every other element will probably have to move to a new position. Can you and your friends agree on where to place it? Next, add in another viewing position from which the composition must "work" aesthetically. How does this change what you have already composed?

This is a fun exercise that I've used in my classes for years. Everyone who has tried it quickly learns that they possess a finely tuned ability to arrange objects so that they bear an aesthetic relationship to each other that most everyone can agree upon. Sometimes I give students a short period of time and ask them to take an entire room as their imaginary garden space, using any props that they find as garden elements. When I return fifteen minutes later, I am greeted with shouts of laughter and a landscape composition of astonishing quality, although it is made out of tables as walls, chairs as benches, torn paper as stepping-stones, wastebaskets as shrubs, coats as pools, and people as groves, arching trees, and arbors.

Try it out for yourself. Sit down with your family over dinner and rearrange the table setting. Or, when you are out with friends at a bar, play with the beer glasses, coasters, and an ash tray. You'll be amazed at your prowess in determining what feels right and what feels wrong. Instinctively, with no formal training at all, you know how to arrange objects in space—you know how to compose a mind journey.

Setting ketchup bottles on a place mat with proficiency is really one step away from placing trees on your lawn without trepidation. Both are focal points, and both require your fine aesthetic eye in order to compose them properly. Once composed, both allow your mind to take a satisfying journey through space.

What are some of the common aesthetic principles that we can use to help us create a focus on our land? In the next section, I will discuss how movement, balance, and scale all affect the harmony of any composition.

Cherry blossoms grace a table setting where each object is carefully placed to create a pleasing aesthetic arrangement for each guest.

Whether we place statues, potted plants, chairs, trees, or rocks in our backyards, we need to understand some of the rules for setting objects in space. The rounded form of the shrub echoes the bulbous shape of the urn, and the texture of the urn seems similar to the textures of the stones, so that despite the different materials, the viewer reads the whole as a composition. Here, at Thuya Garden in Northeast Harbor, Maine, putting a large object in the foreground makes the background landscape appear smaller.

Two weeping blue atlas cedars (Cedrus atlantica "Glauca Pendula") *cascade over a contemplative corner of this backyard garden in a suburb of Washington, DC.*

MOVEMENT IN THE GARDEN

In a good mind journey, your eyes move around the garden space, taking note of the disposition of all the elements within it—the plant material, the fencing, the edgings, the ground cover, any water feature, and even something as small as a bird feeder. Even when none of these elements is in motion, each object holds within it a sense of movement. Whether it is a pyramidal or windswept pine, an upwardly thrusting spray jet or a tumbling sheet of water, a standing figure or a reclining statue, each individual element has a dynamic quality that is important to the overall design of your garden.

There are two kinds of movement that you can use to enliven your garden space: actual movement and virtual movement. Water in the form of fountains, pools, streams, and waterfalls brings *actual movement* into our gardens. We follow its movement as complex patterns of flow and stasis, eddies and ripples, kinetic swirls and syncopated rhythms. The changeable motion of mobiles in the wind, clouds in the sky, smoke, mist, and fog also delight us in this multisensory way.

Yet the virtual movement of a still image can engage us just as deeply, if we can bring calm to the environment around it so that we can contemplate it freely. *Virtual movement* is the motion and dynamics that are implied within the form of a static object or the interplay of several objects together. An angular pine, for instance, suggests the direction and force of wind on trees that stand high on a mountaintop, and offers a dynamic presence in a symmetrical composition. A set of softly rounded shrubs gives a rolling backdrop to a rectangular pool of still water. The water's latency excites; we know that the softest breeze will stir the surface and that one raindrop will send ripples out to the pool's very edge.

Virtual movement is created in the mind by carefully contrasting different shapes and sizes, textures and colors with each other. A static garden—where every element appears to be the same volume, the same height, the same intensity—does not sustain our interest. Our minds are stimulated by the dynamic interaction and contrast between elements. Without a sense of movement—either actual or implied—our minds will make no journey. Because most of the materials we employ in the garden are not obviously in motion themselves, we need to put them together in a way that will suggest movement yet feel balanced.

BALANCE

Objects also need to appear in balance with one another for our minds to feel satisfied with a garden's composition. There are two types of balance: symmetry, or perfect balance, and asymmetry, or dynamic balance.

As a means to organize space in a simple, easy-to-comprehend way, nothing works better than *symmetry:* mirroring one side of the garden to the other. Generations

If you strip the plants from this garden, you will find that its structure is essentially formal and symmetrical. Except for the lozenge-shaped yews that form four corners, the plantings are treated informally, as unmatched billows and drifts of varying colors, textures, and heights.

One way to make a symmetrical garden feel dynamic is to create interest through the design of its details. Color, like the yellows in this garden, can carry the eye back into space. Vertical lines, like the spiky iris in the pool, and the tall trees just beyond the garden wall, carry the eye up and out into space. Repeating forms, like the horizontal lines of the walls, fences, and hedges in the distance, provide a design cadence and rhythm to the composition. Breaking the symmetry, as with the conifer that is placed just off-center outside the garden walls, also energizes what might otherwise be too "perfect" a design.

This symmetrical entry court at the Daitoku-ji Temple compound in Kyoto is made dynamic by the movement implied by the entry path.

have loved symmetry—the ease with which we comprehend it, the perfection of its lines, the clarity of its relationship to architecture, the regularity and balance of its proportions.

Symmetrical garden designs have long held a fascination for garden designers in nearly every culture. Formally laid-out spaces from around the world demonstrate this way of creating a sense of balance in the garden, from the Taj Mahal to Versailles to the Boboli gardens. A dividing line or central axis, such as a water channel or a grass path, unites all sizes, shapes, and position of parts on either side of the compositions.

However, a symmetrical arrangement often allows a designer such a full degree of control that nothing may be left to accident or offered for discovery by the viewer's imagination. Care needs to be taken not to create a space without excitement, which feels static, overcontrolled, and obvious—receiving no more than a quick glance by the viewer, who can understand its composition in an instant. At first glance, for example, a friend's fenced herb garden, with its symmetrical

beds and borders and its axial path to the house, can be "read" (and therefore dismissed) with ease. But I can't stop looking at her garden, since she pays such careful attention to the details of the space: among her feathery pink, white, and red cosmos, she interweaves bright blue delphiniums, yellow lilies, a dovecote, a twig chair, wooden sculptures, a grape arbor, and many other events, all placed as little delightful surprises in the strict formality that she so carefully has set up.

I use symmetrical balance to pull together a set of elements that would otherwise feel unrelated. I have designed a symmetrical perennial border, for instance, to unite our stucco garage on the right and a tall white pine on the left, bringing the two into balance by focusing the view on a center point—an elaborate white birdhouse that unites the two different sides of this composition.

Most of us enjoy a less controlled, more natural look than the strict formalism of a symmetrical composition. But without symmetry, how do you give your garden its needed sense of balance? You can compose your garden using *asymmetry* to create a sense of dynamic balance.

An asymmetrical design is one whose elements do not correspond to each other in any obvious size, shape, or position, yet feel balanced as a whole. The only way to design such a space is to use trial and error—moving your plantings and focal points until they are set just right.

One easy way to think about composing the elements in your garden is to realize that each one is either a point, a line, or a plane. A tree, a statue, and a gazebo are all points, a cobble edging, a streambed, and a pathway are all lines, and a swimming pool, a gateway, and a meadow are planes that, taken

A point is an object upon which your eyes rest and which forms the focus of the mind journey in any garden. This stone lantern is a dynamic point, with its upward-pointing capstone and downward-pointing "roof." The flat-topped stone feels more static, energized by its juxtaposition with the lantern.

Squint and look at this picture of a Japanese entry path to a Zen temple: what "points" stand out in your mind's eye? The repeating form of the clipped round hedges, the bright reds and yellows of the autumn leaves, and the vertical trunks of the pine trees all serve as points that lead your eye through this garden space. Added to this, the linear path with its sudden turn to the left gives another element of dynamism.

together, make up the aesthetic whole that is your garden.

Points. These are focal objects that stand out in the landscape: important trees, sculptures, rocks, or buildings. Within each singular object resides a set of inherent forces that feel static (at rest) or dynamic (in motion). A tree may feel inherently dynamic, like a windblown coastal pine, or static, like a pyramidally pruned yew. The first leans way out, pushed by gales to point diagonally over the sea, as dynamic as the directionality of an arrow. The second stands solid, symmetrical, and squat, pointing upward as well as outward, both balanced and at rest.

You perceive such static or dynamic forces in all the objects around you. Different plants have forms that gesture up, out, or down; they may be billowing, weeping, columnar, or round, for example. Similarly, the shapes of buildings suggest different levels of forces on the land. They may be L-shaped, square, rectangular, or circular; sprawling or compact; primarily vertical or horizontal. The shape of the ground, too, may imply movement if it falls steeply away or rises sharply, feels rounded, flat, or suddenly vertical. These conditions suggest inherent forces within the forms that you must reckon with on your land.

A single object standing alone can hold our interest as a focal point if its design feels intensely dynamic. A chrome-yellow tower that spirals toward the sky, for instance, provides a bright, winding road upon which the mind can journey upward. A Roman bust whose stone eyes seem to look out across the ocean possesses an internal force that can be made palpable by the directionality and vigor of its gaze.

To feel visually related, two points need to be aesthetically linked. We unconsciously link objects of similar shape, form, color, or texture, reading them as a unit. Two massive pine trees along a winding path become a gateway; a statue placed to the left side of a lawn looks across to its twin on the right. We can compose compelling mind journeys through a space when we visually link one point to another.

A focal point can also be composed of many objects that act together to make a singular aesthetic whole. For example, a statue grouping such as the Conservatory Garden's Untermeyer Fountain, by Walter Schott, in Manhattan, is made up of three stone figures that seem to whirl around in a game of "ring-around-the-rosy." Nothing actually moves. Instead, the sculptor gives the appearance of movement by the interrelationship of the points—his figures—and the dynamics of their forms.

Lines. You can organize your garden to create a sense of dynamic balance by using lines to unite disparate areas of the composition. Perspective, diagonal lines, and parallel lines can divide space in a dynamic but balanced way.

Western gardens have traditionally been based upon the compositional technique called perspective: a set of axial lines, such as paths, pools, planting beds, or hedges, which recede into the distance and end in a "vanishing point," like railroad tracks that seem to meet at the horizon. These orthogonal lines have tremendous dynamism, and bring a strong sense of depth to a garden space.

Lines that are parallel to your viewing position can carve out space as a series of overlapping planes. The view of a landscape of foothills and mountains seems farther away than it actually is: we see a detailed foreground—the space before the foothills; a less distinct middleground—the space after the foothills; and background—the abstract distant mountains.

Eastern tradition uses horizontal lines to "layer" space: to create a sense of foreground, middleground, and background that is useful in making a small space seem much larger. Imagine a hedge at the end of your property line: behind it is background space, in front is foreground space. If you add another hedge between you and the first hedge, then you have created an additional sense of depth by suggesting more separate spaces—you would sense that your garden space divides into foreground, middleground, and background space.

Sometimes you can make a small space feel larger by using diagonal lines to organize your garden. A diagonal line—one that extends from one corner to the opposite corner in a four-sided figure—is a dynamic force in a garden. Your eye will

What better place for trysting than a hidden bower in a beautiful garden? From our vantage, this path is like a moving sidewalk that takes our mind's eye back into space. From the vantage of the couple, the same path acts as a viewing threshold for looking out on the adjacent grassy garden of sunken terraces.

Shoden-ji in northern Kyoto is a mountain temple that takes advantage of its height with its borrowed scenery garden of raked gravel and azaleas. Pruned as soft hills in a 3-5-7 arrangement, these shrubs provide interest in the foreground and repeat the form of Mt. Hiei, Kyoto's tallest mountain. The granite edging in the foreground, the whitewashed wall in the middleground, and the roof of the gate in the background carve out space as a series of lines that are parallel to the viewing position.

always follow a diagonal line in preference to a line that is parallel or perpendicular to your view. But watch out— diagonal lines are powerful. Once your eye alights on a diagonal, it steps onto an escalator, rushing back in space to the stopping point; there's no going back. A diagonal line renders any other element around it subordinate to the vigor of its forces.

Planes. Just as our minds pick out singular points and follow orthogonal, horizontal, and diagonal lines, so too do we take note of simple planes—triangles and rectangles—as visual organizers of our garden spaces. These planes may be composed of points or lines or a combination of both. Imagine a formal rose garden in a hedged garden room. The colorful rosebushes are the garden's points, the paths are the lines, and the rectangular planting beds are the planes; together these make a formal composition that is easy for a viewer to understand.

We also perceive the rose garden's hedged enclosure as a visual plane, both in its vertical dimension—the elevation of each wall of the hedge—and in its horizontal dimension—as an overall rectangular plan for the garden. If we add a gateway through the hedge, we add another plane: a frame for our first view into the garden.

With an asymmetrical composition, we still perceive planes in space, but rather than reading them as squares or rectangles, we read them as triangles. The best way to understand this is either to test the concept yourself by moving the objects around on your table landscape or by trying it in your garden. Using the simplest of garden elements for illustration, try placing a bench in the middle foreground, a bird feeder on a pole in the background to the left of the bench, and a cement birdbath in the middleground to its right. Your mind will mentally link these three points as in a follow-the-dots picture, drawing in the lines between them so that their triangular form suddenly pops out—you see it as a whole, as a plane. If you squint when looking out over a natural landscape, you will often read it as a series of overlapping triangles in space, sometimes equilateral, but more often isosceles.

Balancing Forces. Every separate object carries a force and directionality that can be expressed in your garden. Drop a pebble into a pond and watch the water ripple out until it hits the shoreline. Now pretend that your house—or your rock outcropping, or your garden bench—is a pebble. The aura around each element ripples out into the landscape until it hits the aura of another object.

Using points, lines, and planes, you can balance forces on your site that feel askew. If your site slopes downhill to the east, then you may want to plant some tall trees in the downhill corner that gesture up to the west—points that offset and counterbalance the sloping nature of the site. If your focal point is a statue-in-the-round, then you could choose to place it in a circular-hedged garden room, to displace its aura onto the surrounding landscape. If your house is L-shaped, you may want to make the L into a square by constructing a similarly shaped wall opposite the house. Through design, we can impart harmony to forces that feel off balance.

The Balance Between Void and Solid. Another way to balance forces is to actively design the space between them. This "empty space" is actually a dynamic element of your design, for it animates the objects that it surrounds. Think of a Zen garden's rocky islands, which seem to float on a raked gravel sea. The raking pattern that simulates watery ripples and waves adds a pattern and texture that animate this otherwise empty field of white gravel. The points—the rocky islands—become active participants in the design, through animation of the space between them.

Our sense of balance is often determined by the proportion of open space to filled space. Buildings, groves, and planting beds need pools of space around them as relief spaces. It helps sometimes to scrunch up your eyes and note the disposition of solids and voids in your garden composition. What is the proportion of open to filled space? Does the open space seem to flow or does it feel chopped up, discontinuous, or left-over? Does the space that is filled with objects feel cramped, crowded, or unbalanced? Do the two create a harmonious whole?

Scale can be understood only in relation to an object of familiar dimension. Without the car in the aerial view of this Virginia estate, we would not sense how big or small the area really is; similarly, the leaves of the mountain laurel give a sense of scale to what could otherwise be an intimate or an immense mossy landscape.

SCALE: INTIMATE AND IMMENSE LANDSCAPES

The scale of an object—how big or small it is relative to other objects around it—can make an element stand out as aesthetically compelling or allow it to fade into the background. Objects that are tiny or huge tend to hold our attention longer than something scaled to our own size. Images that appear smaller or larger than human dimensions permit us to see the world from a new perspective, one that appears *intimate* or *immense,* depending on our point of view.

We love the intimate scale of the dollhouse and the terrarium because we feel huge in proportion to them, while in our minds we become tiny in order to inhabit them. We may spend hours studying an ant farm or aquarium, imagining ourselves as diminutive beings riding on the backs of worker drones or seahorses. Many love the miniature landscape created by the moss, rocks, and highly pruned plants of a Japanese garden. The underscaled plantings of an alpine garden fascinate collectors worldwide and delight the rest of us. A burgeoning hobby for model railroad enthusiasts holds a similar kind of appeal: creating tiny outdoor landscapes for miniature trains to run through.

When you use intimate objects in a non-intimate landscape, you must find a way to make them stand out, to help your viewer take note of the diminutive in the midst of the more normal, human-scaled elements all around. When you place a child's playhouse in a large backyard, for instance, you might include a small-scale fenced garden all around it, to give its tininess an appropriate sense of place. Another way to set off the intimate as special is to contrast it with something immense.

Most of us love vast, towering landscapes because of their very hugeness, rendering us tiny when set against their size. As children we were fascinated by dinosaurs because of their gigantic scale. Mount Rushmore, with its huge heads of presidents carved into stone, continues to fascinate visitors from around the world. Sunflowers, four-foot gunnera leaves, distant views, overscaled statues, all feel compelling in the gardens we create.

How do you employ overscaled objects in your garden compositions? First, scrutinize your site for all big objects—huge trees, vertical ledge, large rocks, or distant views—to turn them into focal points for your designs. Recently, I taxed the limits of a backhoe when I asked my contractors to move a seven-ton rock from my client's stone wall to a point fifty feet away and then to stand it up on end as the centerpiece of a backyard rock garden. A massive piece of granite measuring eight feet high by four feet wide, this magnificent stone is set so that you can see it through the front door glass, from the entire living room and upper floors, and from a viewing deck facing onto the rocky landscape. The clients call it their "moon-viewing stone" because it seems to both attract moonrays at night and to direct your view out and up to that silver disc in the sky.

Next, try playing different scales off against each other. If you do, you'll find that wonderful and paradoxical effects will occur. For instance, in a tiny garden space adjacent to a brick townhouse, I placed two oversized stone animals from a private sculpture collection that the owner had acquired. When I suggested making these the centerpieces of the garden, the client said no, certain that they were too large for that small area. I explained that when you put large objects into a small space a paradoxical effect occurs—the space feels far larger with them than without them. To simulate this effect, I made cardboard mockups of these sculptures, and propped them up where I hoped to use them in the garden. Seeing these surrogate shapes in place, the client understood my point and approved my plans. Today, these larger-than-life-sized creatures sit happily in their appointed setting, and make this intimate space feel immense.

When you place a large element in the foreground and a similarly shaped but smaller element in the background, you carve out space, making it feel larger than it actually is. Conversely, when you place a small object in the foreground and a huge object behind, you flatten space, making it seem smaller. You can try this on your own property, using one small and

How big is this cottage? The choice of plantings, each with tiny leaf or blossom, does not give its size away. How lucky the bird who resides within!

one large cardboard box. Standing in one particular viewing position, try moving the boxes around to test different relationships with each other. You'll find that with just two carefully placed objects, you can make your small yard seem immense or your large yard seem intimate.

Why is this useful to gardeners? It's because we delight in spatial riddles. Intimacy and immensity are wonderfully para- doxical in their effect upon the viewer's understanding of relative scale. Do you feel dwarfed or colossal in a miniature golf course? Do you feel tiny or huge when you view a house on a faraway hill? Your body remains human-scaled, but your mind makes the adjustments in milliseconds to let you wander freely as a different-sized being. When it comes to understanding scale, imagination may be more accurate than reality.

Mass plantings of just a few species offer a unity of scale, form, and texture that can create delightful spatial riddles.

Designing a stepping-stone path involves understanding a few rules of thumb. Choose flat fieldstones that are generally a foot to eighteen inches wide, several inches deep, and flat-topped. Set them a fist's length apart so that the visitor's pace is slow and deliberate. For viewing thresholds or pivot stones (where several paths come together), use larger stones so that your visitor can pause with both feet on a single stone. Place stepping-stones so that one can comfortably walk with a right-left gait and position them so that each shape complements the stone next to it: concave next to convex, and so on. You can submerge a stepping-stone in the ground cover or set it an inch or two above it—the effects are completely different.

Setting Rocks

I SERVED MY ROCKSETTING APPRENTICESHIP in Kyoto, Japan, in the atelier of Professor Kinsaku Nakane. When he would come to the site to set rocks, Professor Nakane would have me watch, with great care, the placement of each individual stone and each rock grouping. In this way I learned stone composition, intellectually and perceptually. But it was not until I set stones for myself that I really understood how to place objects in space. I had to feel them, know their weight, texture, markings, and personality before I knew how to set them properly.

And there *are* ways to set stones properly. Ancient Shinto religion taught that rocks are abodes of the gods and so must be accorded due respect. Early Japanese "secret texts" talked of taboo and auspicious placement of rocks and other landscape elements in a landscape: for instance, according to David Slawson's *Secret Teachings in the Art of the Japanese Garden,* bad luck would come to the master who "set upright a stone which naturally was flat, or vice versa; violations of this will surely bring evil fortune." Woe to the designer of badly set rocks!

Imagine facing a hundred tons of boulders, some weighing as much as a Mack truck. Your task is to set each one in place so that it looks balanced yet dynamic, so that it reads as part of a larger composition, and feels good perceptually and spiritually. How do you begin?

First, you decide on the image you would like to create. For no one, not even the greatest garden master, can design a garden—any kind of garden—without a picture or a sustaining metaphor in mind. Stones hearken back to nature—an imagery that feels familiar, rich, and deep. To use natural imagery, you must observe nature carefully; understand how rivers work, where stones are eroded away and where they remain, how sand builds up behind an island, and the myriad designs of waterfalls. The beauty of a rock garden derives not simply from copying nature, but from abstracting its most aesthetic properties. One attempts to concentrate a vast scenic landscape into a size that the viewer can grasp.

Having decided upon your imagery, laid it out on paper, and marked it on-site, you then must select the first rock to set.

Choosing the biggest rock, or a set of stones that will make up the largest landscape feature, is a good place to start. You study the stone and decide how it wants to sit on the site: some stones wish to stand upward, others lie flat, a few may even be set diagonally. It helps to understand a stone from an anthropomorphic viewpoint: to know where its head, its foot, its front and back are located. And having decided all that, then the question becomes, how deeply shall it be set? The old rule of thumb—passed down from apprentice to apprentice through generations—is that a rock should be set up to its "waist." Another, more pragmatic point of view is to set a rock as it was found in the wild: its soil markings suggest how it tumbled and came to rest in a balanced, and often pleasing, position.

But having selected a rock, and chosen its head, foot, front, and back, you now must get it into the ground. Depending on the size of the site, you'll need two strong people, or a tripod, a Bobcat, backhoe, or crane to move it from the pile to its proper place. If the rock is chained or wired, tethering it so that the rock sits upright when lifted is an art in itself. And then, having dug the hole, you must understand another art: the art of shimming—placing small stones under the main stone so that its face is shown at just the proper angle.

The ferns, moss, and the Fatsia japonica shrub that surround this water basin are all water-loving plants. Because the visitor is expected to cleanse hands and mouth here before entering the tearoom, the basin rests upon an overflow drain formed by placing rocks loosely in a hole and covering them with a few inches of small-gauge gravel.

The next step is to decide how to relate a set of disparate rocks so that together they create a satisfying aesthetic composition. Think of the stones as being abstract points in space.

• If setting one rock alone, you must select a strong, graphic stone that can hold the viewer's interest as a focal point, riveting attention to itself and the space around it. Each stone should represent a particular landscape feature: a triangular rock suggests a mountain peak, a flat-topped stone symbolizes a plateau, and a low, flat rock "floats" like an island.

• If setting two stones as a related pair of points, one rock should be subordinate—in height, shape, or location—to the other. One way is to set them as a single unit: a "master" rock with a "subordinate" rock, or a "mother-and-child" stone composition. Another method is to carve out space by visually relating two different-sized objects in your garden space. If you place a large vertical rock in the foreground of your garden and a smaller vertical rock in the background, you'll create the illusion of great distance between them; when you do the opposite, and place a small stone in the foreground that relates to a huge stone in the background, your space will feel visually contracted. Try this in your own backyard. You can substitute statues, birdbaths, lanterns, trees, or shrubs for rocks—the effect is the same. When you place two stones together, you have an opportunity to animate your garden space.

• Set three points in space as a scalene (nonequilateral) triangle. This is the most typical form of rock arrangement in Japan and China, as the number three is traditionally associated with infinity, and the three points could be said to represent heaven (a vertical rock), earth (a horizontal rock), and humanity (a diagonal rock). One of the ways that we "read" a garden is by seeing three points that relate to each other as a triangle in space. Our eyes take in three vertical objects and read them as a unit: the highest point of a waterfall, a stone lantern, and a tall water basin, for instance.

Try picking out the points in your garden in this way. You may find that you are missing one leg of the triangle—that is the spot to place another rock, a sculpture, or a beautifully

This serene meditation garden—formerly a swimming pool—at the Bloedel Reserve in Washington state shows a method for raking gravel or sand. Because one footstep would destroy both the image of islands in a raked gravel sea as well as the sense of paradox and scale, the raker must jump onto each rock or set of rocks, and, starting at the back, rake carefully around them. Rakes are heavy, weighing as much as seventy pounds.

formed tree. Make sure that these triangular points are in a kind of asymmetrical balance called occult balance—they should feel dynamic yet peaceful at the same time. Ultimately balanced as a composition, the points feel dynamic in their component parts.

• Large groupings of stones are generally composed in threes, in fives, or in sevens: three azaleas pruned to look like rounded stones, five islands in a raked gravel sea, seven rocks that stand upright, suggesting a crowd of people. Odd numbers give a sense of incompleteness, so that the mind doesn't stop taking in the beauty of the corresponding forms.

The old Zen story of the tea master who asks his apprentice to clean the tea garden explains the idea behind one last rock-setting principle: *suteiishi*—the thrown-away or strewn rock as part of the garden composition. It seems that this apprentice worked with all his might to clean the tea garden perfectly; not a speck of dust lay on the path, nor a stone was out of place. The master sent him back to do it again, stating that it was not good enough. Again and again, the apprentice cleaned the garden, but it was never up to the master's standards. Finally, the master reached over to the Japanese maple tree and tweaked one of its branches: several leaves fluttered down to alight on the path. Now, said the master, the garden is perfect. The moral is that we need small imperfections to understand the true perfection of nature.

And so it is with rock setting. At the end, after your composition is "complete," scatter some small stones so that the whole feels incomplete, natural, and just right. Throwing away rocks may be the highest art of all.

A garden in Rockport, Maine, that opens out onto the ocean will need a big idea that supports the climate, growing conditions, and geography of the place, as well as the pursuits, interests, and dreams of its owner.

Chapter VI
The Inward Garden
Dreaming the Big Idea

YOU ARE NOW READY TO DESIGN your inward garden—to map out a schematic plan for a garden on your land. Having been through five steps of the seven-step process, you now have all the components of your garden revealed—your images laid bare. You have thought about your goals for your garden, visualized your beloved places from childhood, gathered information from your inward and outward sites, analyzed the primary elements, and noted the compositional features of your personal stroll and mind journeys. How does this mixture of ideas and images take form as an inward garden—a design that you can transfer onto your land?

Ironically enough, your garden must go further inward for a time. You need to allow the ideas and images from this book to submerge into the quiet recesses of your imagination. Those reveries, meditations, or daydreams that float back up to the surface of your mind will have merged, both as a whole and also as a sum of parts: they will have transformed themselves into a design for your inward garden.

This important design step is the heart and soul of the creative process. It requires that you cede all control over to your imagination and learn to trust in your creativity. With a rich and detailed inward garden design, your outward garden

Sometimes, as in this garden in Nova Scotia, one big idea will organize the whole.

will, over time, become a carefully crafted work of art that represents your garden dream.

THE BIG IDEA

Any work of art is composed of at least one or a series of *big ideas*—the themes or concepts that organize your garden into a coherent whole. A big idea is really one big image or a set of related images that suggest the form and layout of your garden.

We think up big ideas every day of our lives. They form the solutions to the big problems and small quandaries that occupy our lives—an eleventh-hour brainstorm for that important presentation, a sudden idea that gives a different method for reasoning with a disgruntled customer, an abrupt vision of what color to paint the dining room, a flash of inspiration about the line to a poem. In each case, something that had been unresolved feels like it "clicks into place" and frames our thinking in a new way from that point on.

You can't force a big idea. Each one comes in moments of "down time"—when you are not actively concentrating on a project or an activity, but are engaged in mundane, often repetitive acts: folding laundry, riding the subway, mowing the grass, sipping coffee before going to work, tending your garden.

A big idea gives structure to your images and unity to the features on your site. Without it, you will not have created a coherent design for your garden. A recent client wanted to design a garden for his new house in a subdivision. He studied his site's sun exposure during different times of the year, noted the wind's direction, and selected different rocks to use in his design. He marked out paths with sticks, and created mulch mounds, making sketch after sketch that left him unsatisfied. He worked on a plan for more than two years. Finally, he called me in to consult on a design. I found that what he lacked was a big idea to galvanize all of his thinking and hard work.

The client's site provided potent clues. His house, a contemporary glass-and-wood structure, was surrounded by mature beech and pine trees. In my mind's eye, I began to see the image of a hut sitting within a circular glade in a forest. This early image formed the big idea I was looking for—I felt I now knew how to design the whole garden. I decided to create a series of ever-enlarging circles—mini-glades—of garden spaces that would work their way out to the edge of the forest. Each little glade, to be formed of belts of broad-leaved evergreen shrubs, would feel like a harbor and would be visually linked to its surrounds with a special "event" happening in it: a huge rock standing on end that we had found on-site; a "pool" and "rivulet" of moss; a hollowed-out stone; a round-terraced garden room. Stepping-stone paths would link areas and provide continuity throughout the garden's journey. My client agreed with my design, and we installed the garden. Now less than a year old, the initial structure seems right. As the plantings fill in over the next few years, I will know just how well the garden has fulfilled its promise. Without the initial big idea to stimulate my thinking, neither my client nor I would have known where to begin.

Big ideas do not require big sites. As you find when visiting diminutive cloister or herb gardens, central city pocket parks, or the tiniest of *karesansui* meditation spaces, the smallest gardens are often the most effective showcases for a well-executed big idea. Inversely, as Le Nôtre demonstrated in Louis XIV's vast formal landscape at Versailles, one big idea—the dominance of man over nature—could organize a garden that seemed to stretch all the way to the horizon.

Many large properties break down space into a series of distinct subspaces, each of which requires a different garden concept to make it interesting. In ancient Rome, villa gardens sited on hillsides were designed around a set of courts and colonnades, each specially designed to catch different sun angles and wind directions. Renaissance gardens, such as Villa Lante at Bagnaia, north of Rome, demonstrated a central unifying design feature that linked many terraced levels, each of which possessed a different design theme. English landscape gardeners of the eighteenth century found that by carving out a series of spaces using "belts" and "clumps" of trees, they could feature different mythological, historical, or allegorical features in the form of grottoes, temples, obelisks, statues, or follies. These acted as eyecatchers as well as contemplative reference points, all set along a long strolling path. Smaller English gardens of the turn of the century, such as those designed by architect Edwin Lutyens and garden artist Gertrude Jekyll, divided space into separate garden enclosures that allowed the former to paint different pictures with plants. The pair learned that, as long as each "room" was effectively screened, there could be space in a small area for formal pools and bog gardens, rock gardens, and woodland glades.

USING IMAGES IN DESIGN

I find that the imagery that informs my designs comes as a result of three ongoing activities: careful analysis of my site, quick trial-and-error sketches, and sudden inspirations that will pop into my head at a quiet moment of my day. Over the years, I have learned that I must pay attention to each one. Let me illustrate this point by describing a recent challenging assignment.

The site was a fifth-floor lightwell that faced the lobby of a ten-story office building in downtown Boston. The client was the head of a major financial concern. The problem was to design a viewing garden in the eight-hundred-square-foot narrow rectangle of this rooftop space. While providing an opportunity to bring nature into the middle of the city, the landscape solution also needed to be bold and graphic, a dramatic natural focal point that would light up this fifth-floor lobby.

My team and I met with the client and learned of the depth of his feelings for contemplative gardens. Born and bred in New England, he loved its landscape, its coastline, and its sea. Within the company, he has sought to instill an ethic of excellence and creativity at all levels. Whatever I designed for the garden needed to reflect his background and beliefs, and suggest—metaphorically—the aspirations of this company.

After the initial meeting, we set to work studying both

Viewed from the lobby of a corporate office building, this rooftop garden aims to bring nature into the work life of its occupants. Rooftops create notoriously difficult environmental conditions for growing. In this case I had to overcome poor air circulation, low levels of light, tricky drainage issues, and stringent loading capacities with a design that was evocative, elegant, and ever changing.

the apparent technical constraints and the design possibilities. Each constraint served to limit the design choices I had. The load-bearing capacity of the roof, for instance, eliminated the possibility of including large granite stones in my design, an element that the client wanted. After studying the range of alternatives—hollowing out real stones, using artificial stones, or sculpting glass, aluminum, or wooden "stones"—and doing a series of schematic designs based upon these different solutions, I wasn't convinced that any of them were appropriate. To me, using contrived stones meant that we were cutting the spirit out of them, and I just couldn't do that.

Another problem was the overwhelming presence of the surrounding buildings. I knew that for people to feel free to contemplate, they would want to concentrate on a focal point undisturbed by sudden movement, light, or other people in the background. The many windows surrounding the rooftop needed to be screened somehow, to keep the visitor's viewpoint on the garden level, not above it.

One early morning, daydreaming a few moments before facing the usual morning chores, I suddenly hit upon the solution: design a towering, powerful bamboo grove for this difficult space. Bamboos are lightweight plants that grow tall, and would solve both the weight limitation and screening problem in one elegant and simple solution. Walking into the lobby, the visitor would be faced with a verdant grove of forty-four *Phyllostachys nuda* bamboo clumps. Their thirty-foot-high canopy dramatically screens out the surrounding buildings, and provides a tall vertical screen to a miniature horizontal landscape of billowing broadleaf "hills" and a mossy "island" surrounded by a "sea" of white granite gravel; all designed for interest at the ground level and to incorporate my client's much-loved seacoast aesthetic.

During the different seasons, my garden would change—with subtlety. I wanted to provide my viewers with a continually modulating feature: a set of different focal trees that are replaced by the garden crew every few weeks, providing a changing middle-story element—selected for its form and structure, its flowering habit, and the color and texture of its foliage—that suggests the changing seasons in the natural world outside the garden's walls.

In the summary paragraph I wrote for the client, I tried to describe my design intentions: "This new rooftop garden will provide both staff and visitors a vision of the beauty of nature that suggests the interplay of opposites which make up our world, using design elements that are structured and natural, vertical and horizontal, dark and light, soft and hard. Amidst this stands the focal tree, a symbol of the paradox of continuity and change, firmly rooted to a singular floating island—a vision of the company's special status in the landscape of the financial world."

This design is my most elegant and most audacious garden yet built. It illustrates my mode of thinking as garden designer. Had I chosen to attack only the many site issues, I never would have made the leap to a sound design. Had I studied only compositional solutions, I never would have used the site limitations to suggest a fresh design approach. Working simultaneously on technical problems and conceptual solutions is an important attribute of all good garden design. Perhaps most important of all is inspiration. With it, you'll know the big idea that will soon take form as your inward garden.

THEMES THAT SUGGEST SOME BIG IDEAS

Figuring out your garden's big idea is the most exciting and creative part of the design process. Yet for the novice, the concept of dreaming up a big idea can be intimidating. In the following section, I will outline a set of themes that have guided me in my own search for organizing ideas for my clients' gardens, and will illustrate these with examples from my own and others' projects. The structure of your site and landscape, sensory effects, art imagery, and philosophical ideals can offer clues that help determine the conceptual basis or the overall structure of your garden's design. Already from reading this book, your mind may be teeming with new images that could suggest a particular big idea.

THE GENIUS OF THE PLACE: IDEAS THAT EMANATE FROM THE SITE

Each site has, as Alexander Pope wrote, its own "genius"; its gestalt; its big idea. Sometimes this genius is a particular feature around which the whole seems to revolve: a distant view of the ocean, a stand of trees, a downward-sloping backyard, or just a small flat area of grass—an archetypal space. Sometimes its genius is more impressionistic: a feeling of vastness, of tininess, of cragginess, of melancholy. Step back from your site and ask, what big idea does it portray?

Your site provides a set of opportunities and constraints that can be used to advantage in determining the garden's big ideas. Opportunities—a cosmic tree, a bowl-shaped uphill slope, a stream next to a meadow—are often good starting points for big ideas. A cosmic tree can become the focal point around which the whole garden is centered. The uphill slope can become a rock garden full of intricate plantings. The stream can become the focus of a meadow garden walk and bring visitors down wooden steps, across plank bridges, and up again, all planted with water-loving plants and replete with frogs, tadpoles, and minnows.

Constraints will pare down your range of ideas. My own most creative solutions come when I have the most onerous limitations on a site; my worst constraints end up becoming my best opportunities. One client owned a small corner lot on two busy streets in an urban location. She had three small boys and

Your property represents a history and a living force that existed long before you took ownership. You can choose to respond to your land as a singular place unrelated to the geographical features around it, or you can place it in its proper context, as a continuity in time and space that reflects its setting and provides direction as to the appropriate changes that you may choose to make. Statesman, architect, and president Thomas Jefferson studied his Monticello land well before siting his structures and gardens on it.

A strong ornamental pattern on the ground, such as this geranium-filled parterre, adds a bold feature to your site.

needed to make a safe play area for them, and hoped to create a private place to eat, and some planting beds. The site gave no clues. It was flat, it had no wonderful trees or plantings, and was surrounded by other houses built close together. Its only asset was the Victorian house that sat upon it. I needed a big idea that would find opportunity in its many constraints. I decided to bring the architecture of the house out into the garden space by enclosing it with handsome wooden screens, fences, and pergolas, stained to match the painted details on the house. These different structures gave a harborlike privacy and security to the site, and provided a decorative backdrop for the series of little brick paths and terraces, planting beds, and small lawn area. Although this site was a challenge, the garden

proved to be one of my best, thanks to its rather dire constraints. The opportunities and limitations of your own site may provide some potent clues for your own big ideas.

Another key to finding inspiration for big ideas on your site is to ask yourself how radically you want to alter what already exists. Do you want to subtract elements by "editing" your site in order to better reveal the structure that is already there; or do you hope to add new elements to your site in order to reinforce its existing structure; or apply a whole new structure to your site? Let's look at these different possible site modifications.

Editing Your Site. Sometimes you conceive of a big idea when you imagine taking out some of the elements on your site to make a cleaner, simpler layout that provides a strong image for your garden. I call this "editing your site."

One of my favorite gardens resulted from removing the overgrown shrubs that covered a wonderful rocky ridge, in order to expose it as a kind of miniature landscape. This craggy, fern-laden ledge was rife with tiny archetypal places: cavelike crevices, precipice-promontories, and mini-mountain peaks, all found in a harborlike ring that embraced the adjacent terrace and garden. After stripping away the old vegetation, we laid down swaths of haircap moss to link the upper and lower portions of the land, and added a few boulders to balance a water fountain at the crux of its curve, where "Andrew" sat—a joyously cherubic statue from whose stone vase poured a tiny stream of recirculated water. The garden is simple and elegant, edited carefully to reveal the geologic structure of the land. Older gardens, like this one, often need such editing.

Adding Structure to Feature What Is Already There. Some sites need a big idea simply to pull into place the disparate elements that are already present. A clearer path system, prominent gateways, substantial enclosures, or specialty plantings all can serve to unify a set of features that seem otherwise unrelated. One client built a carefully crafted lodge on his property that overlooked his wooded site, which featured different terrace levels, ornamental trees, and rock outcroppings. He

The young boy featured in this delightful fountain was christened "Andrew" by his owners. When overgrown junipers were removed, I discovered a miniature mountainscape of ledge, and planted moss, azaleas, and ferns to retain a diminutive scale.

This twelve-foot-high Japanese lantern in Boston's Public Garden received a new base: a forty-ton megalith that acts as both lighthouse and landmark for the Swan Boats that float across the Lagoon.

hoped to make a garden that would display these features to advantage. We worked on and off for many months, drawing up a series of informal designs that never quite seemed to fit his needs. Then the family left for a year's sabbatical in England, and spent each weekend visiting gardens. By the time they returned, the client knew exactly what he wanted: not an informal layout but an extremely formal one, with parterres, low walls and steps, and a sunken garden, all built on an axis with the features that he had hoped to display. Although it took this client many years before he found the appropriate big idea, he ended up with a personal garden that matched both his site and his dreams.

Sometimes you need to augment the structure of your site by providing a focal point that is visually linked with its surrounds, but adds something new. At Boston's Public Garden, where the famous Swan Boats glide across a softly curving lagoon, I was asked to design a new base for a twelve-foot Japanese lantern that had been given to the city some fifty years before. After studying the other landscape and focal features on my site, the different types of lantern bases in Japanese tradition, and the technical problems of working on filled land, I came up with four different designs. My favorite was also the most daring: a single forty-ton rock that would act as a promontory on which the lantern would perch like a lighthouse or a beacon over the Lagoon. I received approval for this design from the many different agencies involved in maintaining this Boston landmark, and we proceeded to place a 15-by-9-by-5-foot-high boulder in the Public Garden. It sits proudly across from the rocky island and the footbridge, adding a new element to a venerable landscape, and providing a noble base for the cast-iron lantern that sits upon it.

Giving a New Structure to Your Site. Sometimes a site has no interesting features at all. If you bought a new house on a recently cleared piece of land, for instance, all the best landscape features may have been bulldozed away. I find this to be the toughest kind of garden to design, for without physical features to take my cues from, I must find a source for big ideas

other than the site—either my own ideas or those of my client.

Yet a flat, cleared site offers one huge opportunity: an ability to start from scratch. With no site constraints to work around, you can dare to create nearly any idea that comes into your head, as long as the scale, the topography, and the climatic conditions fit the site.

In Japan, designers believe that the purity of their big idea should not be compromised by existing site conditions and constraints. Thus, they will often bulldoze all features of a site in order to build a completely new garden upon a "blank slate," bringing in a whole new set of elements and plantings that bear no relationship to existing land. This notion is anathema to many American designers, who believe that sound ecological planning and design related to the site should be the primary consideration for any garden's design. In buying a new home, you sometimes inherit a site that has been cleared and that may provide you with rich opportunities to design an original landscape.

ABSTRACTING THE LANDSCAPE AS YOUR BIG IDEA

Another way to find a big idea for your design is to think about abstracting different aspects of your regional or local landscape. Miniaturizing, distilling, or re-creating key physical features from famous places, distant lands, or local settings—a concept used most often by the Japanese—can be a provocative big idea for the design of your garden. A good example is one of the most visible projects I have been associated with: Tenshin-en, the Garden of the Heart of Heaven, at the Museum of Fine Arts in Boston. As its project coordinator and U.S. design associate, I wanted to challenge its Japanese designer, Professor Kinsaku Nakane (the garden master with whom I had apprenticed in Kyoto) to relate to the New England landscape while creating a Japanese-style garden for the site. The day before we set the stones, I chartered a flight in a small plane over the region, so that Professor Nakane would gain a sense of New England's diverse geography and aesthetic qualities. After a long flight from Rhode Island to the Maine

A child dips her hands in Tenshin-en's water basin at Boston's Museum of Fine Arts.

coast, across the White Mountains of New Hampshire, down the Connecticut River valley and back over Mount Monadnock to Boston, the garden master felt ready to tackle the stonework. Without violating the intent of his original plan, he set the stones as he saw them from on high: in this quarter-acre dry landscape garden, one sees elements that call to mind the region's rocky coastline, deep valleys, soft hillsides, and craggy mountainscapes, abstracted and re-created to remind viewers of the beauty and diversity of this region, yet all the while looking like a Japanese-style garden. The intent, in Professor Nakane's words, was to create within the garden's confines ". . . the essence of mountains, the ocean and islands . . . as I have seen them in the beautiful landscape of New England."

Tenshin-en is an interpretation of two cultures, combining the depth of meaning of Japanese garden symbolism with a feeling of beauty and repose that comes from the New England landscape. The measure of our success in effectively abstracting our region's nature came one day when a pair of ducks flew

186

I designed this garden for the small backyard of a specialist in Japanese art. Her favorite Kyoto landscape was the famous sixteenth-century Daisen-in garden, an L-shaped garden in which a dry mountain river rushes under a wooden bridge, eventually terminating in a wide gravel sea. Working with local stones and washed river stone, I reinterpreted her image to fit her Northeast setting.

187

over the garden. The miniature landscape of azalea hills and dales, and mossy islands set in a "sea" of raked gravel, so convinced the pair that they tried to make a water landing and ended up flat on their beaks.

Ecological Ideas. Each region's gardeners can look closely at their natural landscapes to abstract them for use in their own gardens. Illinois prairie meadows, Arizona desert landscapes, Virginia azalea gardens, Colorado Rocky Mountain hillsides, and California coastal-scrub borders—to name a few—are inspiring a new interest in regional garden design that is spreading throughout the country, part of a growing desire to feel that our designs reflect ourselves and our surroundings. More and more American regionalists are writing books that suggest ideal plants for their own particular locale, climate, soil, and geologic conditions.

The specific ecology of a setting provides a rich arena for finding big ideas. You can make a bog, open field, hillside, or woodland garden; brookside, sunny marsh, seaside or sandy bank garden, depending upon the ecology of your land.

I once built a garden on a three-acre parcel of old New England farmland that was to be host to a new house and

Daisies that have self-seeded into ledge suggest the beginnings of a rock garden.

188

Cherries in bloom on rolling Virginia farmland provide a big idea for an orchard garden on this beautiful site.

A xeric plant is one that requires only a small amount of moisture to live. Drought-tolerant plants, native to desert regions like Santa Fe, New Mexico, are coming into popularity in areas of higher precipitation as one way of conserving scarce water resources.

gardens. Juniper and red cedar had grown in the site's flat, sunny areas—as is apt to happen on grazing land that lies fallow—and large white pine trees stood high along its upland slopes. Wildflowers had self-seeded along a marshy rivulet, which drained into an old spring-fed pond formerly used as a drinking source by farm animals. After consulting with my clients, my big idea for this garden was to refine and make slightly ornamental these farmland features, linking them as a series of different gardens around the new house. Over time, we constructed a juniper garden, a pine-needle-and-moss ridge, a wildflower-and-perennial hill, a marshy brook garden, and a newly dredged swimming pond, all of which derived from the specific ecological conditions that we found on-site.

Native Plantings. Native flora can also provide the impetus for a garden's big idea. Many gardeners today are designing with a palette of native plants for their hardiness and distinctively "American" look, which seem to extend directly from the larger landscapes they occupy.

These might be called "wild gardens": groupings of wild plants associated as they grow in nature and containing the species native to the garden's region. Such a garden need not make up a complete ecological grouping, but may comprise only those plants that you find most aesthetically pleasing or botanically interesting. The idea of a wild garden is to make a picture that is reasonably correct as to plant relationships and reminiscent of places in nature that you love.

North American grasses have developed an especially strong following as drought-tolerant alternatives to customary Kentucky bluegrass and Bermuda grass lawns (which, in fact, were introduced from other parts of the world). New varieties of pasture and prairie grasses, although less fine-textured and green than traditional lawns, require only half the watering and mowing. The use of vast areas of ornamental grasses, both native and foreign, can evoke the vastness and looseness of America's wide-open prairies. Dry-tolerant plants are employed throughout most of the southwest and much of California for a look that is considerably different from the lushness of the traditional English perennial border. The big idea of featuring elements from our own landscapes is a refreshing alternative for our contemporary garden designs.

Sensory Effects as the Big Idea

As we discovered when we inventoried our inward sites in chapter 3, sensory effects play a major role in evoking images that can be used in planning our gardens. The effects of light, color, texture, scent, sound, plantings, and even a sense of humor may be helpful in suggesting conceptual ideas for our designs.

Gardeners today are showing considerable interest in designing specialty gardens that appeal to a particular sense organ—scented and herb gardens, butterfly and bird, edible and vegetable, and bog and water gardens, all of which are well documented in the current literature. In this section, I will touch on a few other significant sensory big ideas pertaining to light, color, and texture.

Light in the Landscape. One big idea that I often employ in my garden designs is to intensify the different qualities of light that exist on my site and make them the focus of my design. A particularly difficult site was a tiny townhouse garden surrounded on three sides by four-story buildings in Boston's historic Beacon Hill. With all direct light blocked by these structures, and the only open side to the north further shaded by a massive linden tree, I had to tackle the light problem head-on and make it part of my design solution. I decided to turn the deep quality of the shade into an asset, rather than to try to alter the conditions there. I planted tall green Japanese maples to scale down the height of the buildings and to filter and break up the remaining available light, thereby giving a leafy, shimmering quality to the space. I made a granite-and-bluestone sitting terrace in the most private and shady part of the site. This was linked by a walkway to a viewing terrace, where I placed three overscaled stone features as focal points. I then planted shade-loving hostas, Solomon's seal, ivy, and ferns in deep shades of green and blue, adding spotlights of lime-green hosta and plaits of golden ivy as glittering contrasts that lighten up the deep, dark space. My big idea—to intensify the feeling of deep, cool shade in this garden—worked best when I planted these golden streaks of "sunlight" as contrasts that

The shallow roots of sempervivum have been netted together as a floral painting adorning a deck in Mendocino, California.

appear to illuminate the darkness of the ground plane.

Award-winning landscape architect A. E. Bye uses the effects of shadow and light as one of his major organizing design principles. In recent projects, he has moved vast quantities of earth to form undulating rills of grass that are edged with towering trees, a combination that both captures and intensifies light on the rolling terrain and casts long vertical shadows from the trees across it. Thanks to his sensitivity to landscapes and light, Mr. Bye's vast gardens of grass feel like rippling waves upon a sea.

Seasonal Displays of Color. Your garden can be designed as a series of seasonal displays of color, an organizing factor chosen by Gertrude Jekyll and other English perennial gardeners at the turn of the century. At her home at Munstead Wood near Godalming, Miss Jekyll arranged her plantings according to blooming period, which took plantings out of the realm of the natural and placed them in the realm of high art. Miss Jekyll suggested that flowers that bloom at the same time should be arranged close to each other, creating the Spring Garden of bulbs, sweet cicely, pale primroses, lilac iris, lemon wallflowers, white anemones, and many other plants of "tender coloring";

A large rose garden in Sussex creates the effect of a grand English manor. The first garden roses may have grown in the Middle East, spreading by way of ancient Greece and Rome to all of Europe and eventually to America. Originally grown mainly for their medicinal properties, today roses are planted for their beauty and fragrance.

the June Garden, with an iris-and-lupine border; and the Garden of Summer Flowers, with common annuals such as scarlet geraniums, yellow calceolaria, and blue lobelia.

Today, in this country, autumn and winter gardens are enjoying a resurgence of interest. Autumn gardens, with their intense leaf colors, fruits, and end-of-the-year flowers—including chrysanthemums, asters, and sedums—are increasingly being designed as seasonal displays, to be enjoyed during that period of the year when one normally puts the garden to bed. Winter gardens are designed with plants that display bright berries, seedpods, and long-lasting flower heads, and feature the structure and bark of trees silhouetted against the barren landscape of snow, clouds, or flat winter sun.

Color Schemes. Gertrude Jekyll also taught gardeners to make "gardens of special colouring": creating a series of garden rooms of different hues. At Munstead Wood, a visitor walked from the Orange Border of African marigolds, coreopsis, and rudbeckia daisies, to the Grey Garden of plants of silvery foliage, to the Blue Garden of perennials of the purest azures; coming to the Gold Garden with its many plants of gilt-leafed varieties—including gold yews and hollies, and the golden plane tree, with various yellow-flowering annuals and perennials, and the free-growing perennial sunflowers. Entering the Gold Garden, she wrote, "even on the dullest day, will be like coming into sunshine." The last room of the series was the Green Garden, where shrubs of bright- and deep-green coloring and polished leaf surface predominated, with only a few white flowers ever in bloom. In an era of grand estate gardens and bevies of gardeners, such planting triumphs were still possible to create and maintain.

A Continuous Cacophony of Color. Nowadays, many of us do not have the space to create a series of small garden rooms of one particular color or seasonal display. We need our flower borders to show continuous bloom throughout the gardening season. When we do segregate colors or seasons, we tend to tuck a "white garden" into a shady corner, or create a "summer garden" along a sunny border of the yard.

Many of us demand that our gardens "work" throughout the gardening year by using a mixture of plantings together: flowering shrubs and trees, and herbaceous perennials mixed with brighter and more floriferous annuals. More and more gardeners today are building "cottage gardens" that seem to satisfy some of our need for color display through the seasons in the limited spaces most of us have to work with. These small-space gardens—a traditional English vernacular style of gardening that consists of a seemingly casual mixture of vegetables, flowering plants, fruit trees, vines, and shrubs—derived from those created around small English cottages. They can contain a wild mixture of colors, textures, sizes, shapes, and plantings, all growing freely together in the small spaces around an outbuilding or residence. Making cottage gardens allows for personal expression in the use of plants.

Margaret Hensel, landscape designer and author of *English Cottage Gardening for American Gardeners,* thinks this reaches far

An opium poppy in full bloom (Papaver somniferum).

This joyful planting of roses and valerian (Centranthus ruber) *within a wall shows a way to create a vertical garden in your backyard.*

deeper still. "What I saw in England that transposes so well to this country was that people were creating their dreams, their fantasies through making their gardens. They weren't just taking pictures out of a book, or looking at someone else's garden and saying 'I want that,'—they were creating from their heart." She describes a woman who rented a vacant lot next to her house and filled it with plants. Friends thought she was crazy to invest in something that was not her own. "What that said to me was: here was someone who was looking deep within herself and seeing the beauty and harmony of her vision and bringing it into reality. Why this is particularly timely during this decade is that the world is in such a state of flux, politically, socially, and spiritually, that I think that people, through cottage gardening, look deep within themselves and say, 'I can have a part in transforming the world.'"

Color Fields. Some contemporary landscape architects are working with color as a painter would, designing with an image based upon juxtapositions, patterns, textures, and fields of color.

Plants can be used as architectural massings of bold color

Butchart Gardens in British Columbia uses fields of color to organize many of its gardens. Here, the designer has chosen to fill a long bed with blue salvia and orange and golden African marigolds, using their relationship as complementary colors to create a dramatic floral display.

A topiary garden of oversized chess pieces in Oxford, England, brings a smile to the faces of its viewers.

forms that feel harmonious, yet spontaneous, intuitive, and impulsive, according to landscape architect Sheila Brady, a practitioner of this art. A planted field of color, on the ground or on a canvas, produces an emotional response that comes from a juxtaposition of hues and textures that directly affects the way we feel. She suggests that we try massing together plants like perovskia, with its transparent quality and soft violet color; lythrum, an invasive plant but one with a strong, vertical magenta hue that works well with grasses; daylilies of various colors, both for their strong massing and foliage after flowering; and acanthus, for its strong vertical accent, its glossy foliage, and soft pink-violet coloration. For contrast, she employs the bold red of the common rose mallow in an otherwise soft field of color. According to Ms. Brady, "When I put all this collection together in a meadow—it feels so musical, so varied in color, texture, and heights."

Ms. Brady finds that ornamental grasses, in large swaths, act as graceful musical features of a garden throughout the seasons. Her favorites are the purple moor grass, transparent and beautifully delicate; red switch grass, which looks wonderful as a large mass, yet feels dainty and soft; fountain grass, which acts as an accent that moves beautifully in the wind; and feather reed grass, which she loves for its strong vertical habit that stays very compact—a good choice for smaller gardens. Planted in clumps, these garden fields remain surprisingly low in maintenance.

Each plant is like a stroke of paint on the canvas of Ms. Brady's landscapes. Unlike painting, though, her gardens do not provide a static image—their sensory qualities change with the seasons.

Gardens and a Sense of Humor. To an outsider, the world of gardening may often seem overly serious, if not more than a bit pedantic. The layperson, hearing others' encyclopedic knowledge of plants and their Latin names, and discussions of soils, climatic zones, grading, engineering, and garden history, may feel that designing a garden is not for the light at heart. There are, however, professionals who are inspired to design their gardens by using their sense of humor.

At first glance, Robin Parer's garden near San Francisco appears to be that of a very serious collector, with its sixty varieties of old roses, two hundred and fifty varieties of hardy geraniums and erodiums, as well as companion plantings of spring-flowering shrubs and perennials. She holds proudly both her North American Plant Council–designated collection for the genus Geranium and Erodium, and her membership in the Hortisexuals, an informal group of gardeners in the San Francisco area who come together to discuss horticulture. Their working motto is "No plant is safe!"

Robin's garden sits chockablock with plants on a steep hillside strewn with tiny paths, which she mulches deeply with redwood sawdust and wood shavings—the softest path I have ever trod upon. My favorite stopping place is her rose-covered gazebo, which cantilevers over the garden's deepest, innermost corner. From there, I entered her vegetable garden, walking beneath a sculpted iron arch whose sinuous sides were formed of two curvaceous naked women—a rear view if ever I saw one. Robin explained that on a recent trip to Ephesus, she saw a statue of Artemis, the Greek goddess of hunting and childbirth, sculpted wearing a necklace of breasts. She decided to ask two sculptor friends, Marcia Donohue and Jana Olson Drobinsky, to reinterpret this fertility symbol for her garden, in order to help her plants grow.

Passing underneath and turning back to look, I encoun-

The style of your house will often suggest a style for your garden. This Georgian house in Williamsburg, Virginia, almost demands an austere, symmetrical garden around it.

tered a frontal view of the same women, replete with fifteen concrete breasts, each surmounted by a red marble and ringed in pennies. Nearby, surrounded by lettuces, a sign reads, Titillation. Inscribed over the arch in iron tendrils are the words Lotsa Plenty.

FINDING GARDEN IMAGERY IN THE ARTS

Many years ago, my garden master told me that "One art means all arts." This means that I can find useful design concepts in every art form, if I am open to perceiving them. The arts, including related fields such as architecture, music, literature, and aesthetics, can be one of your best sources for big ideas.

Taking Your Cue from Architecture. Often, you can take your garden's big idea from the architectural style of its accompanying house. In fact, with certain types of houses, it may be imperative that you do. A friend called me recently to ask about how I would handle the front garden of a historic Greek Revival house, complete with Corinthian columns, classic

Having lived in Paris and Rome in his twenties, sculptor Augustus Saint-Gaudens chose to use classical elements to unite house and garden when he created Aspet, his home in Cornish, New Hampshire.

proportions, and stately facade. She had just finished a consultation with a landscape designer who wanted to build a circular driveway, create a mixed bed of shrubs and perennials in an island planting, and place tall trees in a line along the sidewalk to screen the house from the street. This seemed like the wrong approach to me. I felt that the house should be the highlight of the landscape, and that all plantings should be discreet, formal, and symmetrical to emphasize the classic nature of the architecture. I suggested that she keep the front lawn as a meadow of grass surrounded by a white picket fence—a simple ground against which her house would stand out.

If you owned a Jeffersonian Georgian mews house, your garden, enclosed by tall brick or serpentine walls, would necessarily be of formal, if not period, design. To use modern materials, to plant a wild garden, to use asymmetric principles of design, would belie the beauty of the more appropriate herb, box, or azalea plantings; the formal walks and stone terraces; the centrally located fountains; and Georgian benches.

Other styles of houses may demand less formal, more eclectic solutions. Deep within a redwood grove in northern California sits a shingle-style cottage with tiny leaded windows and a topsy-turvy chimney that has teapots and creamers mortared between bricks. The owner set out to make a garden that the house "deserved." Her big idea was to make a Hansel-and-Gretel fairy-tale experience in this giant forest. She and her landscape designer, Beryt Oliver, created a series of winding paths and diminutive planting beds that meander in and around the towering trees and little house, all set on the banks of a winding brook. They chose to contrast the formal (elaborate brick walls and low boxwood parterres) with the wild (narrow cobbled paths that let one wander through head-high lush camellia bushes to the ferny banks of the stream). "I don't own the house," the owner declares. "The house owns me!"

Sometimes, though, your long-standing desire is to create a style of garden that doesn't really go with your house. For instance, how can you install a Japanese garden next to a New England cape in such a way that they both still look good? The

You never know where a big idea will emanate from. Daydream daily, flip through magazines, be aware of the landscapes around you, and you may find that one day, the idea for your garden will suddenly rise of its own accord.

answer is to visually separate the two, leaving a space or an enclosure between them that aesthetically marries these disparate settings. Try to keep all vantage points oriented toward one view or the other, not both. And enjoy them both for what they are—a delightful mixed metaphor.

Musical Metaphors. Perhaps because my earliest aesthetic training was in music, it continues to provide important metaphoric ideas for my garden designs. Its structure, its emotional content, and its ability to evoke atmosphere and mood make composing music very much like designing a garden.

When I interview clients, I ask them about their taste in music—what composers or pieces they love. If I can, I'll then listen to these compositions for clues. I look for an overriding musical concept: Will the garden be felt as a symphony? A tone poem? A concerto, an aria, a children's tune? Is it a pastoral theme (as in Beethoven's Symphony no. 6) or a balletic tone poem, such as Aaron Copland's *Appalachian Spring,* or an emotional idea like Mendelssohn's *Songs Without Words?* Establishing a musical big idea provides me with the mood and atmosphere that will typify the garden I wish to create.

Carrying the musical metaphor even further, I might design the form of my garden's composition: will it be in strict sonata form, a theme-and-variations garden, a medley of unrelated compositions, or a simple, recurring round? Each has its strictures and its opportunities. A theme-and-variations garden might take the same few elements—a stream and a stone path; trees, shrubs, and perennials—and design them as a "rill" garden whose planting combinations and stonework alters perceptibly as the water proceeds downhill. A medley garden, however, might be a set of hedged garden "rooms," each different from the next: one filled with variegated plantings, another stuffed with topiaries, and yet another laid out as a verdant meadow. Each form is a metaphor for thinking about the garden in a new way.

A musical metaphor can also answer many compositional questions. How do I orchestrate a walk through this garden? Will the plantings suggest the sounds of flutes and harps? Brass and snare drums? Folk or country music? What is the tempo—adagio (gracefully slow), allegro (in a brisk, lively manner), or presto (at a rapid tempo)? Is the garden in a major or minor key? What is its beat: waltz time, march tempo, syncopated, mixed times, or in plain four-four?

An example of a musically inspired garden may be found at Bok Tower Garden in Lake Wales, Florida. In 1923, Edward Bok, an author and the editor of *Ladies Home Journal,* set out to make "a spot which would reach out in its beauty to the people, and fill their souls with the quiet, the repose, the influence of the beautiful." Influenced by his grandfather, who was said to have transformed a grim North Sea island ten miles off the Dutch coast into a haven for birds, Bok chose the highest spot in peninsular Florida to build a lovely sanctuary, for birds and for people as well. He invited the landscape architect Frederick Law Olmsted, Jr. (whose illustrious father designed New York's Central Park) to create a garden on Iron Mountain, a sandy hill of ferrous rock covered with pines and scrub palmettos. As work progressed, Bok decided to add a carillon tower, evoking the ones he remembered from his boyhood in the Netherlands. Designed by Milton B. Medary, the "Singing Tower" and its grounds were dedicated by Grace and Calvin Coolidge, and opened to the public in 1929.

Today Bok Tower Gardens is a 130-acre musical offering, located near U.S. 27 in Lake Wales, six miles from Cypress Gardens. Olmsted laid out its grounds as a serene retreat for strolling, viewing, and listening to the music that wafts from the tower across the trees every half-hour throughout the day. The garden's design itself can be likened to the form of a sonata, with an introduction, exposition, development, and recapitulation. Our introduction to the garden occurs miles away, when we spy the tower looming far above its surrounds on the pinnacle of Iron Mountain. After driving through miles of orange grove, we arrive at the garden and choose one of several winding bark-mulched paths to ascend the hill toward the tower. On the way we pass dark-trunked live oak trees supporting high canopies hung in swaths of Spanish moss, spring-green lawns for picnicking, soft walls of camellias, gardenias, and azaleas, and iron benches—all establishing the recurring, expository theme of Bok Tower Gardens.

At the top of the hill, the garden's musical idea is developed further by additional elements: an exedra, a semicircular seat for conversation, which provides a vista out onto Florida's landscape in the distance; and a close-up view of the Singing

After you start gardening you'll find that you can't stop seeing the world as an aesthetic unity. Poet Wallace Stevens wrote, "Just as my fingers on these keys / Make music, so the self-same sounds / On my spirit make a music, too."

Tower itself, this time reflected in a long, irregular pool. The tower's 205 feet of pink marble and tan Florida coquina shimmer among an array of ferns and palms. It thrusts powerfully toward the sky, a delightful Art Deco period piece carved with images of Florida flora and fauna, rising from an island surrounded by a glistening moat and iron gates—but closed, alas, to visitors longing to enter the seven-roomed tower to view the carillon bells above.

"Our carilloneur, Milford Myhre," says Jonathan Shaw, president of the Bok Tower Gardens Foundation, "is careful to create in his programming not just diversity, but also a psychological effect on the listener. I think he considers it an emotional more than an intellectual experience." Visitors listen to the music of Bok Tower directly in the out-of-doors, rather than under the shelter of a large shed, as, for example, at Tanglewood, in Lenox, Massachusetts, or at the Chicago Symphony's Ravinia Park. Benches built of various materials are scattered throughout Bok's landscape, always designed to fit

only one person, or an intimate two. After one listens to the carillons for a few minutes, the tower—the subliminal "orchestra" and the natural focus of attention—recedes in importance as other elements of the composition come into play: a swan preening on an island in the pond, a spider spinning its web against a backdrop of camellia blossoms, a child leading her parent down a gently curving path to some mysterious destination.

"Our policy," says Shaw, "is to turn off all power equipment a minute or two before and after the bells are played." This strategy has an ineffably harmonious effect; there seems to be no disjunction between hearing the bells and feeling the corresponding beauty of the landscape. Garden visitors lower their voices, even the birds become hushed . . . and then the fifty-seven tuned bronze bells peal out, as a solo voice, a quartet, a small orchestra, a symphony. All around is central Florida's languorous subtropical atmosphere. Sitting or strolling, steeped in moisture, music, and beauty, your senses open to the world; your mood alters as the program unfolds; and each piece

New Place in Stratford-on-Avon—Shakespeare's birthplace—features a knot garden following Elizabethan patterns in a layout of low hedges of box, santolina, and hyssop, but planted in modern summer bedding plants.

makes you feel triumphant (Handel), melancholy (Satie), tumultuous (Lerinckx), or joyous (Mozart). When the music ceases all sounds disappear, and for several miraculous moments one attends only silence. Then, the birds begin to cluck and twitter and to sing out their songs once more.

Philosopher Susanne Langer explains the relationship of emotional content and the arts in her seminal book *Feeling and Form*. When we listen to a moving musical performance, she writes, we sit transfigured in an "audible passage filled with motion" that creates an order of "virtual time" set apart from normal time; a "semblance" of reality, of "otherness, transparency, self-sufficiency . . . as separate from the sequence of actual happenings as virtual space from actual space." Gardeners too strive to create this semblance of reality; our illusory worlds, one might say, express emotion through the form and details of our compositions. Using music as the metaphor, we can bring this understanding to the design of our own gardens.

Literary Gardens. Sometimes, my clients ask me to design a garden that has a literary or iconographic theme. During an early interview with a new client—an author—I asked what her favorite children's books were. She suggested I read *The Treasure* by Uri Shulevitz. This picture book describes a tale of a poor man who dreamed that he would find treasure in a faraway place. After journeying through forests and mountains to get there, he discovered that the treasure was buried right under his own stove at home. The moral of the tale is, sometimes one must travel far to discover what is near. The images of this story became the conceptual basis for my design. I created a diminutive built world, forests, mountains, and a treasure of flowers that would spring up along the garden's path. Viewed from my client's kitchen window, this allegorical garden told the story of her own rich imagination and family life that she had created in her home.

Another client, a professor of Shakespearean literature, sought to express her current work in the form of a garden. With the iconography from her book as my guide, I designed a Shakespearean garden in her tiny fenced-in backyard, symboliz-

ing—by means of landforms, stone lanterns, and rocks—many of the places that witnessed heroic deeds in the Bard's plays. My contractors and I created miniature castles, rocky promontories, islands, boats, and mountaintops to walk beside, all viewed from an intimate brick terrace.

Drama in the Garden. Another design metaphor that I find useful is a theatrical one: creating drama in the garden. Plants and garden objects can play the part of actors on a garden stage. By first selecting your cast of characters and arranging them into a variety of poses, you can dramatically—and visually—relate them.

As with the tabletop exercise in which you arranged objects in space, it is your job as designer to carve out spatial relationships, to create tension between objects, and to know how to relate plants that are flat or vertical, round or spiky together into an aesthetic whole. Ask yourself which plants you know that fill such categories, look good with each other, and bloom simultaneously or at different times. Use dramatic plants—ones that are overscaled, have a strong architectural quality, or enjoy spectacular foliage or unusual structure, such as a weeping, vertical, or horizontal plant.

Horticulturist Marco Polo Stufano, of Wave Hill in New York, extends this philosophy to all types of plantings, from wild gardens to woodland gardens to perennial borders. The trick, he feels, is to make a planting look natural, yet have a coherent structure. He suggests that you set the major elements in place, starting with the trees; then proceed to the shrubs, and work your way down to the flowering herbaceous plants only after the larger woody material is in place. He contends that hundreds of seemingly unrelated plants can look good together if the bones of your garden provide a good dramatic backdrop.

Aesthetic Problem Solving. Sometimes my big idea for a garden comes from an aesthetic problem I am given to solve. My design for the 1993 New England Spring Flower Show provides a good example. My client was the Isabella Stewart Gardner Museum—a Victorian house-museum built in the style of a Venetian palazzo. To promote its then-current

The Isabella Stewart Gardner Museum was built as a house-museum in the style of a Venetian palazzo. One of my greatest pleasures is to arrange plants in the Court—a four-story, formal atrium space that houses some of Mrs. Gardner's favorite artifacts and a splendid collection of plants, carefully tended in an on-site greenhouse.

A garden chair at the Isabella Stewart Gardner Museum.

exhibition on Japanese screens, I chose to design a garden that intermingled Oriental and Occidental motifs. With the help of the horticultural staff, I created a rectangular courtyard that suggested the museum's own interior garden space, enhanced by museum objects and its signature plantings—cineraria, baby tears, calla lilies, and jasmine trees. We then hung three "Japanese" scrolls—interpretations created by layering samples of the finest silks and damasks—asymmetrically over the strict formality of the garden's ground plane, in order to emphasize the eclecticism of this institution's wonderful collection. We received several awards for this unusual garden, which successfully resolved problems of balance, contrast, and placement—all exciting aesthetic challenges.

For the 1994 Flower Show, I worked with a different intellectual challenge: to design an exhibit for the same Boston institution that related to Greek art and myth. I decided to organize the design to reflect classical cosmology: ancient Greeks believed that the earth *(Gaia)* was a disc that floated upon the river of Ocean *(Okeanos)*. This was depicted by the brilliant blues of seventy cineraria planted in a mass of "water" around a colorful "island" of spring flowers. The sun *(Helios)* was thought to traverse the heavens like a charioteer, and so I created a vertical arch of gold by raising eight weeping jasmine trees onto stands. To add an educational component to our garden, I used mythological stories in classical literature to explain the origin of the names of the plantings we used— narcissus, iris, hyacinth, oleander, myrtle, ivy, crocus, and primrose. As all good gardens do, the design worked on two

This beautiful entrance path into the Saiho-ji Temple garden supports the philosophical tenet that inspired this eleventh-century landscape. First built as a Buddhist "Pure Land" garden, it changed due to the ravages of nature and civil wars to become a lovely stroll journey around the Kokoro Pond.

scales: the big-idea scale (the conceptual level) and the smaller, detailed scale.

Sometimes I set up a problem to solve within a rigid structure, or with a particular set of rules, or a limited number of forms. Thus, this kind of big idea derives from an intellectual and visual challenge, one that requires a clear and precise design response on my part. In a current project for an art consultant, for example, I decided to solve the complex site problems with a set of simple geometric forms that repeat throughout the garden. We decided to use square bluestone stepping-stones, large circular pools of black stones, and rectangular bridge stones as our organizing elements. Using just these three forms, and shrubs and perennials planted in wide swaths, we created a spare but enticing journey over a bowl-shaped site. The stakes are high in such projects—anytime a rule is broken or structure altered, the whole can fall apart—but they provide valuable intellectual and aesthetic challenges for the designer.

Philosophical Gardens

The greatest challenge that a designer chooses to meet may be to create a garden based upon a philosophical big idea. Setting out a conceptual system, a religious ideal, or an aesthetic philosophy that guides the design of your garden can either suggest simple, tangible organizational ideas or allow you to come up with your own abstract interpretations.

Persian gardens, built as cool, watery oases closed off from the harshness of the desert that surrounded them, derived their features directly from the teachings of the Koran. According to this holy book, the garden symbolizes paradise—an earthly manifestation of the garden that the faithful enjoy with Allah in the hereafter. References to paradise in the Koran mention the "fruits and fountains and pomegranates," the "spreading shade," the "cool pavilions," and "fountains of running water"— everything that the inhospitable desert landscape was not. Organized as *char bagh* ("four gardens"), these landscapes were customarily divided into four sections, with a pool—the Spring of Life—or a pavilion in the middle, marking their intersection.

The religio-philosophical tenets of Islam provided a clear map of the Persian garden's layout and design features.

The garden at Saiho-ji in Kyoto was designed around a more ephemeral big idea. This four-and-one-half-acre verdant landscape is one of the earliest Japanese gardens still extant. The lower garden was built in 1190 as a place to worship Amida, the omnipotent Buddha, who was said to live in *gokurakujo,* the Buddhist paradise—an ideal landscape where it is perpetually spring, full of flowers, sunlight, and songbirds. The original layout was destroyed over time by wars, flooding, and earthquakes: what we see today feels like an ancient paradise garden overrun by mosses.

The upper garden, said to have been laid out by the famous priest/gardener Muso Kokushi, suggests the ideal of *yugen,* a Zen Buddhist concept translated variously as "tranquillity," "mystery and depth," or "lingering resonance." Perhaps most evocatively expressed by the monk Shotetsu in 1430, *yugen* ". . . may be suggested by the sight of a thin cloud veiling the moon or by the autumn mist swathing the scarlet leaves on a mountainside." The dry waterfall that seems to cascade down this bony slope was thought to be Muso's object of meditation—a powerful rock setting softened by the lichens and mosses that flourish on this moist west-facing hillside. Saiho-ji's influence leaves a "lingering resonance" in the visitor's heart and mind; after all my travels, it remains my favorite garden in the world.

DRAWING OUT THE INWARD GARDEN

Dreaming the big idea gives you the imagery, feeling, and form that make up the design of your garden. You should take one more short step before you start to build it: make a plan that acts as a visual guide during the construction process to draw out your inward garden design.

I call this a "master image plan"—a schematic design that records the big ideas for the different areas of your garden. Such a plan holds your images on paper and lets you see them in relation to the other ideas you have for your site.

First, record all your big ideas onto your garden plan, giving an evocative name to each, and adding as much description as possible. For instance, you might want a "Birch Allée" with fifteen-foot trees planted five feet apart, with a grass path underfoot, leading to a "Birchbark and Twig Arbor" in the distance. This is an accurate verbal description of your dream.

Next, see if you can give this big idea form by drawing it to scale on your plan. Don't worry about how your design looks, but how it feels. Draw your birch trees from a birds'-eye perspective, showing the size of their trunks and spread of their branches. Dot in a grassy path underneath and show the location and size of the rustic arbor. With this framework of a plan, you can begin to make decisions regarding the size and location of the elements that you have imagined, adjacent plantings and materials, and connections to other parts of the site. Best of all, you can really see how your inward garden will look on your land, testing your assumptions before you go through the labor and expense—and the euphoria—of building your dream.

The double hedges of Rosa mundi *lead to an arbor of whitebeam,* Sorbus aria, *that frames a surprise: a whimsical seat at Kiftsgate Court, Gloucestershire.*

Artist Marcia Donahue of Berkeley, California, created her garden as a purely personal place, with sculpted heads hidden in and among the foliage, like stone outcroppings.

209

Techniques for Getting to the Big Idea

WOLFGANG AMADEUS MOZART, perhaps the most prolific composer who ever lived, is quoted as saying that when "completely myself, entirely alone, and of good cheer—say, travelling in a carriage . . . or during the night when I cannot sleep; it is on such occasions that my ideas flow best and most abundantly. Whence and how they come, I know not; nor can I force them . . ." In order to compose, Mozart made himself comfortable and gave himself over to reverie, to reflection, to daydreaming. If we are to design personal works of garden art, we too must find a set of techniques for getting to the big idea.

Daydreaming. I find that if I save time to daydream every morning or evening, I am able to let my mind wander among images and ideas that I may have thought of in a fleeting way during the working day. I then follow these reflections, no matter how silly they may seem, to their obvious conclusion. Sometimes I keep notes; other times, I allow my mind to wander in a state of relaxed attention. This involves enough flexibility on my part to permit the images to emerge, along with sufficient control to watch them and to occasionally direct their flow. If nothing else, daydreaming like this allows me to enjoy my inner life, but often, these few minutes in my day are the source of my most creative thoughts.

Meditation. Sometimes I find that meditation can bring to mind various images. When you calm yourself into a state of relaxation through deep breathing, counting your breaths, or trying to rid your mind of all extraneous thought, you are likely to produce rich and detailed visual images. Recent research has shown that good visual imagery is associated with regular breathing and poor imagery with irregular breathing. According to psychologist Edward Hall, "Fantasies produced through relaxation may themselves deepen and intensify the state of relaxation, which in turn enlivens and extends the images." He goes on to state that a reclining position will tend to increase the flow of imagery—assuming that the person feels relaxed and comfortable in the setting.

Dreamscapes. Landscapes that you have dreamed may provide potent ideas for designing your inward garden. As children's writer Margaret Wise Brown wrote, "Subconscious maturation precedes creative production in every line of human endeavor." Can you tap the richness of meaning of these nocturnal gardens? Carl Jung would say that these arise from a "collective unconscious"; a flow of symbols that have universal meaning. "As a general rule," he wrote, "the unconscious aspect of any event is revealed to us in dreams, where it appears not as a rational thought but as a symbolic image." By noting landscape ideas found in your dreams, you may find a clue to your garden's ultimate design.

Visualization. It can help to take a mental walk through your garden while designing. Visualizing how it feels to enter through its gate, to move along its paths, to stop at its resting points may clarify the aspects of the design that aren't worked through.

Another way to visualize your big idea is to find traces of it in other people's design solutions—by visiting other gardens or by flipping through design magazines and garden books. Often, a glimpse into the way others have handled a problem can suggest a host of new images for the garden designer. Take care not to get too literal with these images, however. Remember, every site—both inward and outward—is different, and transformation is necessary before you can call someone else's ideas your own.

Feeling the Image Through Your Hand. Drawings can often capture the big ideas that you are seeking far better than words. So many of my designs have come to me when sketching casually on a napkin in a restaurant, or working a drawing in progress until its lines feel right.

Drawing can be a direct conduit to your imagination. If you allow your hand to freely move across paper, you can begin to try out images, work out relationships, and draw up ideas for your garden. You can suggest emotions through the energy of your sketches or doodles—darkening a line shows intensity; stippling suggests an expanse or a field; shadowing an area indicates three-dimensionality; and coloring a drawing can show the different uses or feelings that you hope your garden will convey.

Switching Fields. This can often galvanize your thoughts in a new, more creative direction. When one mode of thinking does not succeed for me, I am willing and able to try another. When I'm stuck, I'll read poetry or literature, play the piano or listen to music, go to a museum to look at the work of other artists, or flip through magazines to find visual clues in advertisements, articles, and photographs. When I switch modes for a while, I'll see old ideas in a new guise, or new ideas that spark connections back to my own work. As I've mentioned, I'll ask clients to send me copies or clippings of artwork that have meaning for them, which in turn gives me the very idea that I need to design their gardens. If I know that these images "speak" to my clients, then I can in turn let them "speak" to me about how best to handle different areas of their design.

Naming Places. Evocative words help to suggest the qualities and attributes of the places you hope to create in your garden. When you name things, you can imagine, design, and feel the garden in your mind before you actually build it; you can live with the image for a while to see if it fits the site and your needs. I try to name each image that I am trying to define. I ask myself, what is it like? Is this flowerbed like a wedding cake, or a Persian carpet, or an impressionist painting? Does the deck want to feel like a balustrade, an open room, or a

My mother painted a bird's-eye view of her house and garden—a source of imaginative delight for her nineteen grandchildren.

dock? When you visualize images from a fresh perspective, you can hold them in your mind's eye and design your garden from them.

Continuing to Dream. Don't be surprised when your big ideas evolve and change over time. The longer you live with your site, the more images you will find to enrich it in new and exciting ways. One big idea will give way to another that feels richer, more evocative, more appropriate to your present needs and dreams. As you continue to dream, your garden will develop and evolve into a place that is more and more expressive of your self.

Mozart extolled the virtues of his way of composing. "All this fires my soul, and, provided I am not disturbed, my subject enlarges itself, becomes methodised and defined, and the whole, though it be long, stands almost complete and finished in my mind, so that I can survey it, like a fine picture or a beautiful statue, at a glance. Nor do I hear in my imagination the parts successively, but I hear them as it were, all at once. What a delight this is I cannot tell!" Although most of us will never equal the stature of Mozart in our designs, we can, with these techniques, delight in our art as he does.

Sisters chat under a bower of bamboo leaves in a garden I designed for their family. As they grew, their garden changed: the fieldstone terrace on which they now sit used to be a cobble-edged sandbox.

Chapter VII

Building the Dream
The Euphoric Gardener

Since I started writing this book, I have built gardens for a range of thoughtful clients, each of whom offered me the rewarding experience of working closely together with them to design their inward garden. They all have become dedicated gardeners, quietly obsessed with building their dreams and turning their landscape into personal works of art.

I, too, have become a euphoric gardener, as has each member of my family in his or her own way. Our garden, just three years old, is evolving slowly. In the first year, we cleared and pruned trees, improved the lawn, and built a tree house. In the second year, we installed a pond and waterfall, planted some perennial beds, and our son built forts in the forested area next door. This year, we added water plants to the pond, installed new borders, and created a garden with each of our daughters. Next year, we hope to build some terraces near the house and begin to make a meadow down the hill. We have plans to add new features to our garden that will take us well into the next millennium.

We each find different delights in our garden. Our eleven-year-old son, Max, throws pitches on the lawn, makes forts near the tracks, and cuts the grass. Ten-year-old Lindsey hunts bugs, raises mice, contemplates the carp, and collects knickknacks to put in her own little patch. Seven-year-old Charlotte loves flowers and directs plays in our backyard, using the rock as a castle, the arbor as a house, and the lawn as a stage for her musical productions. John, my husband, just loves it all: he enjoys puttering and planting, trimming the hedges, and watering the flowers; on occasion, he will lie back in the hammock and relax. For me, the garden embraces all the things I love: my work, my dreams, and my family. Our garden has become the creative center of our lives.

A Victorian playhouse, named for the family's ancestral home in Scotland, beckons. Children painted the wooden flowers— permanent plantings that brighten the cold New England winters.

Children's Gardens

WHAT ARE THE MINIMUM REQUIREMENTS for creative play in a garden designed with children in mind? According to Katherine Eberbach, manager of Children's and Family Programs at the New York Botanical Garden, it's not play equipment but special objects and places in which a child finds imaginative delight. Children need "a swing to pump high above the world from. A scrubby area to imagine in. An open space to move freely in. A hill to roll down. Water. A tree to climb. Everything beyond that is a bonus," she states. What children seek out are evocative places that allow them to imagine and to explore without the parent's eye always upon them. This means, Ms. Eberbach says, that often marginal land—scrubby, bushy, moory, grassy slopes, weedy areas that are hidden from view, but close to home—are what children love best.

Ms. Eberbach finds that today's typical city child rarely gets a chance to spend time in nature. One remedy is her programs at the NYBG for children from the Bronx. Besides offering courses on traditional planting techniques, she also stresses ecology and environmental awareness through doing— building a pond or a meadow, testing seeds, mapping areas, tending manure piles, designing a secret garden.

Another program, at the Minnesota Landscape Arboretum, teaches gardening skills to eighty urban and suburban children, stressing stewardship, pride, and self-esteem through managing a vegetable garden. The program's manager, Sandy Tanck, gives students their own fenced plot, with each child's name inscribed in large letters on a sign for all the world to see. It's not for adults to plant their children's gardens, she believes, but to enthusiastically celebrate their harvests.

David Elkind, author of *The Hurried Child*, believes that children choose to garden, not because of books or courses on the subject, but because someone they love is out there digging. "Gardening is a wonderful sharing experience between parent and child. In today's world, with work and school taking up so much of their time, there's so little time left for sharing." Professor Elkind, a gardener himself, believes that gardens have special values: "In growing things, a child learns responsibility, stewardship, nurturing skills, and must come to terms with the vagaries of life, such as when your squash plant dies for unknown reasons. Through gardening you have the opportunity for a lifetime of communication and shared experience with your child."

People have the power to provide a rich experience of space in children's lives by re-creating, in their present-day setting, the places they loved in the past. Parents can instill a love of plants by growing things and including the children in the process. And, rather than grooming their yard, parents should restrain themselves from disturbing the constructions of little hands—from filling in mudholes, pruning low branches, and breaking apart stick forts. Instead, they should understand that each element of the landscape holds meaning. For the space of a few years only, the yard ought to belong to our children.

Nearly every afternoon that I set foot in my garden, I find myself surrounded by children—my own three, and at least four of their friends, who want to "help." And they do— although the holes are never dug deep enough, nor the fertilizer scratched in, nor the mulch applied thickly. But I always let them work with me as long as their enthusiasm holds. When interest in planting wanes, I suggest that they work on one of their "special forts": at the edge of the cliff, or on the top of the boulder, or under the rhododendrons near my wildflower garden. Nearby, we've cleared a short sledding hill, and created a little terrace with a twig bench from which to view it all.

This year, my daughters decided to make their own gardens, placing an old wooden dollhouse, their spring horse, some discarded wooden shutters as fencing, slate stepping-stones, and a selection of bright annuals (which I planted for them) in their little plots. Next summer, we plan to plant a "Flower Fairies garden," which will include scilla, lavender, periwinkle, narcissus, snapdragons, and all the other "fairies" named in the reissued English children's book of that name.

Most of the time, my children just play. I work alongside them, but frolic in my imagination, reveling in our garden that holds such palpable pleasures for them and such a storehouse of memories for me.

Twin Mennonite sisters play in their Ontario garden. Jung wrote, "The little world of childhood with its familiar surroundings is a model of the greater world. The more intensively the family has stamped its character upon the child, the more it will tend to feel and see its earlier miniature world again in the bigger world of adult life. Naturally this is not a conscious, intellectual process."

In this final chapter, I would like to pass on some principles and perspectives that may help you make your inward dreams a reality. For whatever enjoyment you have received from imagining your garden, your delight will intensify when you actually start to build it.

DON'T BE AFRAID TO START

The hardest part of any garden design is to actually start building it. What people fear is that they don't know enough to begin; what should concern them instead is not ever wanting to stop.

Many potential gardeners are afraid to start building their gardens because they fear making a mistake. They hear friends and neighbors talking about plants, insecticides, and pruning techniques, and they get so scared they won't buy a single plant. An elderly schoolteacher I know mentioned wistfully that she had always wanted a wildflower garden, but that she thought she should know the Latin name and cultural requirement of each plant before she even dug up a bed.

Don't make her mistake. For the past thirty years, she could have realized her dream, if only she had planted her first wildflower. Had even a single stalk of Solomon's seal reappeared in a bed that she had planted, she would have been so thrilled with her success that she would have found the confidence to continue.

Success breeds success in the garden. One interest—such as wildflowers—will soon lead to another interest—perennial borders—which will lead to another—vines—and another—hostas. As your sense of confidence grows, so will your pride in your accomplishments and your courage to try new and different species, styles, and conceptual ideas.

Even as you develop one area of your garden, you'll be thinking ahead to the next section, and, unable to wait that long, you'll build whatever parts you can as soon as resources become available. You'll work and rework the areas of the garden that

A stony streambed forms the centerpiece of this Japanese-style garden near Boston. To create a natural effect, make sure to cover up a pool or channel liner with rocks, small stones, and plants.

216

A simple stone lantern lights up the corner of this Boston-area Japanese garden.

you "finished," because you'll continually find ways to improve them, moving plantings, ornaments, and benches into new locales. Soon enough, you'll design yourself a cutting garden because you'll want flowers throughout the inside of your home as well as outside it.

DO WHAT FEELS RIGHT

Each of us has different resources—of energy, of time, and of money—with which to build our gardens. It is important to pay attention to what feels right. For instance, there are times when building a garden may be too much effort—when it's better to *dream* than to *do*. If you are responsible for small children in diapers, ailing parents, or an unabating and demanding work load, then building your inward garden may just have

to wait for a more serene time of your life. Gardens, like people, require lots of nurturing time, and you may not have the energy or the emotional resources to do it all.

What you may want to do is start small and work incrementally—build a tiny chunk of what will become your whole garden. Choose a critical corner of your yard and make a place for yourself within it. Perhaps you should just plant your cosmic tree, place a bench beneath it, and erect a small fence and place plantings around it—then stop. Or dig out the ornamental pool you planned, line it with concrete or butyl rubber, plant around and in it, buy some fish, and enjoy it. When you work on a small but significant area of your garden, you feel that you've accomplished something your first year. You'll feel rejuvenated and ready to move ahead at the same pace, or faster, or slower, depending upon your resources from that point on. But what you will have gained, besides a beautiful setting, is the confidence to continue building.

Another constraining factor may be money, or the lack of it. Constructing a garden can be very expensive—building one's dream usually is. Even those of us who are do-it-yourselfers must invest hundreds or thousands of dollars a year to create a place that begins to resemble the inward garden we so long to own.

Even the smallest gardens can easily upset our bank balance. Most urban sites require, at the very least, fencing for privacy, a terrace, and intensive plantings—expensive items all, but necessary to provide the owner with an outdoor landscaped space in an otherwise hardscaped world.

MAKE PREPARATIONS

When you build, start with the bones of the garden—its structure—and work your way through to the plantings. Begin by moving all your earth, making retaining walls, steps, and walks, laying out terraces, and constructing fences, arbors, and trellises, all before you commence planting. Building the structure of your garden will entail the largest capital expenditure of the whole process, but done well, will create the most satisfying design.

Another kind of preparation is important before buying your plants: preparing your beds well. Digging out your soil and adding appropriate amendments to it will allow your plants to thrive for years to come. I spent my first years as a homeowner placing beautiful plants into poorly prepared beds, only to watch many of them fail. Since then, I try always to prepare the beds before I buy.

KNOW YOUR PLANTS

After carefully preparing the soil, you need to select plants that can grow in your locale. How do you begin? Choose the plants you love most and *try them out*.

The enormous variety of plants is daunting to the begin-

ner. The only way to learn about plants is to use them; to place them, with your own dirty hands, into the ground. Reading about each plant's cultural and maintenance requirements will help you care for it, but there is no substitute for hands-on experience. By placing a specimen into your garden, you come to terms with its essential qualities.

When you go to a nursery to buy your plants, have a list with you. No matter what time of the year you go, there will be something blooming that you'll want that wasn't on your list. Resist—or at least control—your impulses. Buy three items instead of ten. Whatever it was will be through flowering by the time you get it home and into the ground, and may not fit in with your carefully conceived planting scheme.

One good way to buy plants is to go back to the nursery every month during the growing season and observe what is in bloom. This way you learn new plants and can place them in aesthetic relation to others in bloom until the next month, when a different group of plants begin to show flowers.

I make sure to try out at least five new plants in every garden that I design. This way I learn new varieties, study

Lacecap hydrangea (Hydrangea macrophylla f. normalis) *requires acid soil for blue flower color. In neutral or alkaline soils, they tend to blossom pink.*

219

growth and flowering habits, and get to handle a plant that I may only have read about in catalogues. When I return to the garden the next year, I can chart the success or failure of the new plant in its particular conditions, and learn for the next garden's planting. You may want to try this too—buying five new plants every year and watching their progress over time. This way, you will soon hold a growing repertoire of plants in your hands and in your head, and gain confidence as you make inroads into this vast field of horticulture.

There is nothing wrong with making a mistake in planting design. You wouldn't be human if you didn't. Canadian gardener Susan Ryley, one of the greatest gardeners I know, moves plants around with alacrity. According to Ms. Ryley, after carefully preparing the soil and selecting plants that can grow in your locale, "you have to choose the things you love most and try them out. If you're wrong, you can always move a plant to a new location as long as you tend it afterward. My garden's always in flux," she declares. "Sometimes I have to move something six times before I get it right."

You'll know when you've finally found the right spot for your favorite plant. Soon enough, it will prosper and need pruning or dividing. You may even find that you have to move it again.

MAINTAIN WHAT YOU'VE CREATED

Gardens require continual care and nurturing. Tender new plantings will need feeding, watering, mulching, staking, dividing, and protecting, so that they can mature to fullness in a short time. You'll need to keep edges trimmed, lawns mowed, branches pruned, leaves raked. As the garden grows, so will your knowledge of how to improve or change it, and you'll be constantly on the lookout for new ideas, information, specimens, or objects to augment it. This is the joy of having a personal place—it is like your childhood fort that needs tending, constant tinkering, and quiet moments for daydreaming. In a sense, your garden comes alive only by the magic of your ministrations throughout its lifetime and yours.

MAKE A RESPONSIBLE GARDEN

We need to be ecologically responsible in our gardens, as in our lives. No matter where you live, you will need to help conserve our nation's water supply. Certainly, the communities in and around our western deserts are usually the first to be affected by scarce water resources, but the potential shortage is also of utmost concern to gardeners from Washington to Illinois to Georgia. Many parts of the country are no longer landscaping, they are *xeriscaping*—landscaping with low-water-use plants. Dry-land perennials and ornamental and native grasses can conserve water while still providing something of the lush ambiance of an English perennial garden. Some horticulturists are studying indigenous plants of other countries with similar climates as imports that would thrive with less summer watering.

Responsible waste management is also of paramount importance to today's gardener. Fifteen states have passed ordinances excluding yard waste from their landfills, and more are likely to follow suit; there simply isn't room in the local dump for trash bags filled with grass clippings and dead leaves. Local botanical gardens are moving to include courses on mowing, mulching, and composting to help gardeners become more responsible with their waste. Within a few years, most homes may well have a composting bin out back, or even in the kitchen itself. Vermiculture—the care and feeding of worms with food waste—creates a high-quality compost for one's perennial beds.

Many gardeners are discovering that the simplest way to manage waste is to select plants that don't generate any: easy-care ground covers instead of lawns; compact shrubs instead of sheared hedges; evergreen trees instead of their leafy deciduous cousins, which create huge piles of photogenic but waste-intensive fallen leaves come Halloween.

We also seem to be cutting down on chemicals and finding environmentally responsible ways to combat pests, weeds, and diseases. A new system called integrated pest management (IPM), researched and promoted by the Berkeley,

Maintaining a garden requires time and effort to get such glorious results. Don't despair if you don't have the energy or resources for a grand beginning: instead, start small and keep learning—the garden will grow as your interest in it does. My mother, Alice Moir, has been working on this garden for the past twelve years.

California–based Bio-Integral Resource Center, aims at suppressing pest populations through a variety of horticultural, biological, and least-toxic-chemical means. IPM's overall goal is long-term problem control rather than the quick fix. Prevention is the key, through proper fertilization and irrigation and by encouraging the natural enemies of insects and other intruders. As people in all walks of life are discovering, an ecologically friendly ounce of prevention is preferable to a poisonous pound of cure.

SEEK PROFESSIONAL HELP WHEN YOU NEED IT

You don't have to build your garden all alone. You probably don't have all the requisite skills to construct dry-stone walls, pollard your plane tree, or mortar a streambed. And you may not feel you have the vision to carry out your ideas single-handedly. I advocate working with collaborators in the field. These should be people who share your values and can help realize the details of your dream landscape through the particular skills they bring to your site.

DESIGN PROFESSIONALS

Garden design is carried out by a variety of professionals. Landscape architects, landscape designers, master gardeners, horticulturists, and some contractors all design gardens of different degrees of artistry, scale, and horticultural intent. Certainly their experience, their particular skills, and specialization may help you choose what kind of professional may work best with you. But I believe that their most important attribute is a willingness to incorporate your program and inward images with their own sensibility as a designer.

At a recent lecture, after I had asked the audience to talk about their childhood daydreaming places, I received a question from a woman who identified herself as a "client." She asked, "How can I tell my landscape architect about my daydreaming places?" When I asked her why she couldn't, she responded, "Because he would feel that they are too personal. And he feels

Dogs need gardens too—this West Highland terrier, Checks, has his own run, which I designed for him and as an aesthetically pleasing utility area for garbage and equipment storage.

he knows what is best for my garden." "Then don't tell him at all," I replied. "Choose a different designer."

Many design professionals feel that their role is to tell you what to do with your backyard to make it into a garden. They will walk your site, ask a few questions, go to the drawing board, and return with a beautiful set of drawings of the garden that they can imagine being constructed there. These are often exquisite, costly visions that may be perfectly appropriate for your home. The problem is, the designers are producing *their* inward garden, not *yours*. If you hope to build your inward garden, then your designer must assume a different role: eliciting your personal images, memories, and experiences and transforming them into a garden for you.

When you interview designers, you should make your intentions quite clear. Look at their work to see if the images they have produced in other projects resonate with those that you hold for your garden. Tell them that you have been collecting ideas that you want them to incorporate into a design, and ask whether they have worked in this capacity before. If so, then work with them. If not, find someone else to interview.

The talented and idiosyncratic landscape architect Fletcher Steele was adamant about the way he liked to work with his clients. He wrote,

"[The sensitive landscape professional] refuses to be turned out in the front yard like a dog while his client holds him on a leash demanding 'What would you do here? Make me a pool under that tree.' Instead he wanders into the house to see what kind of books she reads, what kind of furniture and bric-a-brac she gathers about her. He gets her talking about her travels and the places she likes the best and ones she does not like. He probes to discover, not what she has, but what she dreams of having: not what she does but what she would like to do."

Fletcher Steele would have been an extraordinary designer to work with. He understood that the purpose of his work was to help people create their inward gardens, and not edifices dedicated to himself. But he also brought something else: a remarkable talent for linking someone else's images to his own to produce beautiful gardens on the land. This is what a designer should bring to the process of building your inward garden: a vision of what can be, which is matched with the talent and experience to make it happen and combined with the humility to base the design on your own images. The result should be a true collaboration between peers, built on respect for the wisdom offered by *both* sides—the client and the designer.

LANDSCAPE CONTRACTORS

Gardens often require highly skilled craftsmen to build them. If you are fortunate enough to find a sensitive, caring, and patient contractor, then building your garden will be one of the high points of your life. If not, it could prove to be one of the most disappointing. Your contractor needs to understand that this is not just any garden job, but one that is unique both in his and your experience. Your first interview question might be, "Do you understand that you are building me a dream?"

I have learned to work only with contractors that I can trust completely and that trust me—both sides need to feel that they are benefiting from the collaboration. On your side, you want the most experienced, most painstaking and detail-minded contractor that you can afford. On his (or her) side, the contractor needs to be paid well for his talents. This means that you must get prices nailed down early and clearly so that you can get on with the process of building your dream. Nothing can destroy the harmony of a garden like an adversarial relationship over money.

I have been working with the same contractors most of my professional life. Together, we have learned our craft by honing our different abilities in a range of sites, while faced with a variety of clients and their needs. I will set the image and the context, draw the plan, and deal most directly with the client, while my contractor will gather the materials, set the grades, and make sure that what we build works technically. Before we begin any construction, I'll go through my images and ideas in detail, both in plan and on the site, soliciting all parties' opinions and suggestions. Then, we build the garden together, as a team.

Much of gardenmaking is work of the back and the hands—moving objects around until you get them right. This means that you'll need a contractor who is open to change because his contract allows him some leeway for making alterations. And if he is a craftsman at heart, he'll always want to persevere until the garden feels finished, both to you and to him. If your relationship is good with your contractor, your inward garden will thrive as it takes form.

TAKE YOUR TIME—YOUR GARDEN IS YOUR PERSONAL WORK OF ART

Constructing a garden can be a long and delicate process. Every time you make a significant change to your site, you should live with the new condition for a while to reflect on what you've learned before tackling the next problem. You will be surprised at how your "set ideas" about your design will change as you live with the effects of your design decisions.

Eight years ago, I started working with a client who said he wanted a Japanese garden. He had visited Japan several times and showed me the kinds of gardens he loved. Each image showed the same elements: mossy streams, rivulets, and carp ponds. He was a person clearly drawn to water: he lived on a protected harbor near Boston and had a small cottage overlooking the sea in the Caribbean, where he conducted much of his business. He was a collector of fish, water plants, and begonias, and kept fish ponds, tanks, and grow lights throughout his house. He was a do-it-yourselfer when he had time, and had a limited budget to spend each year. So we began work.

His quarter-acre site was to the leeward side of his renovated seaside cottage, whose shingled, towered mass protected the plantings from the elements. The land sloped slightly downhill from street to house and faced west, rendering most of the site very sunny, but with shade to the south, where large trees cast their shadows on the garden.

The first year we worked out the plan: at the street side, a waterfall into a small pond, which broke into two tributaries that flowed on each side of his long, narrow property. These would come together in a deep koi pond, over which a large deck would cantilever, in the ell of his house. The second year we hired a bulldozer and moved earth—making his site more bowl-shaped—and excavated the watercourse. During this dirty phase of the work, the client laid boardwalk to move from driveway to house.

The third year, we poured concrete and mortared rocks on top of and into the water channels. The fourth year we brought in natural fieldstone to set about the site, and constructed paths of flat stepping-stones that took the visitor on a journey through the site. We made a promontory for looking at the waterfall, set sitting rocks as focal points, and constructed small bridges for crossing the streams. The fifth year, my client changed jobs and took a month off to construct a fence and gate on the street side, building a viewing platform that linked both sides of the garden and the huge, cantilevered deck that acted like a large threshold onto the garden.

Finally, from the sixth year through the present year we have been planting. We began with our large trees and structural plants—Eastern red cedars, black pines, and a cherry, with massings of mugho pines, Japanese junipers, and heathers on the sunny side; and Japanese maples, junipers, and azaleas on the shadier side. Since then, I have added various interesting plantings and replaced those that didn't thrive: now ornamental grasses, iris, bulbs, low-growing perennials, and ground covers are taking over. My client finished the plumbing and pump system for the garden and started the water flowing in the streams. The result is a wonderful garden, completely unique, constantly evolving, and growing richer with age.

What I liked about working with this man was his unabashed passion for gardens, his honesty about his financial constraints, his savoring of the process as we slowly carried out his design, his necessary and abundant patience, and his continuing delight in the product. His garden isn't grand, its details

The Rose Garden's serpentine paths pose an enigma to the viewer. Its designer, landscape architect Fletcher Steele, wrote, "I want all my places to seem the homes of children and lovers. I want them to be comfortable and if possible slightly mysterious by day, with vistas and compositions appealing to the painter. I want them to be delirious in the moonlight . . . I believe that there is no beauty without ugliness and that it should not be otherwise. Both are capable of stinging us to live. Contrast is more true to me than undeviating smugness. The chief vice in gardens . . . is to be merely pretty."

are not finely crafted, but it is all his, and people respond to it. They can sense the fun we had in making it.

My advice to everyone building a garden, then, is to control your urge to hurry through the construction process. Building your inward garden is a lifetime project, not something that can be "accomplished" in a year. Instead, enjoy fully each small alteration that you make and live with it for a while. As you learn from your successes and failures, make changes that improve the garden. Add ornaments, try new plantings, start new gardens. And have fun. For you will have become, almost without knowing it, a euphoric gardener.

Paper birch trunks are events in their own right. When you place them together in a grove, the effect is so bright as to be startling.

Naumkeag's Blue Steps are a tour de force built by landscape architect Fletcher Steele as a means for his client to reach her cutting garden from her high-vantaged house. Deep azure fountain pools are flanked by four flights of stairs, whose white railings echo the white of birch trunks—a vertical backdrop to the curving step design.

How Does Your Garden Grow?
A Whimsical Garden That Grew Over the Years . . .

Alice Moir's garden is rich with fanciful details that she has gathered or created herself over her lifetime. A folk artist, rug hooker, quilter, and gardener, my mother brings the same painterly eye to each endeavor. Every nook and cranny appears filled; each step brings another event to enjoy.

A Simple, Elegant Plan
with a Few Well-Chosen Plants

A recently finished garden that I designed for an art consultant in the Boston area shows a different vision of the world. The client's love of geometric form—squares superimposed on circles—combined with a delight in spare, elegant lines are evident in every detail. The garden reads like an abstract painting, and, viewed from deck or garden hut, appears spacious and soothing despite the small size of the lot.

POSTSCRIPT

THE GARDEN DESIGN of which I am most proud is the Linda J. Davison Memorial Path in the Arnold Arboretum of Harvard University, the oldest botanical park in the country. Still in progress, this garden is being built to celebrate the life of an extraordinary person who died prematurely, and to provide a place of solace for her relatives while creating a contemplative setting for others to enjoy.

The donor of the garden and my direct client was Linda's husband. Rather than erecting a memorial plaque or planting a tree in her name, he decided that he wanted to make a contemplative place in her favorite area of the arboretum, the Rhododendron Dell. This area houses a beautiful collection of specimens from the Ericaceae family, including a thousand hybrids and cultivars of rhododendron, the plant that Linda collected and volunteered to propagate at the arboretum until her death.

I knew this particular place well. It had long been one of my children's secret places and a ritual stop on our weekly trips

A rhododendron in full bloom marks one entrance to the Linda J. Davison Memorial Path at the Arnold Arboretum in Boston.

to this wonderful urban garden. At the base of a steep, rocky hillside covered with hemlock trees is a rocky brook that winds its way under ancient rhododendron bushes overtopped by taller hemlocks and pines, and is bounded by two internal roads that meet at its entrance. We would come to play at this fast-eroding streambed, making stickboats, bridges, and little huts at its edge.

My responsibilities were unusual for a designer. First, I was to design a personal place for someone I had never met. Second, I needed to make a meditative experience in a public and well-used parkland setting. Third, I hoped to make the area feel safe yet secluded in order to promote my contemplative agenda. Fourth, I had to ensure that the garden would be durable and easy to maintain. Finally, I had to design all new elements to fit the surrounding natural features, originally laid out by Frederick Law Olmsted, the grandfather of landscape design in America.

My big idea was to maintain the feeling of this dell, but add a stroll journey of paths and places that flowed alongside the little brook. I wanted the journey to begin under the deep, dark tunnel of towering hemlock trees at the entrance, signaled by a huge stone engraved with the name of the path. Just after entering, visitors could choose a stone path down to the water's edge that would lead to a newly excavated reflecting pool and waterfall, or take a pine needle path that wandered in and among the rhododendron specimens. Along the way, strollers would pass huge pudding-stone boulders that functioned as focal points and as viewing positions. Then they would arrive at a contemplative place of large stones set out as a habitable meditation spot located at the promontory formed by the curve of the stream. A log bridge beyond was built to link one side of the stream to the other.

Woodland perennial plantings at the feet of rocks and along the path help light up the dappled shade, where visitors delight in our careful orchestration of all the elements: the flashing brook, the bright flowers, the massive stones, the little paths, and the filtered light through canopies of rhododendron and hemlock. Having built the first quarter of this garden, we have transformed in a subtle but wonderful way the use of this portion of the arboretum.

Gardens—indeed, all natural settings—are animated by rituals. While this particular place took much of its spirit from the history and form of its landscape, it became a true garden when we celebrated the soul of the woman for whom it was built. One Sunday in early spring, her parents, husband, relatives, and friends all came to walk the path that bore her name. I led them through what had been built and spoke of my images in creating the design. We stood silent at the edge of the water to reflect on her life, and found meaning in the ever-flowing sibilance of the stream and strength in the spirit of the place. That day, the path was sanctified by the collective memories, feelings, and images held by those who loved her; it was no longer my design, but had become her inward garden made manifest.

Today and every day, her path is revivified by the children, parents, and strollers who have discovered it as a place to play and dream in this quiet corner of a large city. I like to think that together, her spirit and my imagination are passed on to the next generation, annexed to all the young souls as an image of their own inward gardens, bringing a smile to their faces and joy into their hearts.

Isn't this what all of us want at the end of our journey—to give and take delight from each other and from our surrounds in this place, in this life, in this world? What better way but to build our own secret place so that we may pass on to others the feelings and forms that reside within our souls, animating our small piece of this garden that we call Mother Earth.

John Milton wrote in *Paradise Lost,* "Accuse not Nature, she hath done her part; Do thou but thine." Go out and design, for yourself and for the earth, your inward garden.

Blossoms grace the contemplative path that winds through the Arnold Arboretum's Rhododendron Dell. Large rocks double as focal points and seats for viewing the adjacent Bussey Brook. Frequented by nearby residents for ritual strolls, it forms a place of peace for others, who leave behind offerings of flowers upon the stones.

Drawings and Plans

Archetypes

Concept sketches

In beginning the process of designing your garden, use these sketches of the archetypes to remind you of how different spaces might make you feel as well as how they might be formed.

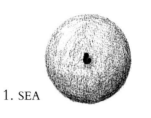

1. SEA

2. CAVE

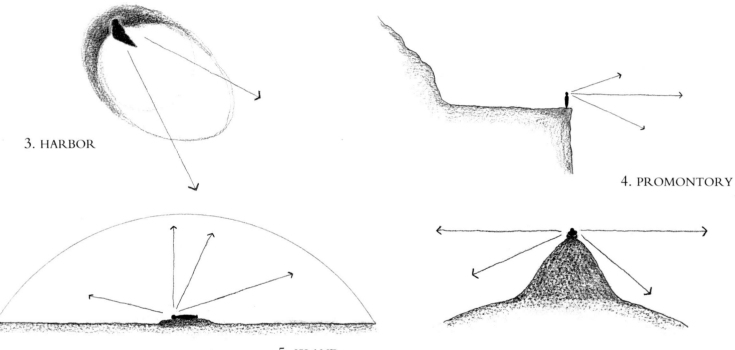

3. HARBOR

4. PROMONTORY

5. ISLAND

6. MOUNTAIN

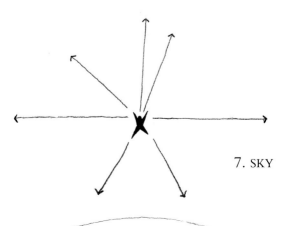

7. SKY

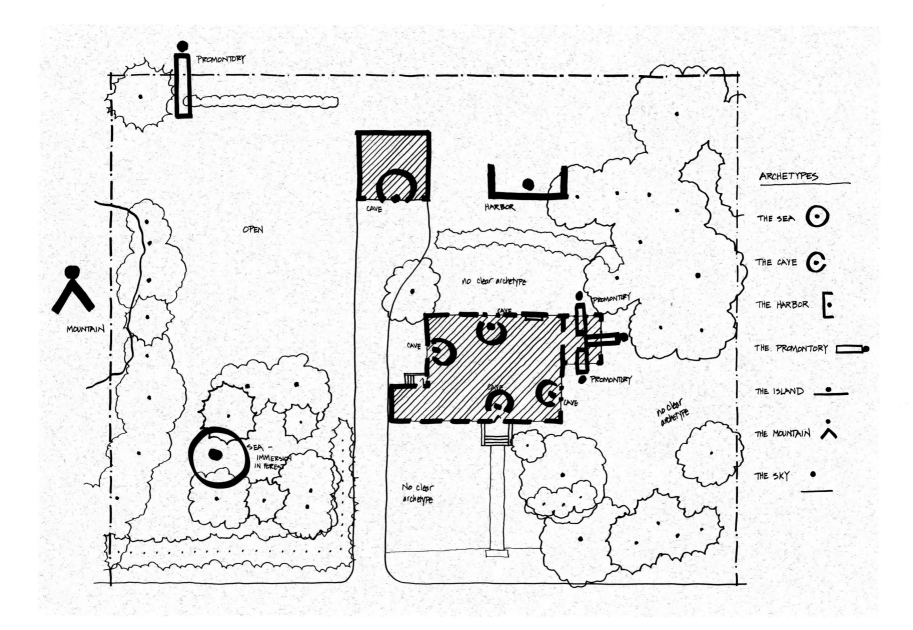

Archetype Diagram

A mortgage survey or other site plan provides a simple layout drawing of your land. Using it as a guide, walk around your site, and discuss the different archetypal places that you feel are in evidence. In what areas do you feel a sense of withinness, inside to outside, enclosure, at the edge of, awayness, upness, or beyondness? Using the following diagrams, record these archetypal places on your mortgage survey. Keep this as a reference during the rest of your design process.

235

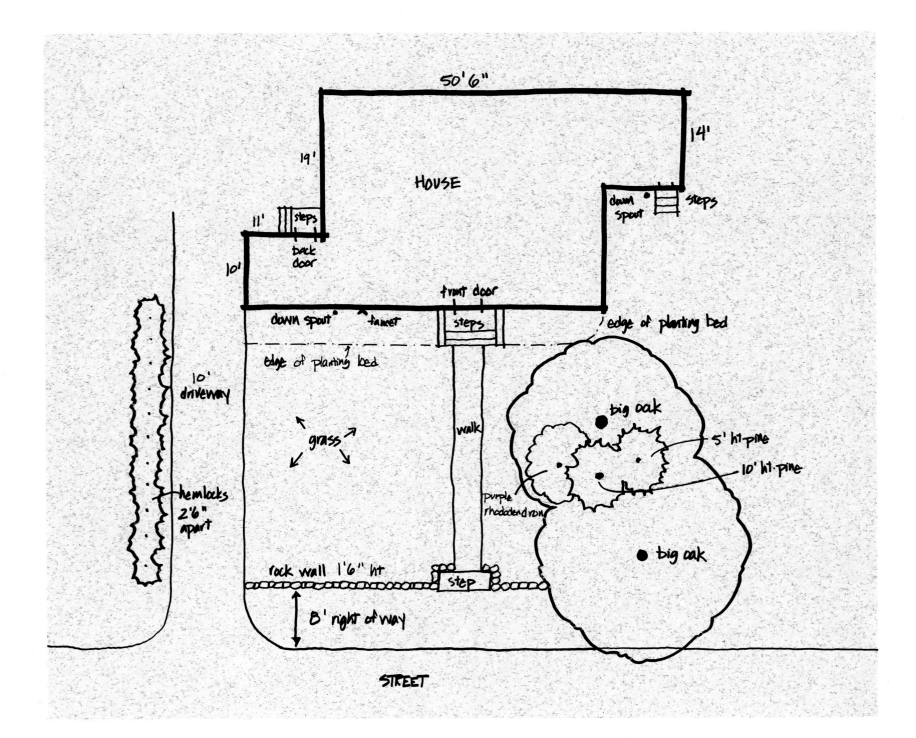

50'6"

14'

19'

HOUSE

11' steps

back door

10'

steps

down spout

down spout faucet

front door

steps

edge of planting bed

edge of planting bed

10' driveway

grass

walk

big oak

5' hi pine

10' hi pine

purple rhododendron

hemlocks 2'6" apart

rock wall 1'6" ht

step

big oak

8' right of way

STREET

236

Setup for Measuring Site

To design your garden using my method, you will need some equipment. At a stationery store, buy an architect's scale for drawing your site accurately, a medium-width roll of tracing paper, a few soft lead pencils, a white vinyl eraser, graph paper divided into eight lines per inch, drafting tape, and either a 50' or 100' measuring tape. You may also want to buy a circle template for drawing trees, and a medium-sized triangle for drawing right angles. Then find a plywood board or Plexiglas panel measuring approximately 2' x 3' on which to mount the graph paper for recording your measurements on-site.

Large or irregularly shaped sites, or sites with a variety of slope conditions, are often too complex for a homeowner to measure without professional help. Ask a registered surveyor or engineer to provide a survey that includes your property boundaries, locations of house and other structures, tree locations, contours at one-foot intervals, and other significant features on your property. This, then, will become the base plan for your garden design.

If you have a small or relatively flat site, you may be able to measure it yourself with acceptable accuracy. First, choose your scale. I have found that a good starting point might be to use $1/8"=1'-0"$ scale for sites of a quarter-acre to a half-acre and $1/4"=1'-0"$ scale for anything smaller than a quarter-acre. You might find that you want to change scales as you work through different parts of your garden.

Tape graph paper to your board, transferring your mortgage survey information onto your graph paper at the scale you've chosen. Square your house to the lines on the graph paper. Cross-check your drawing with actual site measurements.

Using the graph paper as a guide, locate your trees, shrubs, beds, paths, driveway, and other significant features in relation to the house. When you have completed your site survey, redraw this information on tracing paper. This drawing forms the base plan for your garden design.

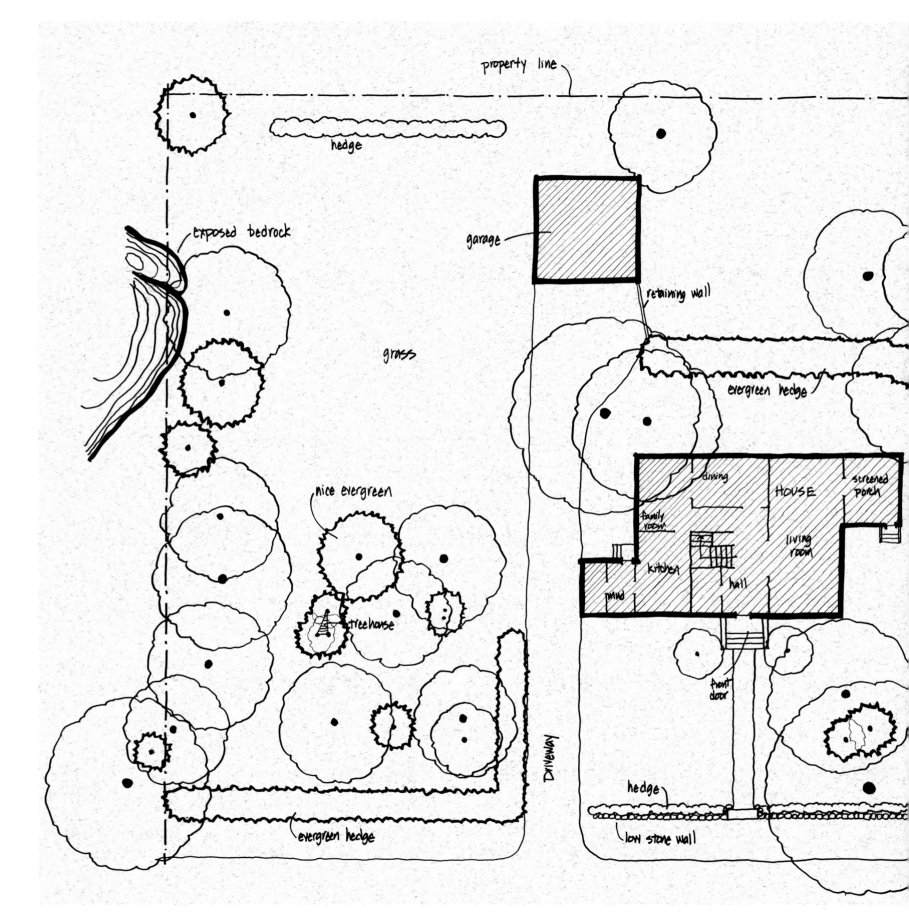

property line

hedge

exposed bedrock

garage

retaining wall

grass

evergreen hedge

nice evergreen

HOUSE

dining

screened porch

family room

living room

treehouse

kitchen

hall

mud

front door

DRIVEWAY

hedge

evergreen hedge

low stone wall

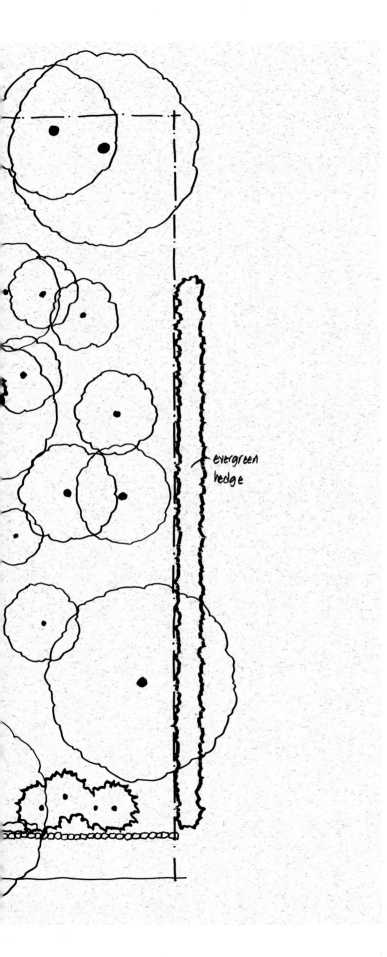

evergreen
hedge

Base Plan

Our half-acre site is on a bluff overlooking the city of Boston some eight miles away. Our house, a gray stucco "hunting lodge" built in 1926, faces west. Behind our house, the land slopes down to the east in a series of terraces that we recently cleared of brush in order to build our garden. To the north of the house lies a set of huge boulders, one fifteen feet high, that form the boundary of our property. The south of the house is wooded, with a high, deciduous canopy overhead.

Since it is such a diverse site, with many of the archetypal places represented, our land shows some of the conditions that many readers may face as they design their own gardens. I refer to this base plan as I explain my design method through the pages of this book.

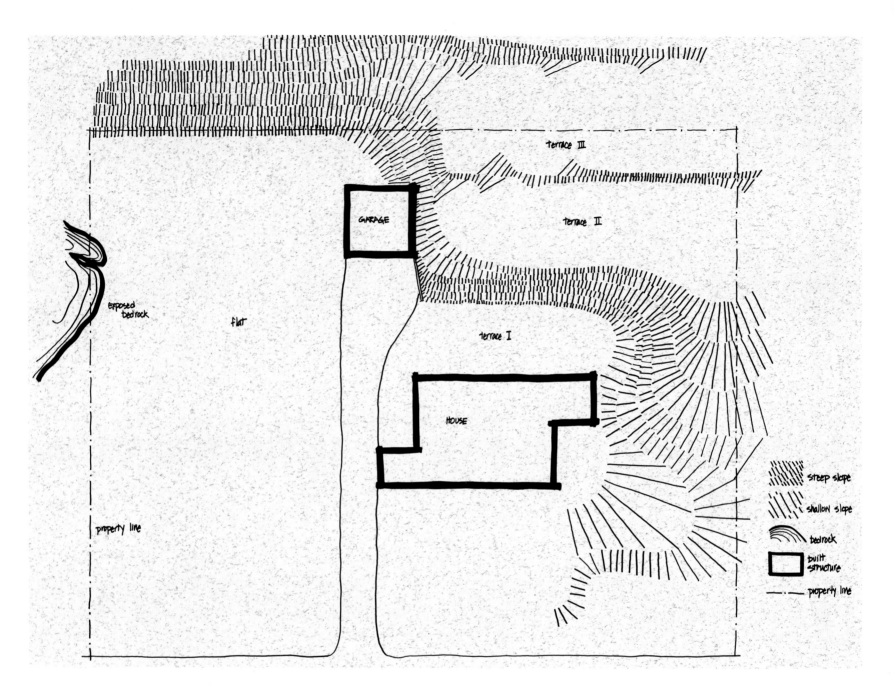

terrace III

GARAGE

terrace II

exposed bedrock

flat

terrace I

HOUSE

property line

steep slope

shallow slope

bedrock

built structure

property line

Grading Plan

Using a stake, a tree, or a person as a reference point, estimate the vertical drop of your land and record it on your base plan. Using one contour line to represent each foot of drop in grade, draw the slope on your graph paper. If the slope was ten feet wide and five feet high, then you'd make five rows of lines, approximately two feet apart each. Then transfer this information onto tracing paper to make a finished grading plan. Fill in between the contour lines with short strokes of the pencil, in the direction that water would flow. Put lines closer together to show a steep slope, and farther apart to show a shallow slope. Place this grading plan under your base plan so that you always know the shape of your land as you design your garden.

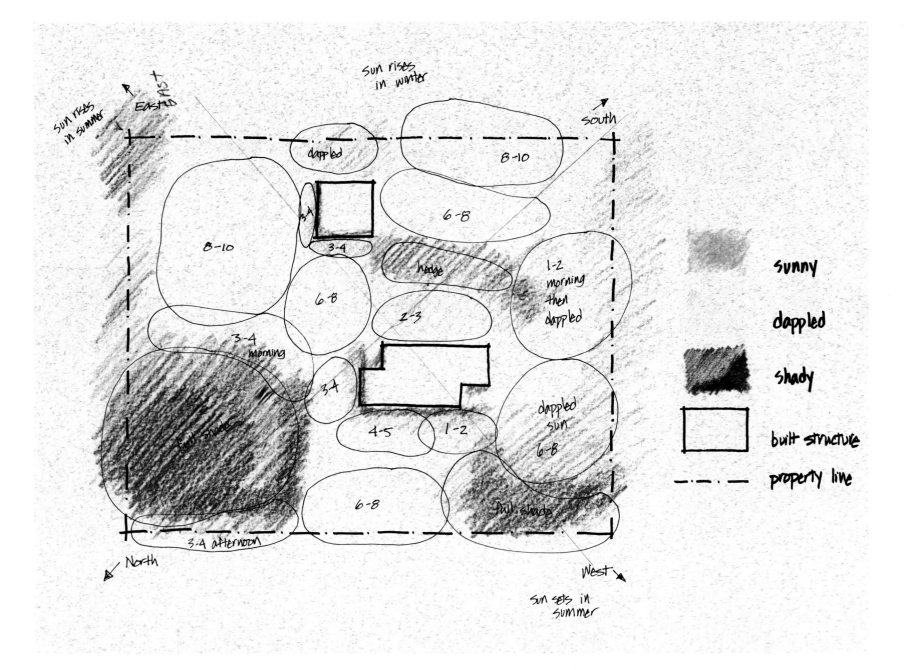

Sun Diagram

On your mortgage survey or your base plan, note the sunny, dappled, and shady sections of your land. You might also find it useful for making plant selections to note the hours of sunlight that your site receives each day, in each season.

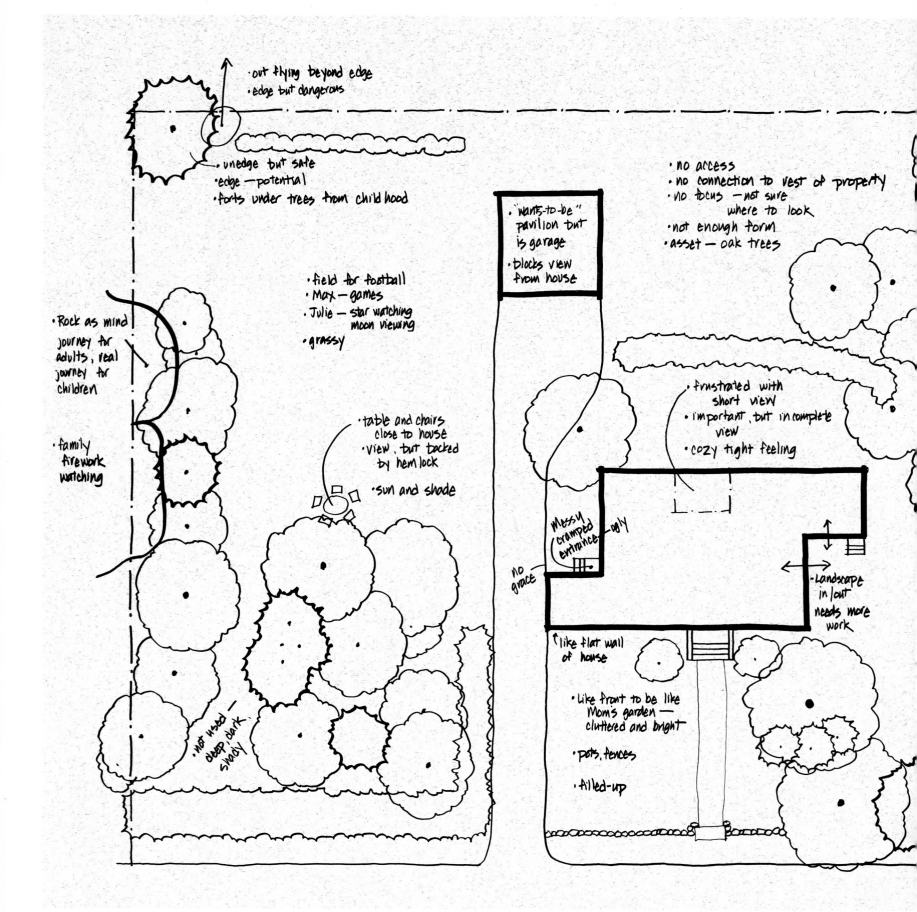

- out flying beyond edge
- edge but dangerous

- unedge but safe
- edge — potential
- forts under trees from childhood

- no access
- no connection to rest of property
- no focus — not sure where to look
- not enough form
- asset — oak trees

- "wants-to-be" pavilion but is garage
- blocks view from house

- field for football
- Max — games
- Julie — star watching moon viewing
- grassy

- Rock as mind journey for adults, real journey for children

- family firework watching

- table and chairs close to house
- view, but backed by hemlock
- sun and shade

- frustrated with short view
- important, but incomplete view
- cozy tight feeling

Messy cramped entrance only

no grace

- Landscape in /out needs more work

- like flat wall of house

- Like front to be like Mom's garden — cluttered and bright
- pots, fences
- filled-up

not used deep, dark, shady

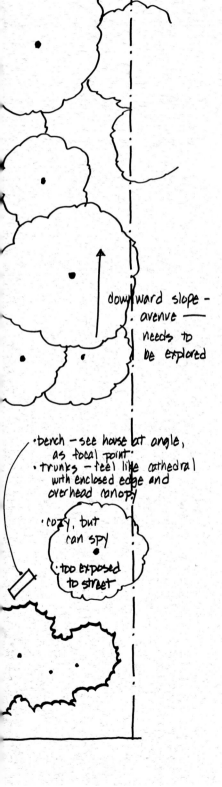

downward slope –
avenue –
needs to
be explored

•bench – see house at angle,
as focal point•
•trunks – feel like cathedral
with enclosed edge and
overhead canopy•

•cozy, but
can spy

•too exposed
to street

Site Analysis Plan

Take each member of the family on a
tour of your backyard and ask each person to
discuss how they use different areas of the site
and what they like or dislike about each one.
Then, on the base plan, make a collage of these
thoughts, opinions, and ideas and refer to it
often during the garden design process. Don't
forget the family pets—note where they like to
lie or perch as well.

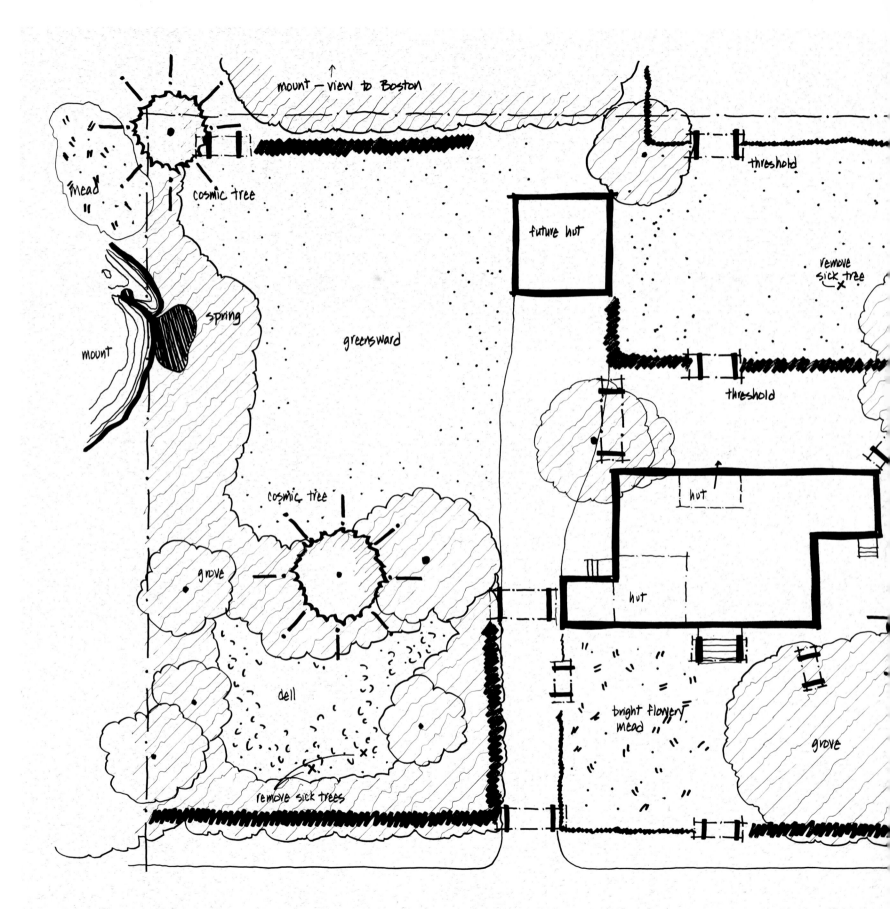

mount – view to Boston

mead

cosmic tree

threshold

future hut

remove sick tree
X

spring

mount

greensward

threshold

cosmic tree

hut

grove

hut

dell

bright flowery mead

grove

remove sick trees

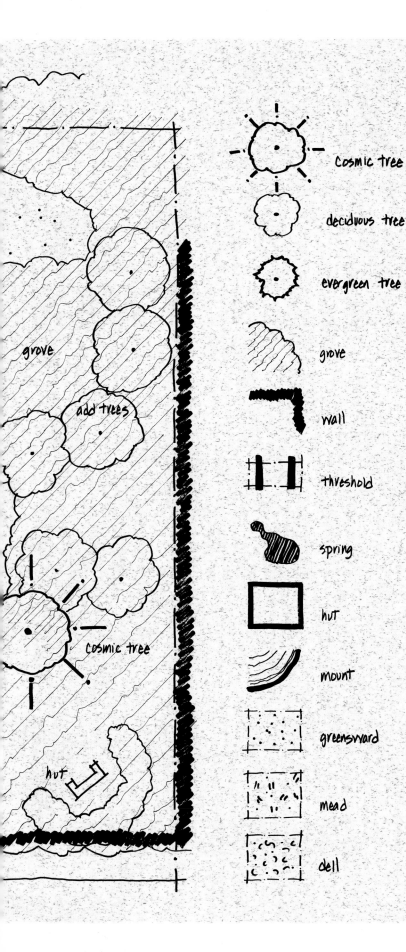

Primary Elements Plan

On your base map, record the different primary elements as they appear on your site. Locate all existing cosmic trees and groves; hutlike spaces both inside and outside your house; enclosures, including walls, screens, beds and borders, and edgings; thresholds, including gateways, terraces, and bridges; meadows, including flowery meads, greenswards, and dells; mounts; and springs on your property. Next, imagine where you might place some of these elements—where do you need a terrace? a flower border? a greensward? This plan marks the beginning of your garden design.

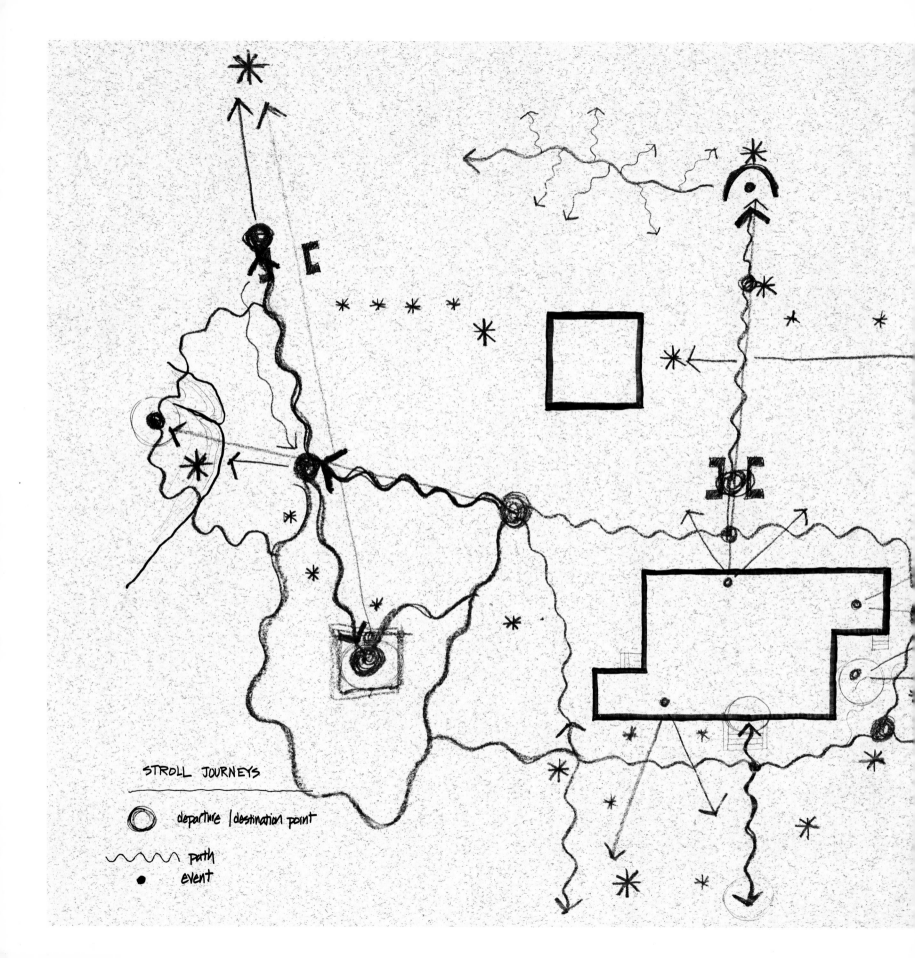

STROLL JOURNEYS

⊚ departure/destination point

〜〜〜 path

• event

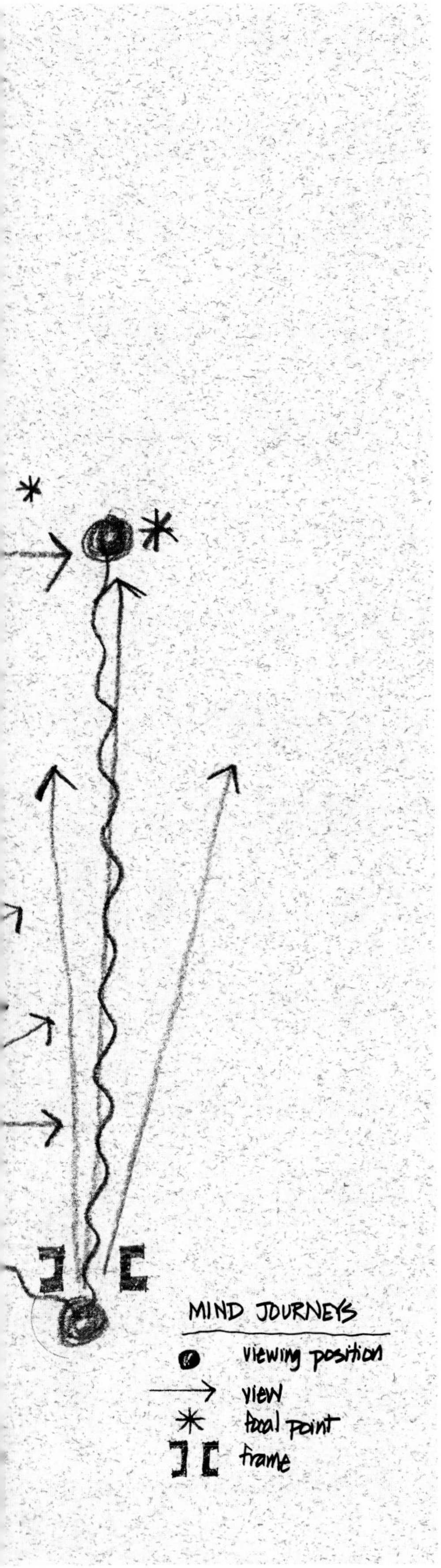

MIND JOURNEYS

● viewing position
→ view
✳ focal point
] [frame

Stroll and Mind Journeys Plan

Now you need to design the ways along which your feet and your mind move through your garden. First, diagram the stroll journeys you already have or would like to create there. Indicate departure and destination points using black circles and arrows. Show the promenades and the walks with a heavy line, and mark the less frequented trails and traces with a thinner line. Show whether the direction of the path is straight or meandering.

Next, show the mind journeys that exist or that you hope to create in your garden. For each journey, mark the viewing position with a black circle, the focus with an asterisk or a star, and the angle of each view with arrows. Indicate each frame using heavy black parallel lines at the point where it occurs in the landscape.

247

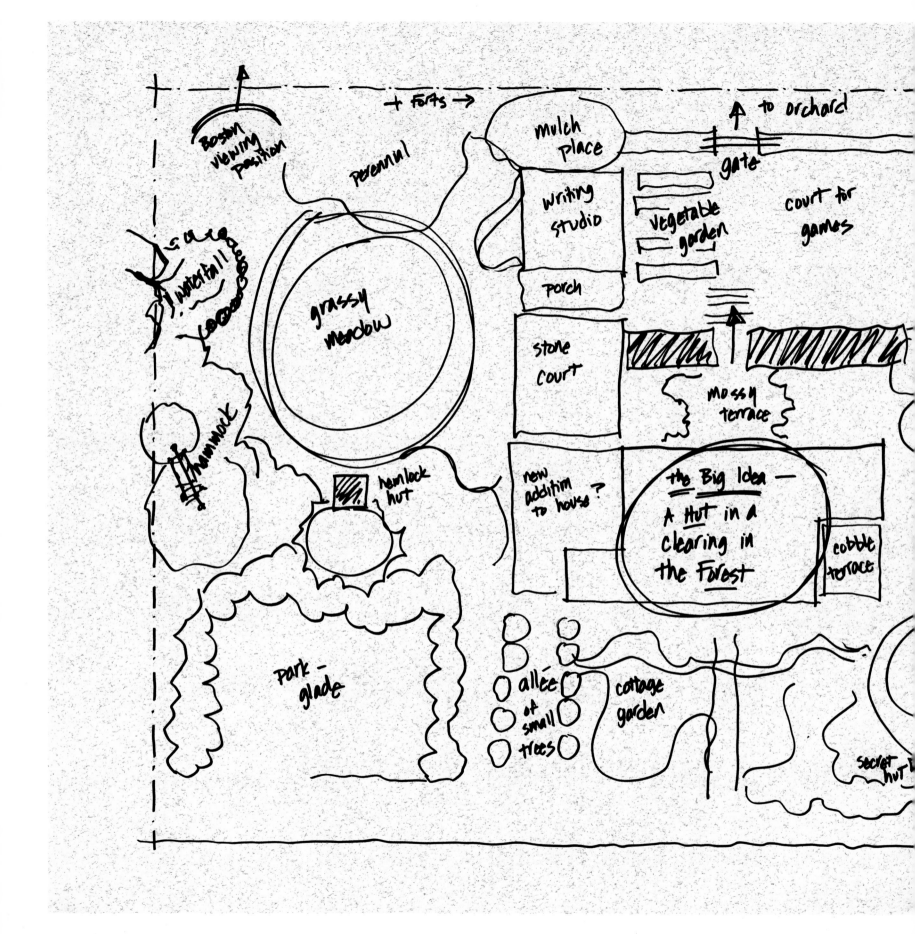

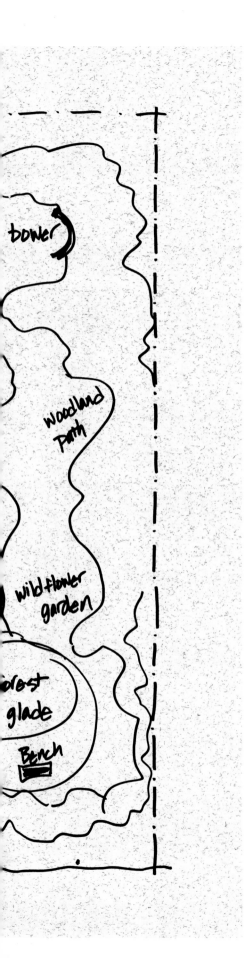

Big Idea Plan

The big idea plan is a schematic record of your big ideas for the different areas of your garden. Using the most descriptive, evocative names you can imagine, record all your big ideas in the appropriate parts of your site. Next, start to give your ideas form by drawing what the plan looks like, either from a bird's-eye perspective or as a series of little sketches. This plan will form the basis for your master design plan.

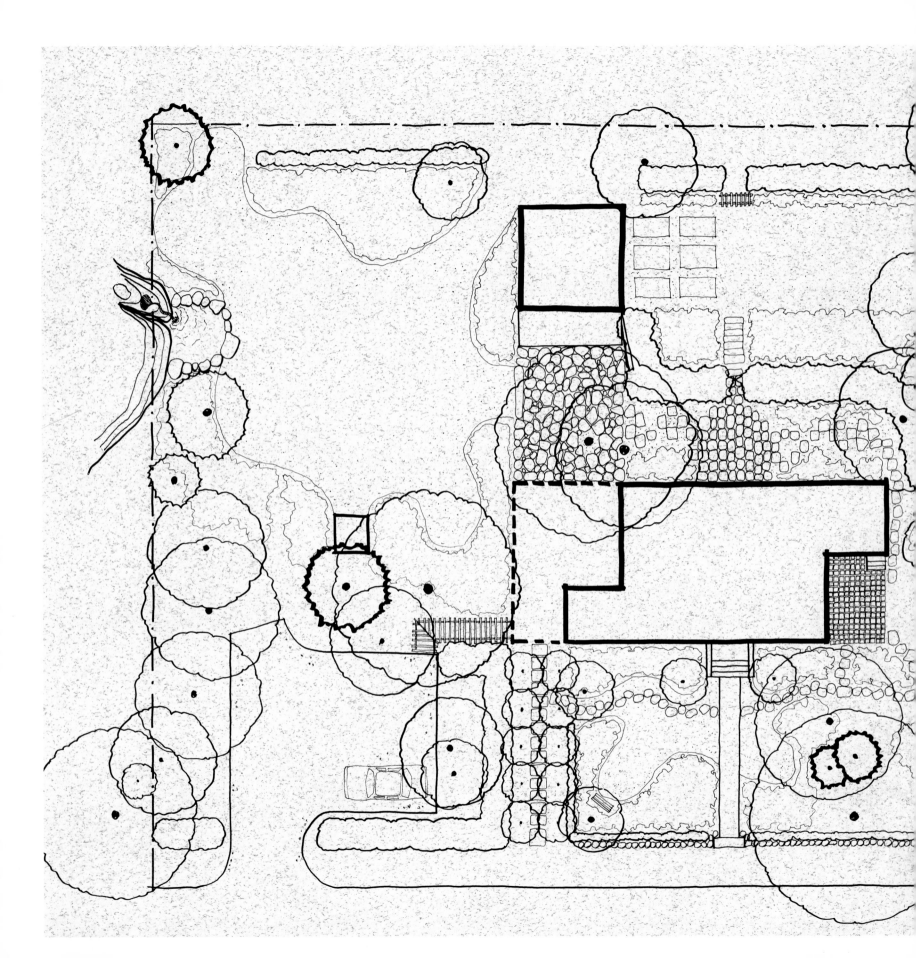

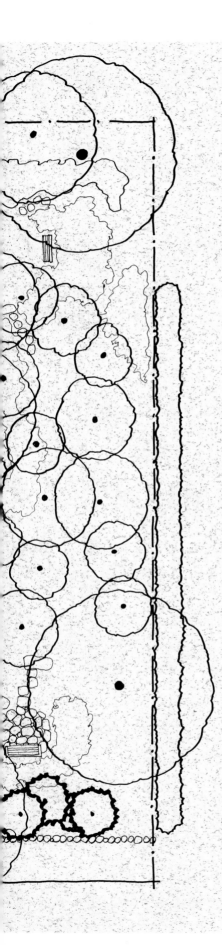

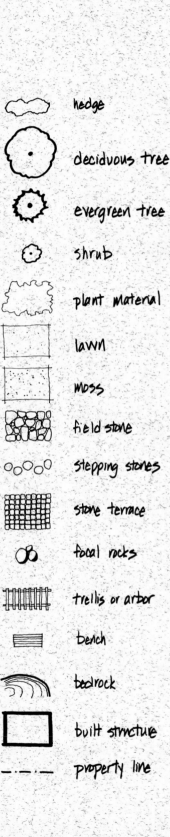

hedge

deciduous tree

evergreen tree

shrub

plant material

lawn

moss

field stone

stepping stones

stone terrace

focal rocks

trellis or arbor

bench

bedrock

built structure

property line

Master Design Plan

This is the plan that gives you enough information to begin to actually build your inward garden. Tracing over the important features of the previous plans, draw a master design plan that indicates new paths, terraces, plantings, benches, hedges, fences, or walls, and focal points as you now imagine them. Make little sketches showing different ways to design each section, allowing your hand to respond freely to the images that appear in your mind. Remember that, over the years, this plan will change as you build and as your needs and your situation—indeed, your life—change.

BIBLIOGRAPHY

I. NATURAL AND SACRED LANDSCAPES

Berger, Pamela. *The Goddess Obscured* (Boston: Beacon Press, 1985).

Crowe, Sylvia, and Mary Mitchell. *The Pattern of Landscape* (Chichester, England: Packard Publishing, 1988).

Devereux, Paul, John Steele, and David Kubrin. *Earthmind: A Modern Adventure in Ancient Wisdom* (New York: Harper & Row, 1989).

Eliade, Mircea. *From Primitives to Zen* (New York: Harper & Row, 1977).

Gadon, Elinor W. *The Once and Future Goddess* (San Francisco: Harper & Row, 1989).

Hamerton, Philip Gilbert. *Landscape* (Boston: Roberts Brothers, 1885).

Higuchi, Tadahiko. *The Visual and Spatial Structure of Landscapes* (Cambridge, Mass.: M.I.T. Press, 1983).

Hiss, Tony. *The Experience of Place* (New York: Alfred A. Knopf, 1990).

Hoskins, William George. *The Making of the English Landscape* (London: Penguin Books, 1986).

Knoepflmacher, Ulrich Camillus, and Georg Bernhard Tennyson. *Nature and the Victorian Imagination* (Berkeley: University of California Press, 1977).

Layton, Robert. *Uluru: An Aboriginal History of Ayers Rock* (Canberra, Australia: Aboriginal Studies Press, 1989).

Lynch, Kevin. *Managing the Sense of a Region* (Cambridge, Mass.: M.I.T. Press, 1976).

———. *Site Planning* (Cambridge, Mass.: M.I.T. Press, 1984).

Norberg-Schulz, Christian. *Genius Loci / Towards a Phenomenology of Architecture* (New York: Rizzoli, 1980).

Olsen, Carl, ed. *The Book of the Goddess / Past and Present* (New York: Crossroad, 1983).

Shepard, Paul. *Man in the Landscape* (College Station: Texas A&M University Press, 1991).

Tuan, Yi-Fu. *Topophilia: A Study of Environmental Perceptions, Attitudes and Values* (Englewood Cliffs, N.J.: Prentice-Hall, 1974).

II. IMAGES, METAPHOR, AND MEANING

Alexander, Christopher, et al. *A Pattern Language* (New York: Oxford University Press, 1977).

Arieti, Silvano. *Creativity: The Magic Synthesis* (New York: Basic Books, 1976).

Arnheim, Rudolf. *Art and Visual Perception* (Berkeley: University of California Press, 1974).

———. *Toward a Psychology of Art* (San Francisco: University of California Press, 1966).

———. *Visual Thinking* (Berkeley: University of California Press, 1969).

Bachelard, Gaston. *The Poetics of Reverie* (Boston: Beacon Press, 1960).

———. *The Poetics of Space* (Boston: Beacon Press, 1960).

Bloomer, Kent C., and Charles W. Moore. *Body, Memory and Architecture* (New Haven, Conn.: Yale University Press, 1977).

Campbell, Joseph. *The Mythic Image* (Princeton, N.J.: Princeton University Press, 1974).

———. *The Power of Myth* (New York: Doubleday, 1988).

Caudwell, H. *The Creative Impulse* (London: Macmillan, 1953).

Eliade, Mircea. *The Sacred and the Profane* (New York: Harcourt, Brace, 1959).

———. *The Two and the One* (New York: Harper & Row, 1962).

Guidoni, Enrico. *Primitive Architecture* (New York: Abrams, 1978).

Jung, Carl G. *Man and His Symbols* (New York: Doubleday, 1964).

———. *Memories, Dreams, Reflections* (New York: Pantheon Books, 1961).

———. *Modern Man in Search of a Soul* (New York: Harcourt, Brace & World, 1933).

Koestler, Arthur. *Insight and Outlook* (Lincoln: University of Nebraska Press, 1949).

Kubie, Lawrence S. *Neurotic Distortion of the Creative Process* (New York: The Noonday Press, 1958).

Langer, Susanne K. *Feeling and Form* (New York: Charles Scribner's Sons, 1953).

Mahler, Margaret S., et al. *The Psychological Birth of the Human Infant* (New York: Basic Books, 1975).

Merton, Thomas. *Contemplation in a World of Action* (Garden City, N.Y.: Doubleday Image Books, 1973).

Miller, Alice. *The Untouched Key* (New York: Doubleday, 1988).

Rykwert, Joseph. *On Adam's Hut in Paradise* (Cambridge, Mass.: M.I.T. Press, 1981).

Santayana, George. *The Sense of Beauty* (New York: Dover Publications, 1955).

Singer, Jerome L. *The Inner World of Daydreaming* (New York: Harper & Row, 1966).

Sommer, Robert. *The Mind's Eye: Imagery in Everyday Life* (New York: Dell, 1978).

Storr, Anthony. *Solitude: A Return to the Self* (New York: Ballantine Books, 1988).

III. GARDEN HISTORY AND THEORY

Agnelli, Marella. *Gardens of the Italian Villas* (New York: International Publications, 1987).

Brookes, John. *Gardens of Paradise: The History and Religion of the Great Islamic Gardens* (New York: Meredith Press, 1987).

Bye, Arthur Edwin, Jr. *Art into Landscape/Landscape into Art* (Mesa, Ariz.: PDA Publishers, 1983).

Cartwright, Julia. *Italian Gardens of the Renaissance* (London: Smith, Elder, 1914).

Clifford, Derek. *A History of Garden Design* (New York: Praeger, 1963).

Crowe, Sylvia, and Sheila Haywood. *The Gardens of Mughal India* (London: Thames & Hudson, 1972).

Fukuda, Kazuhiko. *Japanese Stone Gardens* (Tokyo: Charles E. Tuttle, 1970).

Halprin, Lawrence. *Works by Lawrence Halprin* (Tokyo: Process Architecture, 1978).

Hayakawa, Masao. *The Garden Art of Japan* (Tokyo: Weatherhill/Heibonsha, 1973).

Hensel, Margaret. *English Cottage Gardening for American Gardeners* (New York: W.W. Norton, 1992).

Hisamatsu, Shin'ichi. *Zen and the Fine Arts* (Tokyo: Kodansha International, 1971).

Howett, Catherine, ed. *Abstracting the Landscape: The Artistry of Landscape Architect A. E. Bye* (University Park: Pennsylvania State University, 1990).

Itoh, Teiji. *Space and Illusion in the Japanese Garden* (New York: Weatherhill/Tankosha, 1965).

Jekyll, Gertrude. *Colour Schemes for the Flower Garden* (Suffolk, England: Antique Collectors' Club, 1982).

Jellicoe, Geoffrey, and Susan Jellicoe. *Landscape of Man: Shaping* the Environment from Prehistory to the Present Day (New York: Thames & Hudson, 1987).

Karson, Robin. *Fletcher Steele, Landscape Architect* (New York: Abrams, 1989).

King, Ronald. *The Quest for Paradise: A History of the World's Gardens* (New York: Mayflower Books, 1979).

Kuck, Loraine. *The World of the Japanese Garden* (Tokyo: Walker/Weatherhill, 1968).

Lacey, Stephen. *The Startling Jungle: Colour and Scent in the Romantic Garden* (London: Penguin Books, 1986).

Lawrence, Sidney, and George Foy. *Music in Stone: Great Sculpture Gardens of the World* (New York: Scala Books, 1984).

Lehrman, Jonas. Earthly Paradise: *Garden and Courtyard in Islam* (Berkeley: University of California Press, 1980).

MacDougall, Elisabeth B., and Richard Ettinghausen, eds. *The Islamic Garden* (Washington, DC: Dumbarton Oaks, 1976).

Moynihan, Elizabeth B. *Paradise As a Garden* (New York: George Braziller, 1979).

Nitschke, Gunter. "Ma, the Japanese Sense of Place," *Architectural Design,* March 1966.

Page, Russell. *The Education of a Gardener* (New York: Random House, 1983).

Schwenk, Theodor. *Sensitive Chaos* (New York: Schocken Books, 1978).

Scott-James, Anne. *The Cottage Garden* (London: Michael Joseph, 1979).

———. *The Language of the Garden* (England: Penguin Books, 1984).

Shepherd, John C., and Geoffrey Jellicoe. *Italian Gardens of the Renaissance* (Princeton, N.J.: Princeton Architectural Press, 1986).

Slawson, David. *Secret Teachings in the Art of Japanese Gardens* (Tokyo: Kodansha International, 1987).

Thacker, Christopher. *The History of Gardens* (Berkeley: University of California Press, 1979).

Turner, Tom. *English Garden Design* (England: Antique Collector's Club, 1986).

Wagenknecht-Harte, Kay. *Site + Sculpture* (New York: Van Nostrand Reinhold, 1989).

IV. FAVORITE PRACTICAL REFERENCE BOOKS FOR GARDENERS

Dirr, Michael A. *Manual of Woody Landscape Plants* (Champaign, Ill.: Stipes, 1983).

Hobhouse, Penelope. *Colour in the Garden* (Boston: Little, Brown, 1985).

Hudak, Joseph. *Gardening with Perennials Month by Month* (New York: Quadrangle/New York Times, 1976).

Jellicoe, Geoffrey, and Susan Jellicoe, eds. *The Oxford Companion to Gardens* (New York: Oxford University Press, 1986).

Mabberley, David John. *The Plant-Book: A Portable Dictionary of the Higher Plants* (New York: Cambridge University Press, 1987).

Wilkison, Elizabeth, and Marjorie Henderson. *The House of Boughs: A Sourcebook of Garden Designs, Structures, and Suppliers* (New York: Viking Penguin, 1985).

Yang, Linda. *The City Gardener's Handbook: From Balcony to Backyard* (New York: Random House, 1990).

Locations of Photographs